9.00

GW01513383

Philosophy and Theistic Mysticism
of
the Āḻvārs

Philosophy and Theistic Mysticism of the Āḻvārs

S.M.S. Chari

MOTILAL BANARSIDASS PUBLISHERS PRIVATE LIMITED • DELHI

First Edition: Delhi, 1997

© MOTILAL BANARSIDASS PUBLISHERS PRIVATE LIMITED
All Rights Reserved

ISBN: 81-208-1342-1

Also available at:

MOTILAL BANARSIDASS

41 U.A. Bungalow Road, Jawahar Nagar, Delhi 110 007
8 Mahalaxmi Chamber, Warden Road, Mumbai 400 026
120 Royapettah High Road, Mylapore, Chennai 600 004
Sanas Plaza, Subhash Nagar, Pune 411 002
16 St. Mark's Road, Bangalore 560 001
8 Camac Street, Calcutta 700 017
Ashok Rajpath, Patna 800 004
Chowk, Varanasi 221 001

PRINTED IN INDIA

BY JAINENDRA PRAKASH JAIN AT SHRI JAINENDRA PRESS,
A-45 NARAINA, PHASE I, NEW DELHI 110 028
AND PUBLISHED BY NARENDRA PRAKASH JAIN FOR
MOTILAL BANARSIDASS PUBLISHERS PRIVATE LIMITED,
BUNGALOW ROAD, DELHI 110 007

To the Revered Memory of

Sri Madhurantakam Veeraraghavacharya Swami
with profound respects and gratitude

CONTENTS

Foreword ix

Preface xiii

Notes on Transliteration xvii

List of Abbreviations xix

Introduction **1-8**

Chapter 1 **Life and Works of the Āḻvārs** **9-35**
The Dates of the Āḻvārs 10
The Divine Origin of the Āḻvārs 13
The Life and Compositions of the Āḻvārs 16
The Classification of the Prabandhams 32

Chapter 2 **The Doctrine of Ultimate Reality** **37-67**
The Philosophical Theory of Paratattva 37
Paratattva as Nārāyaṇa 52
Paratattva as Śriyaḥpati 60

Chapter 3 **The Doctrine of God** **69-107**
Divine Attributes 70
Divine Personality 83
Divine Incarnations 90
Divine Activities 103

Chapter 4 **The Doctrine of Individual Self** **109-119**
The Nature of Jīva 110
Jīva and Human Bondage 111
Jīva and Īśvara 116
The Concept of Bhāgavata-śeṣatva 118

Chapter 5 **The Doctrine of Sādhana** **121-141**
The Views of Nammāḻvār on Sādhana 122
The Theory of Bhakti-yoga 126
The Theory of Prapatti 131
Divine Grace and Sādhana 139

Chapter 6 **The Doctrine of Supreme Goal** **143-150**
The Upaniṣadic Theory of Mokṣa 143
The Theological View of Mokṣa 145
The Theory of Kaivalya 147

Chapter 7 **Theistic Mysticism** **151-219**
Meaning of Mysticism 151
Theistic Mysticism as Aspects of Bhakti 153
Philosophical Significance of Mysticism 158
Mysticism of Nammāḻvār 162
Mysticism of Tirumaṅgai Āḻvār 186
Mysticism of Āṇḍāḷ 199
Mysticism of Periyāḻvār 208
Mysticism of Kulaśekarāḻvār 214

Chapter 8 **General Evaluation and Conclusion** **221-245**
The Status of Divyaprabandham as Tamil Veda 222
The Tiruvāymoḻi as Vedānta 225
The Theory of Ubhaya-vedānta 230
The Influence of the Tamil Prabandhams on Rāmānuja and his Successors 234
The Āḻvārs and the Vaiṣṇava Sects 240

Glossary 247

Select Bibliography 253

Index 259

FOREWORD

The celebrated Vaiṣṇava saints of South India, known as Āḻvārs, not only heralded a significant movement of devotion but prepared the ground for a great philosophical system, later crystallized by the eminent Ācāryas, Nāthamuni, Yāmuna and Rāmānuja. They provided the springs from which the waters of ecstatic devotion and intuitive wisdom gushed out to form a mighty stream.

The Vaiṣṇava movement in South India gathered momentum when the Pallavas established their empire here. The Āḻvārs were itinerant saints who contributed to the religious renaissance in the Pallava, Pandya and Chola countries. They witnessed the rise and fall of principalities in these countries and passed through times which were tumultous. But their sole concern was the one Ultimate Reality (*paratattva*), beyond time and space, whom they called Viṣṇu. The twelve Āḻvārs sang the glory of this Supreme Deity in the Tamil hymns collectively known as Nālāyira Divya-prabandham. They moved about extensively and propagated the religious philosophy of total surrender to Godhead. Living between the fifth and eighth centuries A.D., they visited Viṣṇu shrines in Tonda-nadu, Pandi-nadu, Vada-nadu and Sola-nadu and celebrated the glory of these shrines in the Tamil hymnology.

There are frequent references in this Hymnoloy (Prabandham) to the Vedic mantras being recited in the shrines the Āḻvārs visited and of fire-rituals being performed. The Āḻvārs appear to regard the worship of Viṣṇu as well within the fold of Vedic culture. Those were the days when the temple-culture had unmistakable alignment with the Vedic framework. The Pandyas who were avid temple builders were Vedic in their affiliation. They performed great yagas and also built temples like the one at Virakerala vinnagar (Viṣṇu-gṛha).

The Āḻvārs represent the phase of synthesis of the Vedic outlook and the Āgama ideology. The philosophy which the Prabandham contains, therefore, would mark an important phase in the evolution of Indian philosophical thought. Books like Divyasūri-carita (by Garuḍavāhana paṇḍita, said to be Rāmānuja's contemporary) and Guru-paraṁparā-prabhāvam (by Aḻagiya-perumāḷ-jīyar), contain only the biography of the Āḻvārs or legendary accounts of their lives. The first attempt to bring out he philosophical teachings contained in the hymns was made by the Vaiṣṇava Ācāryas of the post-Rāmānuja period in their commentaries on them written mostly in maṇipravāḷa (Tamil language interspersed with Sanskrit), the earliest one being by Tirukkurukaipirān Piḷḷān, a direct disciple of Rāmānuja. Attempts were made in more recent years to present some aspects of the philosophy of the Āḻvārs by a few modern scholars like A. Govindacharya (Divine Wisdom of the Drāviḍa Saints). J.S.M. Hooper (Hymns of the Āḻvārs), K.C. Varadachari (Āḻvārs of South India) and N. Subba Reddiar (Religion and philosophy of Nālāyiram). But these attempts have not been very successful; they fail to carry clarity and conviction to the open-minded but earnest student of philosophy.

The first attempt in this direction to focus attention on the philosophical theories in the works of the Āḻvārs, bereft of religious or sectarian sidetracking, has been made by Dr. S.M. Srinivasa Chari. He has had the advantage of studying the Prabandham and Vedānta under traditional scholars for long years and of being equipped with the modern methods of study and research. A keen student endowed with critical faculty, he has been able to separate the grain from the husk. He has gone into the depths of the Tamil compositions of the Āḻvārs and commentaries on them, to discover the philosophy that is characteristic of the Āḻvārs, and to distinguish it from theistic mysticism.

The Āḻvārs had their intuitive apprehension of the Ultimate Reality (*para-tattva*), of the Godhead within man's approach, of the nature of the soul bound as well as yearning to be freed and of the spiritual discipline that leads the soul to the supreme goal. Dr. Chari has presented all these doctrines comprehensively with remarkable clarity, analytical skill and profound understanding. Scholars who have already been acquainted with his work on the

Philosophy, Theology and Religious Discipline of Vaiṣṇavism, will find the present work a competent supplement to the former work.

While Dr. Chari is in fact a traditional scholar, his approach to the academic and sectarian controversies like that with regard to the value of Prabandham *vis-à-vis* the authority of the Vedānta, distinguishes him as an impartial, critical and rational thinker. The Āḻvārs have at last found an exponent of their philosophy, who can do abundant justice to their inspired utterances, and who can feel sympathetically with themselves. Like the Āḻvārs, who were so called because they dived deep into the ecstatic experiences consequent on direct encounter with Godhead, Dr. Chari has dived deep into their compositions. He now invites us to share his findings.

I am sure we will richly rewarded.

S.K. Ramachandra Rao

Vidyalankara, Sastrachudamani, Vedanta-nidhi,
Sangita-kalaratan Prof. S.K. Ramachandra Rao.

Formerly Prof. Nimhans and Bangalore University,
President Silpa-Kala-Pratishthana and Visiting
Faculty, National Institute of Advanced Studies,
Indian Institute of Science, Bangalore.

PREFACE

This book is devoted to the study of the Tamil hymns of the Vaiṣṇava Saints of South India known as Āḻvārs who lived between the 6th and 8th centuries of the Christian era. Its main objective is to present the philosophical and theological teachings as contained in the hymns and to evaluate the extent to which they have contributed to the Viśiṣṭādvaita Vedānta and Vaiṣṇava Theology as expounded at a later period by Rāmānuja and his successors. Right from the time of Nāthamuni (9th century), the Vaiṣṇava Ācāryas have given great importance to the four thousand hymns of twelve Āḻvārs collectively known as *Nālāyira Divyaprabandham*. They have accorded to it a status equal to that of the Sanskrit Veda as it contains the quintessence of the Vedic teachings. Except for some sporadic attempts to render the hymns into English and a few general studies of some aspects of the teachings of the Āḻvārs, there is no single book in English that presents in a systematic manner the Philosophy and Mysticism of the Āḻvārs comprehensively. The present attempt is intended to meet this requirement.

The poetical compositions of the God-intoxicated Saints comprise mostly devotional songs in praise of the glory of God and do not as such discuss philosophical and theological doctrines in a sequential order. In view of this, it is generally believed that these poems contain little philosophy and are intended to promote the *bhakti* movement. Though such a view may be partly true in respect of the hymns of some Āḻvārs, it is not applicable to the *Tiruvāymoḻi* of Nammāḻvār which comprises 1,102 verses. The philosophical and theological doctrines of the Āḻvār are well- pronounced in the *Tiruvāymoḻi,* while the same are only implicit in the hymns of other Āḻvārs. All the Āḻvārs, however, have dwelt either directly or indirectly on the three fundamental doctrines of Vedānta namely, *tattva* or the Ultimate Reality, *hita* or the means of its attainment and *puruṣārtha* or the supreme goal of life. Their main objective is to disseminate the essential tenets of Vedānta philosophy among the common people through the media of Tamil. This fact is not widely recognised by many modern scholars and hence it is considered necessary to bring to light the philosophical contents of the hymns of the Āḻvārs.

In presenting the philosophy of the Āḻvārs, I have drawn material from their original hymns. There are several scholarly commentaries on the poems which by way of interpreting the hymns also include in them theological ideas that came to be developed in the post-Rāmānuja period. In order to evaluate the basic tenets of Vaiṣṇavism as they prevailed long before Rāmānuja and how the hymns of Āḻvārs have influenced the Vaiṣṇava Ācāryas of later period, I have tried to discuss the Philosophy of the Āḻvārs in the background of the Upaniṣads, Vedānta-sūtra, Āgamas, Itihāsas and Vaiṣṇava Purāṇas. Besides philosophy, the theistic mysticism understood in the sense of ardent longing of the Āḻvārs for a direct vision of God is a predominant theme of some of the *prabandhams*. This important subject has also not received proper treatment in the limited literature available at present. The present book aims to cover it. For the first time such an attempt is being made here to present in English a comprehensive exposition of the Philosophy and Theistic Mysticism of the Āḻvārs. It is hoped that the book will be found useful by scholars as well as students of comparative religion.

In a work of this type, the use of terms both in Tamil and Sanskrit is unavoidable. Wherever they are used, their nearest English equivalent is given. I have avoided quoting the Tamil hymns in the body of the text as these would be difficult to read and comprehend by a person not conversant with Tamil. I have, however, given the English rendering of the verses as far as possible in lucid prose in order to convey the true import of the hymns which is often missed in a literal translation. Wherever necessary, the Tamil hymns and the interpretative statements from the commentaries are given in the footnotes in Roman script with the use of standard diacritical marks adopted for Sanskrit. The compound Tamil words in the hymns are split up to facilitate easy reading.

In the preparation of this book, I am guided primarily by the teaching of the essentials of the Viśiṣṭādvaita Vedānta imparted to me by my spiritual preceptor, the late Sri Gostipuram Sowmya Narayanacharya Swami (1878-1943). I am also guided by the knowledge of *Divyaprabandham* imparted to me by the late Sri Madhurantakam Veeraraghavacharya Swami (1900-1983) under whom I studied *Bhagavad-viṣayam* (commentary on *Tiruvāymoḻi*) which is the major source-book for the philosophy of the Āḻvārs. I am greatly indebted to both these Ācāryas. I have also consulted those few traditional Śrī Vaiṣṇava scholars who are available today in South India and I take this opportunity to express my grateful thanks to them.

I also wish to express my sincere thanks to Dr. V. Varadachari, Dr. V.K.N.S. Raghavan, Sri S.M. Krishnamachar, Sri A.N. Srinivasa Iyengar, Sri E.S. Bhuvarahachar and Dr. N.S. Anantharangachar who have gone through the major part of the typescript of the book and offered useful comments. My special thanks are due to my esteemed friend, Sri S. Srinivasachar who patiently read the entire typescript and made useful corrections. I owe a debt of gratitude to Sri R.K. Swamy, President, Vishishtadvaita Research Centre, Madras who made it possible to publish this book. I should also express my grateful thanks to the esteemed Professor S.K. Ramachandra Rao for evincing keen interest in my work and for graciously writing the foreword.

Bangalore
19 November, 1994

S.M. SRINIVASA CHARI

NOTES ON TRANSLITERATION

Sanskrit (Devanagari) Script

Vowels	a	ā	i	ī	u	ū	ṛ
	e	ai	o	au	aṁ	aḥ	
Consonants							
Gutturals		k	kh	g	gh	ṅ	
Palatals		c	ch	j	jh	ñ	
Cerebrals		ṭ	ṭh	ḍ	ḍh	ṇ	
Dentals		t	th	d	dh	n	
Labials		p	ph	b	bh	m	
Semi-vowels		y	r	l	v		
Sibilants		ś	ṣ	s	h	ḷ	kṣ

Tamil Script

Vowels	a	ā	i	ī	u	ū
	e	ē	ai	o	ō	au
Consonants						
Gutturals		k	ṅ			
Palatals		c	ñ			
Cerebrals		ṭ	ṇ			
Dentals		t	n			
Labials		p	m			
Semi-vowels		y	r	l	v	
Letters peculiar to Tamil		ḻ	ḷ	ṟ	ṉ	

Remarks

1. The Tamil alphabets are not fully phonetic as the Sanskrit alphabets are. These letters indicate different sounds in different connections. Following the way the Tamil words are actually pronounced, these are transliterated by adopting the standard diacritical marks as are used for Sanskrit., e.g. Āṇṭāḷ as Āṇḍāḷ, Caṭakopan as Śaṭakopan, tivyaprapantam as divyaprabandham, vīṭu as vīḍu, Kulacekara as Kulaśekhara, Tirumaṅkai as Tirumaṅgai.
2. ழ (ḻ) is a peculiar Tamil guttural. It is transliterated by using a hyphen below l as ḻ instead of two dots below it as l̤.
3. ள (ḷ) is a Tamil palatal and it is transliterated with a dot below the letter l as ḷ.
4. ற (r) is a hard palatal pronounced after a soft consonant. It is transliterated with a hyphen below r as ṟ.
5. ன (n) as distinct from the consonant ந (n) is transliterated with a hyphen below n as ṉ. The grammatical rule regarding the use of these two letters is not strictly observed.

LIST OF ABBREVIATIONS

ĀH	Ācārya Hṛdaya of Aḻakiyamaṇavāḷaperumāḷ Nāyanār
AiUp	Aiteraya Upaniṣad
ĀP	Ārāyirappaḍi of Piḷḷān (commentary on Tiruvāymoḻi)
BG	Bhagavadgītā
BP	Bhāgavata Purāṇa
BrUp	Bṛhadāraṇyaka Upaniṣad
ChUp	Chāndogya Upaniṣad
DTR	Dramiḍopaniṣat-tātparya-ratnāvaḷī of Vedānta Deśika.
Īḍu	Muppattiyārāyarappaḍi of Vaḍakku Tiruvīdi Piḷḷai (commentary on Tiruvāymoḻi)
ITi	Iraṇḍām Tiruvandādi of Pūtattāḻvār
KaUp	Kaṭha Upaniṣad
Mbh	Mahābhārata
MUp	Muṇḍaka Upaniṣad
MTi	Mudal Tiruvandādi of Poygai Āḻvār
MuTi	Mūṉṟām Tiruvandādi of Peyāḻvār
NacTM	Nācciyār Tirumoḻi of Āṇḍāḷ
NanTi	Nānmukaṉ Tiruvandādi of Tirumaḻiśai Āḻvār
NUp	Nārāyaṇa Upaniṣad
PeriTM	Periyāḻvār Tirumoḻi of Periyāḻvār
PeruTM	Perumāḷ Tirumoḻi of Kulaśekharāḻvār
PTM	Periya Tirumoḻi of Tirumaṅgai Āḻvār
PPS	Periya Parakālasvāmī's commentary on Tiruvāymoḻi

RB	Rāmānuja's Śrī-Bhāṣya (commentary on Vedānta-sūtra)
RTS	Rahasyatrayasāra of Vedānta Deśika
ṚV	Ṛgveda
RRB	Raṅgarāmānuja Bhāṣya on Tiruvāymoḻi
ŚB	Śaṁkara Bhāṣya on Vedānta-sūtra
ŚvUp	Śvetāśvatara Upaniṣad
ŚS	Śabdārtha of Sākṣātsvāmi on Tiruvāymoḻi
TNUp	Taittirīya Nārāyaṇa Upaniṣad
TUp	Taittirīya Upaniṣad
TVM	Tiruvāymoli of Nammāḻvār
Up	Upaniṣad
VD	Vedānta Deśika
VP	Viṣṇu Purāṇa
VS	Vedānta-sūtra of Bādarāyaṇa

INTRODUCTION

Śrī Vaiṣṇavism, the oldest monotheistic religion of India having its roots in the Vedas and Upaniṣads, has passed through several stages of development before it was expounded by Rāmānuja as a full-fledged theological system with a strong philosophical basis.[1] The four important phases that can be discerned in this development are: the Vedic period, the period of the Itihāsas and Purāṇas, the period of the Āgamas and the period of the Āḻvārs or the twelve Vaiṣṇava Saints of South India.[2] Of these the last phase is of special importance because the Tamil hymns of the Āḻvārs, which are the spontaneous outpourings of their divine experience contain rich philosophical and theological ideas related to the three fundamental doctrines of the Viśiṣṭādvaita Vedānta and Vaiṣṇava religion namely, *tattva* or the Ultimate Reality, *hita* or the means of its attainment and *puruṣārtha* or the supreme goal of life. The teachings of the Āḻvārs are not basically different from what is said in the Vedas, the Epics and the Āgamas. Their uniqueness, however, lies in the fact that they are presented for the first time to the common people in their spoken language (Tamil). In view of this, they have been accorded an important place in the history of Vaiṣṇavism.

The names, dates and other biographical details of the Āḻvārs including their works are outlined in the subsequent chapter.[3] The Āḻvārs were born in South India between the 6th and 8th

1. See for details Srinivasa Chari, *Vaiṣṇavism—Its Philosophy, Theology and Religious Discipline*, Chapter 1.
2. The term Āḻvār literally means one who is immersed deeply in the divine experience. It is an honorific title used in respect of the Vaiṣṇava Saints of South India.
3. See Chapter 1.

centuries of the Christian era. They were saints who devoted their entire life to the worship of Viṣṇu as the Supreme Deity. Blessed with spiritual insight and intense love for God, they sang the glory of Viṣṇu and spent their active life in the divine service. They have bequeathed a rich heritage of sublime poetical compositions known as *prabandham*. There are twenty-four *prabandhams*.[1] The number of hymns in each one varies from ten to eleven hundred making a total of four thousand and hence they are known as *Nālāyira Divya-prabandham*[2] or the collection of Four Thousand Divine Hymns. The hymns in general are laudatory Tamil songs in praise of the glory of God in all His aspects. They are intensely devotional in character and represent the spontaneous outpourings of their deep love and experience of God. They have, therefore, gained great religious significance and are highly esteemed by the Vaiṣṇava Ācāryas. They are also recited by the Vaiṣṇavas during worship in temples and at homes on certain special occasions.

These hymns, apart from their religious significance, also contain rich philosophical and theological ideas. As devotional poems they appear to be similar to the devotional songs of other mystics such as the *Tevāram* and the *Tiruvācakam* of Nāyanmārs (Śaiva devotees), the *Kīrtanas* of Tyāgarāja and Purandaradāsa, the *Gīta-govinda* of Jayadeva, the *Bhajans* of Meera and the *Abhaṅgas* of Maharashtra saints. On closer examination, however, the Āḻvārs' hymns can be found to stand on a different footing. They embody the philosophy of the Upaniṣads as interpreted by Rāmānuja together with the Vaiṣṇava theology developed on the basis of the *Vedas*, the Pāñcarātra Āgamas, the Epics and the *Vaiṣṇava Purāṇas*. These compositions of the Āḻvārs are not merely intended to promote the *bhakti* cult, as is commonly believed but they aim at disseminating the knowledge of the Vedānta Philosophy among the common people through the familiar medium of Tamil. This fact can be seen conspicuously in the *Tiruvāymoḻi* of Nammāḻvār which comprises 1,102 verses. The

1. See pp. 36-38.
2. The word *divya* denotes the Supreme Being (*divi sthitam divyam bhagavantam*) and *prabandha* means that which captures Him (*prakarṣeṇa badhnāti*). The Hymns are Divine because they reveal lucidly the glory of God.
See S.S. Iyengar, *Candamihu Tamiḻ Marai*, Vol. 1, Introduction.

Vaiṣṇava Ācāryas regard this work as *Drāviḍa Veda* or *Dramiḍa Upaniṣad* in the sense that it contains the quintessence of the Upaniṣadic teachings. Acknowledging its philosophical character, scholarly commentaries have been written on the *Tiruvāymoḻi* by eminent Ācāryas of the post-Rāmānuja period: Tirukkurukai Pirān Piḷḷān (1068 A.D.), Nañjīyar (1113 A.D.), Periyavāccān Piḷḷai (1168 A.D.), Vaḍakkutiruvīdi Piḷḷai (1167 A.D.), Aḻakiyamaṇavāḷa Jīyar (1242 A.D.) Vedānta Deśika (1268 A.D.),[1] Raṅgarāmānuja (circa 1650 A.D.), Periya Parakālasvāmi (1676 A.D.) and Sākṣātsvāmi (circa 1700 A.D.). Several independent treatises known as *Sampradāya Granthas* (traditional works dealing with esoteric doctrines) contributed between the 12th and 15th centuries have drawn material from the *Tiruvāymoḻi*. Thus, the *Nālāyira Divyaprabandham* in general and the *Tiruvāymoḻi* in particular along with their commentaries serve as important source-book for both the Viśiṣṭādvaita Vedānta and Vaiṣṇava religion, to the same extent as are the Upaniṣads, the *Vedānta-sūtra* and the *Bhagavadgītā*.

The philosophical contribution of the Āḻvārs to the development of Viśiṣṭādvaita Vedānta does not seem to be widely appreciated among modern scholars. This is primarily due to the fact that it is written in classical Tamil and the commentaries on it are mostly in *maṇipravāḷa*[2] (Tamil language interspersed with Sanskrit) which is not easily understood by non-Tamil speaking persons. The literature in English on the subject is sadly inadequate. During the last hundred years, a few sporadic attempts have been made to present the teachings of the Āḻvārs in English. The earliest work is the one written by Alkondavalli Govindacharya under the title "Divine Wisdom of the Drāviḍa Saints" published in 1902. This contains a summary of the selected topics related mostly to the divine glory and attributes illustrated by anecdotes drawn from the commentary on

1. These dates are taken as given in the *Ponviḻa Malar* in Tamil published by S. Krishnaswamy Ayyangar, Puttur (Tiruchy), 1978.
   See also N. Subba Reddiar: *Religion and Philosophy of the Nāḻāyiram*, Appendix VI.
2. The word *maṇipravāḷa* literally means gems or pearls (*maṇi*) and *corals* (*pravāḷa*). It refers to the style of writing in which the Tamil words are interspersed with Sanskrit words, even as gems and corals are strung together alternately in a necklace.

Tiruvāymoḻi (*Īḍu*). The next book appeared in 1929 under the title "Hymns of the Āḻvārs" written by J.S.M. Hooper. It gives a translation of the *Tiruviruttam* of Nammāḻvār (100 verses), the *Tiruppāvai* of Āṇḍāḷ (30 verses) and a few selected hymns of Periyāḻvār, Kulaśekharan and Tirumaṅgai with a brief general introduction and notes. The book of K.C. Varadachari under the title "Āḻvārs of South India" published by Bharatiya Vidya Bhavan, Bombay in 1966 presents a brief sketch of the biography and selected teachings of the Āḻvārs. The next work is the one written by N. Subba Reddiar under the title "Religion and Philosophy of Nālāyiram with special reference to Nammāḻvār" published in 1979 by the Venkatesvara University, Tirupati. It is a voluminous book containing a lot of material not having a direct bearing on the philosophical teachings of the Āḻvārs. One other book jointly contributed by R.D. Kaylor and K.K.A. Venkatachari under the title "God Far, God Near" published in 1981 by the Ananthacharya Indological Research Institute, Bombay claims to present an interpretation of the thoughts of Nammāḻvār without leaning on traditional commentaries thereon. It is rather sketchy and as such does not bring out adequately the philosophical theories of all the Āḻvārs. Recently another book under the title "Tamil Veda" authored jointly by John Carman and Vasudha Narayanan has been published by the Chicago University Press, Chicago. This book is mainly concerned with the study of the earliest commentary written by Piḷḷān in maṇipravāḷa on the *Tiruvāymoḻi* with a view to finding out how the Tamil poetic tradition of the Āḻvārs is fused with the Vaiṣṇavite commentarial tradition in Sanskrit on Vedānta. Though it covers a few theological topics with the purpose of evaluating Piḷḷān's interpretation of the hymns, it does not present the philosophical doctrines of the Āḻvārs comprehensively. Besides these independent works,[1] a few translations of the Hymns of Nammāḻvār in English have been published. In the absence of

---

1. The following books include some material on the Āḻvārs, but these do not discuss their philosophical teachings:
   P.N. Srinivasa Chari: *Mystics and Mysticism*, Madras, 1951.
   D. Ramaswamy Ayyangar: *Peeps into Mysticism*, Madras, 1962.
   Dr. S.N. Dasgupta: *A History of Indian Philosophy*, Vol. III.
   Friedhelm Hardy: *Viraha-Bhakti* (The Early History of Kṛṣṇa Devotion in South India), Oxford University Press, Delhi, 1983.

detailed notes and introduction, these translations which are literal do not bring out fully the philosophical ideas implicit in the hymns of the Āḻvārs.

It may be noted in this connection that the Āḻvārs, as staunch devotees of Viṣṇu have composed the poems against the background of the Viśiṣṭādvaita Vedānta as enunciated in the Upaniṣads, the *Vedānta-sūtra,* the *Bhagavadgītā,* the *Vaiṣṇava Purāṇas* and the *Pāñcarātra Āgamas.* A full and in-depth understanding of the philosophy imbedded in the hymns of the Āḻvārs calls for a knowledge of ancient Tamil in all its idiomatic nuances, deep insight into Vedānta as expounded by Rāmānuja and the underlying tenets of Vaiṣṇavism. It is not, therefore, surprising that many of the books authored by well-meaning scholars have not succeeded in doing full justice to the philosophy of the Āḻvārs. We have on the other hand, an extensive literature written mostly in Sanskritised Tamil by both the traditional and contemporary Vaiṣṇava Ācāryas in the form of commentaries and independent treatises which explain in detail the philosophy of the Āḻvārs. With due deference to these authors it must be said that most of them, being carried away by the devotional aspect of the hymns, have glorified the views of the Āḻvārs, by imposing on the hymns the theological ideas that came to be developed later during the post-Rāmānuja period. A balanced and dispassionate approach to the Āḻvārs' hymns needs to be made in order to understand properly the philosophical teachings contained in them. This book attempts to make such a study.

Scope of the Book

The important topics covered by the *prabandhams* are:

1. The nature of Ultimate Reality
2. Nārāyaṇa as *para-tattva*
3. The theory of Goddess *Śrī* as inseparable from God
4. The divine attributes
5. The divine body
6. The divine incarnations
7. The importance of *arcā* deities
8. The cosmic functions of God
9. The divine *līlās*
10. The nature of the individual self

11. Human bondage and freedom of the soul
12. The longing of the soul for divine communion
13. Aspects of mystic experience of God
14. The concept of *bhakti*
15. The theory of *bhakti-yoga* as means of God-realization
16. The theory of *prapatti* as direct means to *mokṣa*
17. The simpler methods of worship of God
18. The concept of grace
19. The concept of *kaiṅkarya* for Bhagavān
20. The concept of *Bhāgavata-Śeṣatva*
21. The nature of spiritual goal
22. The concept of *paramapada*
23. The theory of *mokṣa* and *kaivalya*
24. The Vaiṣṇava *dharma.*

All these theories are not the innovations of the Āḻvārs. These are found in the Upaniṣads, the Pāñcarātra Āgamas and the Purāṇas that existed long before the Āḻvārs were born. A few of the Āḻvārs, particularly Nammāḻvār, who are said to be born yogis intuited these philosophic truths even as the Ṛgvedic seers did. Others who have had an opportunity to acquire knowledge like Tirumaḻiśai, Kulaśekharan and Toṇḍaraḍippoḍi would have gathered them from the sacred texts. They have had divine inspiration and presented the philosophical theories as arising from their own experience. Hence the *Divyaprabandham* has assumed a special importance for the Śrī Vaiṣṇavas.

The various topics referred to in the Tamil *prabandhams* are not presented as full-fledged doctrines with supporting arguments in a systematic order as in a philosophical treatise. These are found scattered in different parts of the poems. On the basis of this available material, the following pages attempt to present the philosophical and theological theories of the Āḻvārs in a logical sequence under the following headings:

1. The Doctrine of the Ultimate Reality (*Paratattva*)
2. The Doctrine of God (*Īśvara*)
3. The Doctrine of the Individual Self (*Jīvātma*)
4. The Doctrine of *Sādhana* (*hita*)
5. The Doctrine of the Supreme Goal (*parama-puruṣārtha*)
6. The Theistic Mysticism.

The first five correspond to the three principal topics covered in the *Vedānta-sūtra* viz., *tattva, hita* and *puruṣārtha.* Though in the Viśiṣṭādvaita Vedānta, God of religion is not different from the Ultimate Reality of the Upaniṣads, a separate chapter is devoted to the Doctrine of God for the reason that the hymns of the Āḻvārs are predominately theistic dealing with a vivid description of the different aspects of God viz., divine attributes, divine personality, divine incarnations and divine deeds. In discussing this subject, greater importance is given to the theological significance of these aspects of Godhead than the mythological episodes connected with them.

The theistic mysticism understood in the sense of an ardent longing for a direct vision of God is the predominant theme of the hymns of the Āḻvārs. The saints who were inspired by their deep love and experience of God have naturally given expression to their emotional feelings in many ways. In the case of Nammāḻvār and Tirumaṅgai Āḻvār, they have assumed the role of a *nāyakī,* or consort of the Lord and sought to convey their longing for God either through the media of the maiden or through her imaginary mother and companions and sometimes through messengers in the form of the birds or other objects of nature. A large number of the hymns in the poems of Nammāḻvār and Tirumaṅgai Āḻvār deal with this aspect of mystic experience. Āṇḍāḷ, the only female Vaiṣṇava Saint, takes on the role of a milkmaid and pours out her devotional love to Lord Kṛṣṇa. Periyāḻvār and Kulaśekharāḻvār adopt the guise of a mother to express their love to the divine child Kṛṣṇa. These devotional songs containing mystical elements have deep theological significance and they are not 'love poems' and 'mythological folk songs' as some scholars believe. A separate chapter is therefore devoted to this important subject to explain the true nature of Āḻvārs' mysticism and its theological significance.

These doctrines are presented with the hymns as the source material. Though the various commentaries have been consulted, the details found in them are not included in this presentation for two reasons. First, some of the views expressed by the commentators, though apparently valid, are of a later origin, developed in the post-Rāmānuja period. Without questioning the authority of the statements of the traditional scholars, it is preferred to present the teachings of the Āḻvārs in the background of the Upaniṣads, the *Vedānta-sūtra*, the Itihāsas, the Purāṇas and the Āgamas which preceded the age of the Āḻvārs and which constitute the basis for its philosophy and theology.

The second important reason for this approach is that the teachings of the Āḻvārs have considerably influenced Rāmānuja and the later Vaiṣṇava Ācāryas in developing the Vaiṣṇava religion as it is now practised. In order to evaluate the extent of such an influence, it is considered desirable to study the hymns without imposing on them the thoughts and interpretations of later day scholars. This will enable the modern scholars to appreciate the philosophical contents of the Tamil hymns and their contribution to the development of Vaiṣṇavism. It is hoped that this attempt to provide an authentic and comprehensive account of the philosophical and theological teachings of the Āḻvārs including their Mysticism would be found useful by readers not familiar with the Tamil *Divyaprabandham*.

Chapter 1

LIFE AND WORKS OF THE ĀḺVĀRS

The principal Āḻvārs in the chronological order according to the traditional dates and also as acknowledged by Vedānta Deśika[1] and Maṇavāḷamāmuni[2] are:

1. Poygai Āḻvār
2. Pūtattāḻvār
3. Peyāḻvār
4. Tirumaḻiśai Āḻvār
5. Nammāḻvār
6. Kulaśekharāḻvār
7. Periyāḻvār
8. Toṇḍaradippoḍi Āḻvār
9. Pāṇāḻvār
10. Tirumaṅgai Āḻvār.

To these ten are added Āṇḍāḷ and Madhurakavi. The former is the adopted daughter of Periyāḻvār, while the latter is a devoted disciple of Nammāḻvār and hence they are also included in the list. For all practical purposes, they are treated as Āḻvārs and their compositions are also regarded as part of the collection of

---

1. *Adhikārasaṅgraha,* verse 1.
   See also *Prabandhasāra,* verse 17.
   The verse in the *Adhikārasaṅgraha* does not mention the names of ten principal Āḻvārs in the chronological order. But the verse in the *Prabandhasāra* which includes Madhurakavi and Āṇḍāḷ refers to them in the chronological order.
2. *Upadeśaratnamālai,* verse 4.

four thousand Tamil hymns known as *Nālāyira Divyaprabandham*.

The biographical account of these Āḻvārs is given in works such as *Divyasūri-caritam* and *Guruparamparās* which were mostly written in the post-Rāmānuja period, several centuries after the life-time of the Āḻvārs. The *Divyasūri-caritam* is the earliest poetical work composed in Sanskrit in the 11th century by Garuḍavāhana Paṇḍita, who is claimed to be a contemporary of Rāmānuja. Based on this, two other biographical works have appeared at a later period. The first one was written in Maṇipravāḷa style by a Pinpaḻakiyaperumāḷ jīyar (about 13th century) under the title of *Guruparamparāprabhāvam-ārāyirappaḍi*. The second book was contributed by Tṛtīya Brahmatantra Parakālasvāmi (about 14th century) bearing the title of *Guruparamparāprabhāvam-mūvāyirappaḍi*. During the last five hundred years other Vaiṣṇava scholars have written biographies both on the Āḻvārs and the Ācāryas but what is generally accepted are the two works referred to above.

The life sketch of the Āḻvārs as presented in the *Guruparamparās* is full of miraculous anecdotes. In the absence of reliable historical and other credible evidence it is difficult to accept them on their face value. However, we can attempt a brief biographical sketch of the Āḻvārs on the basis of the available material in their hymns and the *tanians* (reverential verses) pertaining to them.

I. *Dates of the Āḻvārs*

Before we outline the life of the Āḻvārs individually we may discuss their origin and dates of birth. Tradition assigns high antiquity to the Āḻvārs, taking them to 4200 B.C. to 2700 B.C. and also regards them as divine incarnations. According to the *Guruparamparās*, the first four Āḻvārs—Poygai, Pūtattār, Pey and Tirumaḻiśai—were born at the end of Dvāparayuga which will correspond to 4200 B.C. Madhurakavi is also believed to have taken birth in the Dvāpara era corresponding to 3222 B.C. Nammāḻvār, Kulaśekharāḻvār, Periyāḻvār and Āṇḍāḷ were born during the first century of Kaliyuga which approximates to 3101 B.C. to 3003 B.C. The remaining three Āḻvārs—Toṇḍaraḍippoḍi, Pāṇan and Tirumaṅgai—took birth in the years of 298, 343 and 399 respectively of Kaliyuga which correspond to 2803 B.C., 2758 B.C. and 2702 B.C.[1]

1. See A. Govindacharya, *The Holy Lives of the Āḻvārs*. See also *Divyasūri* (Āḻvār) *Caritāni*, Appendix II.

Modern scholars have questioned these dates and assigned a period ranging from the 5th to the 9th centuries A.D. on the basis of a few historical evidences.[1] There is no unanimity among them regarding the dates of the Āḻvārs. Dr. N. Subba Reddiar has, however, attempted a critical evaluation of the views of these scholars and arrived at the following dates for the Āḻvārs:[2]

1.	Poygai Āḻvār	713 A.D.
2.	Pūtattāḻvār	713 A.D.
3.	Peyāḻvār	713 A.D.
4.	Tirumaḻiśai Āḻvār	720 A.D.
5.	Toṇḍaraḍippoḍi Āḻvār	726 A.D.
6.	Kulaśekharāḻvār	767 A.D.
7.	Tiruppāṇāḻvār	781 A.D.
8.	Tirumaṅgai Āḻvār	776 A.D.
9.	Periyāḻvār	785 A.D.
10.	Āṇḍāḷ	767 A.D.
11.	Nammāḻvār	798 A.D.
12.	Madhurakavi	800 A.D.

Even these dates lack clear historical evidence. Besides there are few discrepancies in these dates. Āṇḍāl who is the adopted daughter of Periyāḻvār could not have been born earlier than Periyāḻvār. Nammāḻvār who is admitted by the traditional scholars as belonging to a period earlier than the other Āḻvārs except the first four, could not be the last but one in the chronological order. Further, the reference made in the *Bhāgavata Purāṇa* to the birth of the Āḻvārs goes against the views of modern scholars. This Purāṇa states:

> In the beginning of Kaliyuga persons exclusively devoted to Nārāyaṇa and endowed with spiritual knowledge will be born here and there but in large numbers in the land of the Drāviḍas where flow the rivers Tāmraparṇī, Kṛtamālā

1. See S. Krishnaswamy Aiyangar, *Early History of Vaiṣṇavism in South India*, pp. 4-13.
   R.G. Bhandarkar, *Vaiṣṇavism, Śaivism and Minor Religious Systems*, pp. 69-70.
   T.A. Gopinatha Rao, *History of Vaiṣṇavas.*
2. See Dr. N. Subba Reddiar, *Religion and Philosophy of Nālāyiram*, Chapter IX and Appendix VII.

(Vaigai), Payasvinī (Pālār), the holy Kāverī and the Mahānadī (Periyār) which runs westwards.[1]

This verse is quoted by Vedānta Deśika in the *Guruparamparāsāram* predicting the advent of the Āḻvārs in South India. It may be noted that Nammāḻvār and Madhurakavi were born on the banks of Tāmraparṇī, Periyāḻvār and Āṇḍāḷ in a place close to Vaigai, Poygai Āḻvār, Pūtattāḻvār, Peyāḻvār and Tirumaḻiśai Āḻvār near the Pāḻār and Toṇḍaraḍippoḍi Āḻvār, Tiruppāṇāḻvār and Tirumaṅgai Āḻvār on the banks of the Kāverī. While the places of birth are indicated, there is no mention of the period of their birth except in a general way that they will appear in the Kaliyuga. The word Kaliyuga may mean either the early part of the Kali era as claimed by traditional scholars or even during much later years of Kali, as contended by modern scholars. It cannot, however, support the view that a few Āḻvārs were born in Dvāparayuga unless the words 'in Kali era' are interpreted to include the years preceding it.[2]

Some scholars have questioned the antiquity of the *Bhāgavata Purāṇa* and also the validity of this verse which is regarded as an interpolation. There is no substantial evidence to prove this view. The *Bhāgavata* is regarded by all schools of Vedānta as one of the ancient Purāṇas, narrated by sage Śuka as taught by sage Vyāsa. Madhva (12th century) has annotated on it. So also Vedānta Deśika has accepted its authority. It was not composed, as some scholars claim either during the period of Āḻvārs or at a later time since we find the influence of the teachings of the *Bhāgavata* on the Āḻvārs. If the *Pāñcarātra Āgamas*, the Epics and the *Vaiṣṇava Purāṇas* are accorded an antiquity, the Āḻvārs too should enjoy an antiquity since they were born after the advent of these works. If the date of the composition of the *Pāñcarātra Saṁhitās* and the *Mahābhārata* are put down to the early period of the Christian era,

1. BP XI.5. 38-40.
kalau khalu bhaviṣyanti nārāyaṇa-parāyaṇāḥ;
kvacin-kvacin-mahābhāgā drāmiḍeṣu ca bhūriśaḥ;
tāmraparṇī nadī yatra kṛtamālā payasvinī;
kāverī ca mahābhāgā pratīcī ca mahānadī.
2. Some traditional scholars have quoted verses from *Brahmakaivarta Purāṇa* and *Nāradīya Purāṇa* in support of the birth of some of the Āḻvārs in earlier yugas (*Kṛta* and *Tretā*) but these do not appear to be authoritative statements.

then in all probability the Āḻvārs belong to the period ranging from the 5th to the 8th centuries. The references to a few temples such as Parameśvara-viṇṇkaram, Canjeevaram built in 770-780 A.D. by Parameśvara Varman I, places such as Kaḍalmallai (the present Mahabalipuram), the historical personality such as Paḻlavarkōṉ (ruler of Pallavas) cannot be construed to give any specific dates because temples and persons bearing the same names could have existed even in an earlier period. According to the Āgamas, which is the main source of authority for the belief in the presence of divinity in a temple, God can reveal Himself in the form of an *arcā* deity (icon) at a religious centre even prior to the construction of a temple which can take place in stages at a later period.[1] The Āḻvārs often address a God in His manifested form as an icon without the mention of the temples. In view of these facts and also in the absence of adequate internal evidence and inscriptional support, it is difficult to come to an undisputed conclusion in this matter.

The dates of the Āḻvārs are not really relevant for the purpose of the study of their philosophy and religion. The important point to be taken note of for the purpose of our study is that the Āḻvārs were born long before Nāthamuni (823 A.D.) and Rāmānuja (1017 A.D.) who were greatly influenced by their teachings. Similarly, they belong to a period which is later than the period of the Āgamas, the Epics and the older Purāṇas, since their hymns disclose a deeper knowledge of these works.

II. *Divine Origin of the Āḻvārs*

Coming to the origin of the Āḻvārs, the tradition regards them as divine incarnations. The first four Āḻvārs—Pūtattār, Poygai, Pey, Tirumaḻiśai—were incarnations of weapons of Viṣṇu—*gadā* (mace), *śaṅkha* (conch), *nandaka* (sword) and *cakra* (discus) respectively. Nammāḻvār was an incarnation of *Viśvaksena,* the divine angel; Kulaśekharāḻvār of *kaustubha* (the ornament worn on the chest of Viṣṇu). Periyāḻvār, Toṇḍaraḍippoḍi Āḻvār and Tirumaṅgai Āḻvār were incarnations of *Garuḍa* (the divine bird), *vanamāla* (the garland worn by Viṣṇu) and *sāraṅga* (the bow of Viṣṇu) respectively. Pāṇāḻvār is considered as the manifestation of *Śrīvatsa,* the

1. See Chapter 3, p. 117.

mole in Viṣṇu's chest, whereas Madhurakavi is regarded as representing the chief of *Viṣṇugaṇa.* In the case of Āṇḍāḷ, she is taken as a manifestation of *Bhū-devī,* one of the consorts of Viṣṇu.

Apart from the divine origin, the tradition also speaks of a supernatural birth in respect of a few Āḻvārs. Thus, Poygai Āḻvār is said to have sprung from a lotus flower in the tank near the Yathoktakāri Temple at Conjeevaram, Pūtattāḻvār out of *mādhavi* flower in Tirukkaḍanmallai (the present Mahabalipuram) and Peyaḻvār from a red lotus in a well near Mayūrapuri (the present Mylapore in Madras). Āṇḍāḷ was discovered as an infant lying in the flower garden maintained by Periyāḻvār. There are other miraculous episodes associated with some of the Āḻvārs. Tirumaḻiśai Āḻvār was born to a sage named Bhṛgu who was enticed by a celestial nymph during his penance and the baby born out of this union was deserted by the nymph in a jungle but later picked up by a hunter who reared it. Nammāḻvār was born to a pious parents belonging to the Vellala family of Tirukkuruhūr, now known as Āḻvār-Tirunagari in the Tirunelveli district of Tamil Nadu (South India). Right from his infancy he entered into yogic meditation under a tamarind tree in the precinct of the Viṣṇu temple, where he remained in meditation for sixteen years. Āṇḍāḷ was offered in marriage to Lord Raṅganātha, the deity at Śrīraṅgam temple and soon after marriage she was absorbed in the deity. Similarly, Pāṇāḻvār belonging to the lowest caste was carried on the shoulders of the temple priest at the command of the Lord Raṅganātha but as soon as he entered the sanctum sanctorum, he vanished becoming one with the deity. Tirumaṅgai Āḻvār who led a life of a brigand in younger days was transformed into a saint through the marriage with a celestial being who grew up as a handsome young lady in a Vaiṣṇava family.

To a rational mind these stories sound fictitious. Before we brush aside such accounts we have to understand their underlying spiritual significance. According to the theory of *avatāra,* which is distinctive feature of Vaiṣṇavism, Viṣṇu, the Supreme Being, incarnates Himself in various forms for the purpose of protection of human beings by way of establishing *dharma* or righteousness and destruction of the evil forces. He condescends out of His will (*saṅkalpa*) to come down from His heavenly abode as and when the occasion demands, not only in human form but also in the form of other living beings. The *Jayākhya Saṁhitā,* one of the oldest Pāñcarātra treatises, says: "The Supreme Deity, Nārāyaṇa Himself assumes the form of a human being out of compassion and uplifts the world submerged in the darkness of ignorance by extending his helping hand in the form of *śāstra* or sacred texts."[1] Another verse in *Viṣṇudharma* more specifically states: "In the *yuga* of Kali, the Lord Acyuta (Viṣṇu) enters into the respective human beings already born and carries out His tasks."[2] This is known as *anupraveśāvatāra*, that is, God infuses special power into the selected individuals and make them function as sages, saints and preceptors endowed with extraordinary spiritual power to propagate the philosophic knowledge. On the authority of these *smṛti* texts, Vedānta Deśika explains the significance of the advent of ten Āḻvārs at a particular point of time. Thus he says:

> Nārāyaṇa assumed a new series of ten incarnations in the form of *Parāṅkuśa* (Nammāḻvār), *Parakāla* (Tirumaṅgai Āḻvār) and others; just as the clouds gather the moisture from the ocean and then pour it down in the form of rain so essential to the life of all the living beings, the Lord in the guise of ten *avatāras* collected together those essential teachings of the Vedas which are of significance and revealed them briefly in a language (Tamil) which is understood by everyone.[3]

In the light of these explanations, the supernatural birth of some of the Āḻvārs and the miraculous episodes connected with them have some relevance. As the hymns composed by them would reveal, they were all born-saints gifted with extraordinary spiritual insight into the glory of God.

---

1. *Jayākhya Saṁhitā: sakṣāt nārāyaṇo devaḥ kṛtvāmartyamayīm tanum; magnān uddharate lokān kāruṇyāt śāstrapāṇinā.*
2. *Viṣṇudharma* 108.50: *pūrvotpanneṣu bhūteṣu teṣu teṣu kalau prabhuḥ; anupraviśya kurute yat samīhitam acyutaḥ.*
   According to one interpretation, "*purvotpanneṣu bhūteṣu*" is taken as *nityasūris*, the eternally existing souls; during their incarnations as human beings, the Lord enters into their bodies.
   See also VD *Śatadūṣaṇī, Vāda* 65:
   ādibhaktānāṁ ananta garuḍa viśvaksenādīnām avatāra viśeṣaḥ iti purāṇaprasiddhiḥ.
3. See RTS, *guruparamparāsāram*.

III. *The Life and Compositions of the Āḻvārs*

We do not have an authentic and fuller information about the life of the Āḻvārs other than what is narrated in the *guruparamparās.* However, on the basis of the material available in their hymns and the verses written by the early Vaiṣṇava Ācāryas as *tanians* (verses paying obeisance) on the Āḻvārs, we shall give a brief outline of each Āḻvār with a view to highlighting their greatness (*vaibhava).*

Poygai Āḻvār, Pūtattāḻvār and Peyāḻvār

These three are the earliest among the Āḻvārs and are known as "Mudal-āḻvārgal". According to the tradition they were born in the same year and month but on three consecutive days. Poygai Āḻvār, the earliest, was born near a tank in the proximity of Yathoktakāri temple located in Kanchi (the present Conjeevaram). He is so named because of his birth in *poygai* (tank). He is also known as Saroyogi, indicating his birth in a *saras* (tank). Pūtattāḻvār, the second Āḻvār, was born at Kaḍalmallai which is the present Mahabalipuram near Madras. He is so named because of the possession of divine knowledge out of God's grace.[1] He is also known by the name of Bhūta-Muni. Peyāḻvār, the third one, was born at Mylapore, a locality in the Madras city. The term *pey* means one who is possessed and as he was intoxicated with intense love for God, he was called Peyāḻvār. He is also called Mahadāhvaya Muni, signifying his greatness as one who had experienced God.

As devotees of God they were going from one religious centre to the other in search of God with a craving for a direct vision of Him. The story goes that on the night of a particular rainy day they chanced to come together seeking shelter from the heavy downpour of rain in a narrow entrance room of a hermitage near Tirukkovalur, a pilgrim centre in South India. According to the *guruparamparā* account, the place was so narrow that hardly one person could lie down, two could sit and three could stand. The first one to enter the place was Poygai Muni, then came in Pūtattār and a little later Peyāḻvār. While all the three were standing there,

1. *Bhūta* (Sanskrit equivalent of *Pūta*) means etymologically one who has gained *sattā* or sustenance by spiritual knowledge (*bhū sattāyāṁ vāci*).

meditating on God, they suddenly felt the presence of a fourth person who had squeezed in. Being curious to know the person who was pushing them, they saw to their dismay the intruder was no other than God. That they had a vision of God and His glory is brought out in the spontaneous hymns composed by them known as *Tiruvandādi*. In the opening hymn of the *Mūṉṟām Tiruvandādi*, Peyāḻvār exclaims:

> I now beheld the Goddess by the side of my Lord who has the lustre of the blue ocean; I saw the lustrous divine body of golden colour; I perceived the radiant sun-like form; I saw the beautiful discus that glows fiery in the battlefield and the lovely conch in the beauteous hands (of the Lord).

The other two Āḻvārs have expressed in a similar way the joy of the direct experience of God.

Each one of these Āḻvārs has composed one hundred hymns in praise of God known as *Tiruvandādi*. The words *anta* means end and *ādi* stands for beginning. *Andādi* is a kind of poetry in Tamil in which the last word or syllable of the preceding verse becomes the opening word or syllable of the succeeding verse. These three works which constitute the earliest poetical compositions contributed by the Vaiṣṇava saints of South India contain philosophical and theological ideas of Vaiṣṇavism. We shall deal with them separately while discussing the Philosophy of the Āḻvārs.

Tirumaḻiśai Āḻvār

Chronologically Tirumaḻiśai Āḻvār is the fourth among the Āḻvārs born in the same period as the first three Āḻvārs, at a place known as Tirumaḻiśai, also called Mahīsāra (near Madras city). He is also known by the name of *Bhaktisāra* indicating that he is the very personification of intense *bhakti* to God. Tradition speaks of many interesting anecdotes in his lifetime. From his own writings what is evident is that he was well-conversant with other schools of thought including Śaivism, Jainism and Buddhism, that he practised yoga over a long period and acquired tremendous yogic power and that he established conclusively that Nārāyana is the Supreme Deity (*paratattva*). At the outset of the *Nāṉmukaṉ Tiruvandādi*, he explicitly states:

Nārāyaṇa brought forth the four-faced (Brahmā); the four-faced one being the first (creature) himself begot Śaṁkara; being myself the first (seer), have made known this inner meaning (to all) in the form of *andādi*. Do thou comprehend this fully after careful examination and study.

Tirumaḻiśai Āḻvār has contributed two important works: (1) *Nāṉmukaṉ Tiruvandādi* comprising 96 hymns in the same style as the *Tiruvandādi* of the three earlier Āḻvārs; (2) *Tiruccanda-viruttam,* comprising 120 hymns. The first work is the earliest Vaiṣṇava treatise upholding the supremacy of Viṣṇu or Nārāyaṇa as against Brahmā and Rudra who are accorded a subordinate status and it is of considerable importance to the Vaiṣṇava Ācāryas of post-Rāmānuja period. The second work which is an excellent poetic composition full of rhythmic beauty contains important metaphysical ideas of the Viśiṣṭādvaita Vedānta. We shall give the details separately.

Nammāḻvār

Nammāḻvār is the most outstanding mystic saint both in terms of his extensive composition of the hymns and the distinctive contribution he made to the Vaiṣṇava Philosophy and Theology. He is, therefore, held in higher esteem by the Śrī Vaiṣṇavas and regarded as *kulapati,* the founder-seer of Vaiṣṇava community. He is fondly called *'Naṁ Āḻvār'* (our Saint). He was born at Tirukkuruhūr (the present town of Āḻvār Tirunagari in South India) in the vallala community to Kāriyar and Uḍayanaṅgaiyār, who were devotees of Viṣṇu. He was named Māraṉ by his parents. The other names by which he is popularly known are Śaṭhakopaṉ and Parāṅkuśa. He often calls himself in his hymns as *Māraṉ Śaṭhakopaṉ* or *Kuruhūr Śaṭhakopaṉ.*

Nammāḻvār who is regarded as a divine incarnation,[1] was a yogi even at the time of birth. According to tradition, he grew

1. Vaḍakku Tiruvīdipiḷḷai in his *Īḍu* describes Nammāḻvār as a *nitya saṁsārī* or as an individual born with bondage after passing through several births, as indicated in his own hymn *(māri māri pala pirappum pirandu...*II.6.8) but blessed with divine knowledge by God out of His unconditioned compassion (*nirhetuka kṛpā*).
See *Īḍu, Mudal Śriyaḥpati.*

up as an extraordinary child without any of the normal propensities of an infant. When his worried parents took the child to the local Viṣṇu temple, he chose to sit under the tamarind tree in the temple precincts and remained there in deep meditation for 16 years. Later when Madhurakavi discovered his spiritual power, he woke him up from the trance and sought him as his *guru.* Nammāḻvār who had experienced the vision of God then burst spontaneously into Tamil hymns of sublime beauty and mystic profundity. These are known as *Tiruvāymoḻi* or the Divine utterances.[1]

His own writings reveal that Nammāḻvār was gifted with spiritual knowledge. In the opening hymn of his *Tiruvāymoḻi* he says that he is blessed by God with knowledge leading to intense love for God (*matinalam*). He possessed adequate knowledge of the Vedas including the Upaniṣads, the *Rāmāyaṇa,* the *Mahābhārata,* the Purāṇas as well as the Āgamas. This is abundantly evident from the references he has made to the Upaniṣadic thoughts, the Paurāṇic episodes and the various incarnations of Viṣṇu. According to tradition, Nammāḻvār obtained all this knowledge by the grace of God through direct intuition, as in the case of Vedic seers and not by means of formal study under a preceptor.[2] Though he does not quote the *Śrutis* or Scriptural texts, the phrases used in the Tamil hymns convey the import of the Upaniṣadic statements. Nāthamuni extols Nammāḻvār as one who rendered Veda into Tamil (*Vedam tamiḻ śeyda māraṉ Śaṭhakopaṉ*).[3] Though Nammāḻvār was born in a lower caste (*śūdra*), he had the highest respect for the Vedas and the Brahmins who recite them.[4] As a true *bhakta* of Viṣṇu and also as a divine incarnation, caste did not affect either his status as a spiritual leader or the validity of his teachings.

Whether or not Nammāḻvār travelled widely is not known. He

---

1. The word *Tiruvāymoḻi* literally means sacred (*tiru*) words (*moḻi*) emanating from the mouth (*vāy*) of the saint.
2. See Parāśara Bhattar, *Raṅgarājastava,* verse 6.
   sahasra śākhāṁ yo adrākṣīt drāmiḍīṁ Brahma-saṁhitāṁ
   See also Vedānta Deśika, *Pādukāsahasra, verse* I.3
   āmnāyānāṁ prakṛtim-aparāṁ saṁhitāṁ dṛṣṭavantaṁ ...munim.
3. See *Kaṇṇinuṇ-śiruttāmbu,* taniyan 2.
4. See Chapter 8, p. 273, fn. 2.

has, however, sung the glory of the *arcā* deities in 33 shrines. There are references to *Vaḍamadurai* (the present Mathura in North India) and also to *Tuvarāpati* (Dwāraka). Barring these two, the farthest shrine from his native place is Tirupati (Andhra Pradesh). Most of the shrines referred to by him are closer to his native place located in the present Tirunalvali District (Tamil Nadu) and Kerala State. Tradition holds that Nammāḻvār had visions of these deities through his yogic powers.

The greatest achievement of Nammāḻvār in his life is the composition of four works comprising Tamil hymns dealing with Viśiṣṭādvaita Vedānta, Vaiṣṇava theology and theistic mysticism. These are: (1) *Tiruviruttam* comprising 100 verses, (2) *Tiruvāciriyam* consisting of 7 stanzas, (3) *Periya Tiruvandādi* comprising 87 verses, and (4) *Tiruvāymoḻi,* the largest poetic collection with 1,102 hymns.

Tiruviruttam, as the title itself suggests, is devoted primarily to narrate the ardent longing of the soul for communion with God. Nammāḻvār poses himself as a consort (*nāyakī),* who is separated from her Beloved Lord (*Nāyaka*) and expresses his yearning for a reunion with God. The physical and psychological conditions of the consort caused by the pangs of separation are described with a rich poetic imagery along with pathetic appeals to the Supreme Lord, both directly and through the media of the emissaries, seeking His grace for a direct union.

Tiruvāciriyam, named after the *āciriyappa* metre in which the poem is composed, describes briefly the God's personality, His glory, the ways and means of attaining Him and the nature of the supreme goal.

Periya Tiruvandādi is a poem written in the *andādi* style and is called great (*periya*), because it manifests the deep love of Āḻvār for God. It emphasises the greatness of God as the sole saviour of mankind and also as one who is easily accessible to the devotees towards whom He has a loving disposition. It advocates the need to worship Him in all possible ways, despite the incapacity of the human beings to comprehend His greatness and render appropriate divine service. By addressing his own mind, the Āḻvār conveys his ardent craving for direct experience of God.

The *Tiruvāymoḻi* is the largest and most important work of Nammāḻvār. This classical poem comprising 1,102 hymns is divided into ten sections known as *pattu* (centum) of about 100 verses each and each centum again subdivided into ten decads and each decad comprising eleven verses called *pāśurams*.[1] The hymns are basically devotional songs inspired by the experience of God. They speak about the glory of God in all its aspects. On the face of it the main trend of the *Tiruvāymoḻi* looks like an ardent longing of the Āḻvār for direct communion with God (*sākṣātkāra*) culminating in an uninterrupted divine service. According to the traditional scholars, its central theme is that God as the Ultimate Reality (*paratattva*) is the goal of human endeavour and that He Himself also serves as the means of attainment.[2] Each centum of the poem covers a specific subject-matter related to the central theme and the ten verses in a decad deal with specific topics supporting the main subject of the centum. Thus, the entire *Tiruvāymoḻi* is a well-knit philosophical work presenting the five doctrines of the Viśiṣṭādvaita Philosophy viz., Brahman or God to be attained (*prāpya*), the *jīva* or the aspirant seeking God (*prāptā*), the *sādhana* or the means of attainment (*prāptyupāya*), the goal to be attained (*phala*) and the obstacles in the way of its attainment (*prāpti-virodhi*).[3]

These four works are held in high esteem by the Vaiṣṇava Ācāryas. According to some, these represent the four Vedas—*Ṛg*, *Yajur*, *Sāma* and *Atharva*. According to another view which is acclaimed by all the Ācāryas, only *Tiruvāymoḻi* represents the *Drāmiḍa-veda* or *Tamiḻ-maṟai* (Tamil Veda). Nāthamuni, the foremost Viśiṣṭādvaita exponent, describes it as *drāviḍa-vedasāgara*, the ocean of Tamil Veda. Parāśara Bhattar regards it as *Drāmiḍa Brahma-Saṁhitā*. Vedānta Deśika considers the *Tiruvāymoḻi* as *Dramiḍa Upaniṣad* and has written two Sanskrit works in verse under the title of *Dramiḍopaniṣat-sāra* and *Dramiḍopaniṣat-tātparyaratnāvaḷī* giving the purport of the hymns as related to the *Bhagavad-guṇas*. Maṇavāḷamāmuni also acknowledges that

1. Only one decad (II.7) which refers to the twelve names of Viṣṇu comprises 13 verses. The last stanza in each decad speaks of the benefit accruing to one who chants the songs of that decad (*phalaśruti*). Thus the *Tiruvāymoḻi*, which is usually regarded as a poem of thousand *pāśurams*, actually contains 1,102 hymns on account of the 100 extra verses as *phalaśrutis* (one for each decad) and two additional hymns in the decad (II.7) devoted to 12 names of Viṣṇu.
2. See DTR verse 7. *devaḥ śrīmān svasiddheḥ karaṇamiti vadan ekamarthaṁ sahasre....*
3. See Chapter 8, pp. 268-70.

Nammāḻvār rendered Vedas into Tamil (*vedam tamiḻ śeyda meyyan*). The issue relating to the justification of these claims will be discussed in the concluding chapter.

Madhurakavi Āḻvār

Madhurakavi was born in a Brahmin family at Tirukkolur in South India, a few years earlier than Nammāḻvār. According to the tradition, Madhurakavi while he was on a pilgrimage to North India, saw the effulgence of the saint Nammāḻvār and from afar, he wended his way to the source of the effulgence and reached the tamarind tree under which Nammāḻvār was seated absorbed in meditation. He woke him up from the trance. After discovering the spiritual character of the saint he sought him as his *guru* and continued to serve him with utmost devotion. It is believed that he recorded the spontaneous outpourings of Nammāḻvār.

Nāthamuni has extolled the greatness of Madhurakavi in a verse written as a *tanian*:

> Madhurakavi knew saint Śaṭhakopa as the only true guide and preceptor; he knew none else other than him; he became overjoyed by singing the holy Upaniṣadic utterances of Śaṭhakopa. He hailed Nammāḻvār as the supreme master because of his ennobling qualities and benign virtues.

Vedānta Deśika regards Madhurakavi as a saint of exemplary character who has set an illustrious example of the deep devotion of a disciple to his *guru* (*ācāryā-bhakti*).

The only written contribution made by Madhurakavi is the poem of 11 verses in Tamil on Nammāḻvār under the title of *Kaṇṇinuṇ-śiruttāmbu* which also forms part of the *Nālāyira Divyaprabandham*. These verses portray, according to Vedānta Deśika, ten virtues of Nammāḻvār which are similar to the qualities of God in terms of offering protection and salvation to a soul. By chosing Śaṭhakopa as the sole refuge Madhurakavi has demonstrated that deep devotion and service to an *ācārya* (preceptor) is even of greater importance than service to God for attaining salvation. This poetical work of Madhurakavi has provided the doctrine of *ācārya-bhakti* which constitutes the corner-stone of the Vaiṣṇava theology.

Periyāḻvār

Periyāḻvār, also known as Viṣṇucitta and Bhattanātha, was born in an orthodox Brahmin family at Śrī Villiputtur in South India. As his name indicates, he was an ardent devotee of Viṣṇu and deeply engrossed in His contemplation. He engaged himself in rendering *kaiṅkarya* or divine service to the deity at the local Viṣṇu temple. As a part of this service he cultivated a flower garden and used to offer flowers daily to the deity. As recorded in his own hymns and the verses written by Nāthamuni and Vedānta Deśika in praise of Periyāḻvār, he won the distinction of establishing the truth that *Māl* (Nārāyaṇa) is the Supreme Deity (*Paratattva*). The story goes that Viṣṇucitta was called upon by the then Pandya King, Vallabhadeva to expound the quintessence of Veda and win the prize set up for the purpose. Though at first he was hesitant, he decided to go to the court taking it as a divine command. Amidst the other paṇḍitas seated in the royal assembly hall, he recited the relevant scriptural texts and established conclusively that Nārāyaṇa is the *Paratattva*.[1] He thus won the prize offered by the Pandyan King. As a mark of respect and adoration the king arranged for a ceremonial procession for Viṣṇucitta. When he was taken round the main road of the capital city on an elephant, he beheld the vision of the Lord Viṣṇu along with His consort Lakṣmī seated on Garuḍa (Viṣṇu's mount). The Āḻvār who was overwhelmed with joy at the sight of Viṣṇu burst out singing the famous hymn *pallāṇḍu* meaning 'May you Long Live for many years.'

One other miraculous event in the life of Periyāḻvār is the acquisition of a female child who was found in his flower garden. He adopted her as a daughter and brought her up fondly as a God-given gift. She was named Āṇḍāḷ, who was later offered in marriage to Lord Raṅganātha. We shall deal with this story separately.

---

1. See *PeriTM* IV.3.11.
vedānta viḻupporuḻiṉ mēlirunda viḷakkai,
viṭṭucittaṉ virittananē.
See also *Prabandha sāra*, verse 9.

The two important poetical works contributed by Periyāḻvār are: *Tiruppallāṇḍu*[1] comprising 12 verses and *Periyāḻvār Tirumoḻi* consisting of 461 hymns. The first one is a special type of song born out of the overwhelming joy after beholding the vision of God, expressed in the form of a prayer wishing an eternal existence for the Lord. The second one is a beautiful poetic work in which Periyāḻvār enjoys the glory of God in His incarnation as Kṛṣṇa. He poses himself as mother Yaśodā and conveys his love to God in terms of intense motherly solicitude for the child. He also sings the glory of Rāmāvatāra and a few *arcā* deities at selected religious centres. Many of the hymns cover the mystic experience of God. They are also pregnant with philosophic ideas. We shall deal with this subject later.

Āṇḍāḷ

Āṇḍāḷ also known as *Goda* was born at Śrī Villiputtur (South India). According to the Vaiṣṇava theology she is an incarnation of *Bhū-devī,* one of the consorts of Viṣṇu. She was found in the flower garden of Periyāḻvār and was brought up by him with great affection.

Right from her childhood she developed an intense love for God and yearned to marry Him. The intense yearning for union is conveyed by her in her hymns. The story goes that she used to decorate herself with the flower garland kept ready by her foster-father to be offered to the deity at the temple. One day her father noticed this act of his daughter and did not offer the garland already used by her. That night Periyāḻvār had a dream in which the Lord expressed His displeasure for not offering the garland worn by Goda and preferred to accept the one used by her. Periyāḻvār then realised the divine character of his foster-daughter and called her as *Śūḍikkoḍutta-nācciyār,* the goddess who offered the garland worn by her.

When the question of Āṇḍāḷ's marriage was causing concern for Periyāḻvār, the latter was commanded in a dream by Lord

1. According to some Vaiṣṇava Ācāryas including Vedānta Deśika *Tiruppallāṇḍu* is not a separate lyrical treatise but it is part of *Periyāḻvār Tirumoḻi.* Maṇavāḷamāmuni and his followers have accorded a separate status for it.

Raṅganātha to bring her to Śrīraṅgam and offer her in wedding to Him. Accordingly he took her to Śrīraṅgam and presented her to Lord Raṅganātha. As soon as Āṇḍāḷ entered the sanctum sanctorum of the deity, she was absorbed into the idol.

Āṇḍāḷ has contributed two poetical compositions: (1) *Tiruppāvai* comprising thirty hymns; (2) *Nācciyār Tirumoḻi* consisting of 143 hymns. The first one is held in high esteem by the Śrīvaiṣṇavas as the spiritual "song of songs". As the title (*pāvai*) indicates, it speaks of a religious rite (*vṛta*) observed by a bride during the month of Mārgaśīrṣa in the autumn season to secure a person of one's choice as husband. Keeping Lord Kṛṣṇa of Bṛndāvan in mind as her beloved bridegroom, Goda, in the guise of a *gopī* in love with Kṛṣṇa along with other companions implores the Lord to fulfil her cherished desire. The thirty poems portray beautifully the ritual ceremony (*nōṉpu*) observed in the early morning of the winter month, the awakening of companions from sleep, the waking of the persons in the Lord's mansion including His consort and finally imploring the Lord Himself to grant them the boon. But, these hymns, as explained by the Vaiṣṇava Ācāryas, carry much deeper import of a spiritual character. They speak about the nature of the Ultimate Reality and the means of attaining the supreme goal. In view of this philosophical significance *Tiruppāvai* is considered as the quintessence of the Upaniṣads. We shall deal with this aspect separately.

The second composition of Āṇḍāḷ known as *Nācciyār Tirumoḻi* contains the mystic outpourings of Āṇḍāḷ's intense love for Lord Kṛṣṇa seeking a union with the beloved Lord. The various aspects of the mystic experience of God-intoxicated woman—the anguish, the despondency, seeking the help of the God of love (*manmatha*), sending of messengers as mediators, the aggressive behaviour in the absence of favourable response from the lover are all depicted in erotic verses. Some of these hymns are also of theological significance as they focus on the concept of absolute surrender of the soul to God to earn His grace. This point will be brought out in the later chapters.

Kulaśekhara Āḻvār

Kulaśekhara was born in Tiruvancikkuḷam in the State of Kerala (South India). From his own writings it is evident that he belonged to a royal family and ruled over the Chera kingdom, the present Kerala in South India.[1] As an ardent devotee of Viṣṇu he spent most of his time in the company of Bhāgavatas listening to the religious discourses. The story goes that in order to dissuade him from his religious preoccupation and pay more attention to his royal duties, the ministers manoeuvred to bring the charge of theft of a precious ornament of the family deity on the pious Bhāgavatas. In order to prove their innocence, Kulaśekhara voluntarily inserted his hand into the pot filled with a live poisonous cobra which did not hurt him and thereby he exposed the plot hatched by the deceitful ministers. Later he abdicated his throne, moved to Śrīraṅgam and engaged himself wholly in the service of God and Godly men.

Kulaśekhara Āḻvār has contributed only one poetical composition in the name of *Perumāḷ Tirumoḻi* comprising 105 hymns roughly divided into ten decads. The first three decads are devoted to the glory of the *arcā* deity at Śrīraṅgam. He expresses his craving to have the vision of the Lord, the zeal to spend the time in the company of Bhāgavatas and his madness after God. In the next two decads he sings the glory of the *arcā* deities at Tirumalai, Tillai Cittirakūṭam (the present Chidambaram) and Tiruvakkōḍu, a religious centre in Kerala. In the last five decads Kulaśekhara gives expression to his mystic experience of God by contemplating on the selected episodes of the Bhāgavata and Rāmāyaṇa. He imagines himself as Devakī and weeps over her plight at being forced to forsake infant Kṛṣṇa to protect him from the murderous hand of Kaṁsa. He also poses himself as Kauśalyā and pours out the motherly affection towards Rāma as a child. He also imagines himself as Daśaratha and laments over Rāma's exile in the forest.

In these hymns two important doctrines, which are vital to Vaiṣṇava theology have been brought out. These are: the service to God (*Bhagavat-kaiṅkarya*) and service to the Lord's devotees (*Bhāgavata-kaiṅkarya*). We shall discuss these theories in a later chapter.

Toṇḍaraḍippoḍi Āḻvār

Toṇḍaraḍippoḍi, also known as Bhaktāṅghrireṇu was born in an

1. See *Perumāḷ Tirumoḻi* II.10.
kollikāvalaṉ kūḍalnāyakaṉ koḻikkōṉ kulaśekaraṉ.

orthodox Brahmin family at Tirumaṇḍaṅguḍi in Tamil Nadu (South India). Right from the childhood he developed an intense devotion to Viṣṇu. With a keen desire to offer divine service to Lord Raṅganātha at Śrīraṅgam, he took up the pious occupation of cultivating a flower garden and offered daily *tulasī* leaves and flowers to the deity. It is said that this devotee was one day captivated by the beauty of a harlot named Devadevi, who accidently came to his garden. He found in her an irresistible charm and fell into her trap. By the grace of God, he was later rescued from the degraded life and made to repent the grave error committed by him. Thereafter, he dedicated himself not only to serve God but also His devotees. He sincerely believed that he is a devotee of devotees of God and called himself as *Toṇḍaraḍippoḍi* which means one who enjoyed besmearing his head with the dust of the feet of devotees. In one of his hymns he prays to God to wake up and make him His humble devotee, who is ever keen on doing service to His ardent worshippers.[1]

Toṇḍaraḍippoḍi has contributed two poetical works: (1) *Tirumālai* comprising 45 hymns; (2) *Tiruppaḷḷiyeḻucci* consisting of ten verses. The first work is described as sacred garland (*mālai*) of poems offered to Lord Raṅganātha. In these verses the Āḻvār refers to the ephemeral character of the human life and also the worldly and heavenly pleasures, the need to control the sense organs, the ways of overcoming obstacles to attain God, the need of reciting the names of God to get rid of the sins and the importance of service to God and Godly men. A few verses reveal the plight of the Āḻvār himself when he had become a slave to his sense organs.

The second one, as the title indicates, is a celebrated song of the early morning meant to awaken Lord Raṅganātha from His yogic slumber (*yoga-nidrā*). Naturally, the verses contain a poetic description of the dawn—the sun rise, the gentle breeze, the fragrance of the fresh blossoms, the movement of birds, the buzz of bees, the desire of celestial beings to offer worship etc. They also refer to the various glorious acts of God during His incarnations.

1. *Tiruppaḷḷiyeḻucci*, verse 10.

The concept of *Bhāgavata-kaiṅkarya* or service to the devotees of Bhagavān (Viṣṇu), which is developed into an important doctrine in later Vaiṣṇava theology, finds its strong roots in the hymns of Toṇḍaraḍippoḍi. We shall discuss this in a later chapter.

Tiruppāṇāḻvār

Following the traditional chronology, Tiruppāṇāḻvār comes after Toṇḍarāḍippoḍi and earlier than Tirumaṅgai Āḻvār. He was born at Woraiyur near Śrīraṅgam in South India in a family belonging to a low caste. He was stated to be a musician as well as a poet deeply devoted to Lord Raṅganātha. Because of his caste, he was not permitted to enter the precincts of the temple, in accordance with the religious custom then prevalent. However, as a person of pious and highly devotional character he used to sing the songs in praise of God by sitting on the banks of the river Kāverī facing the temple. According to the traditional account, it so happened that one day a temple priest named Lokasāraṅga Muni hurled a stone at Pāṇaṉ as he was found obstructing the pathway to the river. Pāṇaṉ, who was in a state of ecstacy, was hurt and after realizing his mistake in not responding to the shouting of the priest, he repented. That very night, Lord Raṅganātha who was moved by the sincere devotion of Pāṇan and who also does not discriminate between His devotees on the basis of caste, commanded the priest in his dream to bring the saint inside the sanctum. Following the divine command, the priest carried Pāṇaṉ on his shoulders and took him inside the temple so that he could offer worship to Lord Raṅganātha. This incident is celebrated by the fact that the saint is named *Munivāhana* or the one who was carried on the shoulders of the Muni. On entering the sanctum, the saint was so captivated by the enchanting beauty of the deity that he expressed it in his hymns. While he was in a state of trance he is believed to have vanished, becoming one with divinity.

Pāṇāḻvār has contributed only one short poem of ten significant verses under the title of *Amalanādipirāṉ*. These hymns describe the grandeur of every part of the divine body of Lord Raṅganātha—the feet, the apparel, the navel, the waist girdle, the chest, the neck, the mouth with red lips, the eyes and the entire body as a whole. The beauty of the deity appeared so bewitching to the saint that he gave expression to his joy in the following last words uttered by him: "My eyes having beheld Thee cannot verily see anything else." Even this shortest composition of ten hymns is not without philosophical ideas. As explained by Vedānta Deśika,[1] every hymn brings out the important attributes of God. The word *amalaṉ* (blemishless) used at the outset and which is adopted as the title of the work, signifies one of the essential attributes laid down by Vedānta for determining the Ultimate Reality. We shall discuss this matter later.

Tirumaṅgai Āḻvār

Tirumaṅgai, also known as Kaliyaṉ and Parakālaṉ, was born at Tirukkuraiyalur in Tamil Nadu (South India) in a family of tribal brigands. In his younger days he was well-trained in archery and in recognition of his valour and skill in this art, he was made the chieftan of a group of villages with Tirumaṅgai as headquarters under the sway of the Chola King. He thus earned the title of Tirumaṅgai-mannaṉ or the Chief of Tirumaṅgai, which remained his name even after he became a saint. There is an interesting story about how a person leading a life of brigand in younger days became later an ardent devotee of Nārāyaṇa and an Āḻvār (mystic saint) of extraordinary eminence. According to the traditional account, which is also substantiated by a few biographical details given in the hymns, Tirumaṅgai came to know about a very handsome heavenly nymph named Kumudavalli, who was an adpoted daughter of a Vaiṣṇavite native doctor. He married her on a condition stipulated by her that he should become a true Vaiṣṇavite both by conviction and deeds and for this purpose he should also feed daily 1,008 Vaiṣṇavas for a period of one year. He managed to fulfil this expensive promise by indulging in highway robbery. One day while he was engaged in such an occupation, he chanced to come across a newly married couple. He attempted to rob the jewellery worn by them. As he was trying hard to remove the ornament on the toe of the bride, he realised that the young couple were none other than the Lord Nārāyaṇa and His beloved consort. With a keen desire to trans-

1. Śrī Deśika in his *Munivāhanabhoga*, a commentary on *Amalanādipirāṉ*, points out that these ten stanzas convey the meaning of *Aṣṭākṣara*, the eight syllabled *Nārāyaṇa Mantra*.

form Kaliyaṉ into a saint, Lord Nārāyaṇa imparted to him the spiritual knowledge. The first ten hymns of the *Periya Tirumoḻi* speak how Tirumaṅgai was transformed after learning the meaning of *Nārāyaṇa Mantra* which is acknowledged by the Śrī Vaiṣṇava Ācāryas as the most important *mantra* containing the quintessence of Vedānta. With his becoming a Vaiṣṇava saint, Tirumaṅgai gave up his vocation as a chieftain and engaged himself in divine service by visiting the various Vaiṣṇava religious centres all over India right from Badrīnāth in the North to Tirukkuruṅguḍi in the extreme South. These visits which cover nearly 86 centres are immortalised in his monumental work, *Periya Tirumoḻi.*

Tirumaṅgai-mannaṉ, one of the most learned Tamil poets, has contributed six poetical compositions. These are:

(1) *Periya Tirumoḻi* with 1,084 hymns of high literary excellence.
(2) *Tirukkuruntāṇḍakam* with 20 verses.
(3) *Tiruneḍuntāṇḍakam* with 30 verses.
(4) *Tiruveḻukūṟṟirukkai* as a single long poem in 47 lines.
(5) *Śiriya Tirumaḍal* consisting of 155 lines.
(6) *Periya Tirumaḍal* consisting of 297 lines.

These extensive poetical works constitute a major part of the *Nālāyira Divyaprabandham.* They not only exhibit the poetical genius of the author but also convey important theological teachings of Vaiṣṇavism. We shall cover them in the appropriate chapters dealing with the concerned doctrines. For the present we may take note of a few general features of these poems.

Periya Tirumoḻi is the most important work of Tirumaṅgai Āḻvār. It is a composition of a large number of devotional verses generally on the greatness of the several Vaiṣṇava shrines, the *arcā* deities installed therein and in particular the numerous auspicious attributes of God as experienced by the mystic saint. Besides the detailed references to God and His attributes, there are a large number of verses which speak about human suffering caused by bondage and the ways and means of overcoming it leading ultimately to the attainment of God. As Vedānta Deśika describes, the *Periya Tirumoḻi* provides a deep insight into the spiritual knowledge (*arivu taruṁ periya Tirumoḻi*).[1]

---

1. *Prabandhasāra,* verse 13.

Tirukkuruntāṇḍakam and *Tiruneḍuntāṇḍakam: Taṇḍakam* literally means a staff used as a support while walking up a hill. In the context of the poetry, it refers to a particular type of poetical composition addressed to God as comparing Him to such a support or in other words, a source of sustenance for the soul. The words *kuru* and *neḍu* signify the length of the compositions in terms of the number of verses and the number of meters adopted in the poems. The main theme of the *Tirukkuruntāṇḍakam* is that the soul is wholly dependent on God who is the sole supporter and it can hope to escape the suffering by means of sincere prayers and worship to Him. The *Tiruneḍuntāṇḍakam*—which is a longer poetical composition portrays the mystic experience of God by the saint. Here the Āḻvār speaks in the guise of a *nāyakī* or consort of God who is separated from her beloved Lord (*Nāyaka*). He conveys his mental anguish caused by separation from God in the mystic language through the media of the mother of the *maiden* and also directly as maiden.

Tiruveḻukūṟṟirukkai is a single long poem of 47 lines. It deals with the concept of absolute surrender of the soul to God who out of his supreme saving power can rescue it from bondage. The nature of God, the means of attaining Him and the supreme goal to be attained are all briefly presented in this poem.

Śiriya Tirumaḍal and *Periya Tirumaḍal*: The term *maḍal* refers to a traditional custom in which the man or woman who has been in love with his or her lover takes a vow to secure the person loved, by openly demonstrating in public his or her love to the person concerned. The custom generally followed for this purpose in the ancient Tamil country was that the person affected would take a ride in a street on a palmyra stem using it as a horse, so that the lover having been exposed to public scandal, realizes his mistake and comes back to the aggrieved person. Tirumaṅgai Āḻvār adopts this concept of *maḍal* in expressing his intense love for God to arouse the compassion of the latter to the former so that he can obtain communion with Him. Here the love expressed towards God is of a spiritual type expressing the soul's longing for union with Him. It is an aspect of *bhakti* expressed in the mood (*bhāva*) of a maiden towards her lover. The mystic saint assumes the guise of a *nāyakī* or consort and conveys the inner feelings caused by separation from the *Nāyaka,* the Supreme Lord. The two *maḍals* portray the mystic feelings of the saint towards

God. We shall deal with this subject in detail in the chapter on the mysticism of the Āḻvārs.

IV. *The Classification of the Prabandhams*

We may recapitulate the works of the Āḻvārs in a chronological order:

1. Poygai Āḻvār	: *Mudal Tiruvandādi*	100	verses
2. Pūtattāḻvār	: *Iraṇḍām Tiruvandādi*	100	"
3. Pey Āḻvār	: *Mūṉṟām Tiruvandādi*	100	"
4. Tirumaḻiśai Āḻvār	: *Nāṉmukaṉ Tiruvandādi*	96	"
	Tiruccanda Viruttam	120	"
5. Nammāḻvār	: *Tiruviruttam*	100	"
	Tiruvāciriyam	7	"
	Periya Tiruvandādi	87	"
	Tiruvāymoḻi	1,102	"
6. Madhurakavi Āḻvār	: *Kaṇṇinuṇ-Śiruttāmbu*	11	"
7. Kulaśekhara Āḻvār	: *Perumāḷ Tirumoḻi*	105	"
8. Periyāḻvār	: *Tiruppallāṇḍu*	12	"
	Periyāḻvār Tirumoḻi	461	"
9. Āṇḍāḷ	: *Tiruppāvai*	30	"
	Nācciyār Tirumoḻi	143	"
10. Toṇḍaraḍippoḍi	: *Tiruppaḷḷi-eḻucci*	10	"
	Tirumālai	45	"
11. Pāṇāḻvār	: *Amalanādipirāṉ*	10	"
12. Tirumaṅgai Āḻvār	: *Periya Tirumoḻi*	1,084	"
	Tirukkuruntāṇḍakam	20	"
	Tiruneḍuntāṇḍakam	30	"
	Tiruveḻukūṟṟirukkai	1	"
	Śiriya Tirumaḍal	77½	"
	Periya Tirumaḍal	148½	"[1]

The above enumeration is in accordance with the views of Maṇavāḷamāmuni and his followers. There are twenty-four *prabandhams* of varying size, making a total collection of 4,000 hymns, known as *Nālāyira Divyaprabandham.* Vedānta Deśika and his followers do not acknowledge *Tiruppallāṇḍu* as a separate

1 The *Śiriya Tirumaḍal* and *Periya Tirumaḍal* are actually two long single poems but they are split up ino 77½ and 148½ verses by the followers of Teṅkalai sect to make up a total of four thousand hymns.

poem but treat it as part of *Periyāḻvār Tirumoḻi*. The *Śiriya Tirumaḍal* and *Periya Tirumaḍal* are split up by him into 40 and 78 verses respectively instead of 77½ and 148½. In order to make up the total of 4,000, he adds the *Rāmānuja-nūṟṟandādi*, a Tamil *prabandham* comprising 108 hymns composed by Tiruvaraṅgattamudanār in praise of Rāmānuja. The justification for doing so is that it is similar to *Kaṇṇinuṇ-Śiruttāmbu*, which is a poem in praise of an Ācārya. Thus, in either case the total number of *prabandhams* with 4,000 hymns to be collectively called as *Nālāyira Divyaprabandham* remains unchanged.

The twenty-four *prabandhams* have been divided into four parts. The *Tiruvāymoḻi* of Nammāḻvār with 1,102 hymns forms one part. The *Periya Tirumoḻi* with 1,084 hymns of Tirumaṅgai along with *Tiruneḍuntāṇḍakam* (30 verses) *Tirukkuruntāṇḍakam* (20 verses) constitute another part. The *prabandhams* of Periyāḻvār, Āṇḍāl, Kulaśekharan, Toṇḍaraḍippoḍi, Pāṇāṉ, Mathurakavi and *Tiruccanda Viruttam* of Tirumaḻiśai are grouped together under the title of *Mudalāyiram* forming the third part. The rest of the *prabandhams* are categorised as a separate part under the name of *Iyarpā*. The basis on which this division into four parts is made is not clear, though the Vaiṣṇava tradition has offered some explanation. The general belief is that the entire *Divyaprabandham* is an exposition of the three Vaiṣṇava *mantras*—*aṣṭākṣara, dvaya* and *carama-śloka*—containing the essence of the esoteric doctrine of *Vaiṣṇava sampradāya*. The division of the four thousand hymns into four parts is accordingly made following the order in which these esoteric doctrines are contained in the *prabandhams*.

All these poems are commented by the Vaiṣṇava Ācāryas. While only two Ācāryas—Periyavāccān Piḷḷai and Periya Parakāla-svāmi—have commented on all the *prabandhams* in maṇipravāḷa, several others have written scholarly commentaries on *Tiruvāymoḻi*. The first one known as Ārāyirappaḍi (6,000 *granthas*)[1] was writ-

1. The word *paḍi* or *grantha* is a unit of 32 letters. It was customary to indicate the length of a maṇipravāḷa commentary on *Tiruvāymoḻi* in terms of the number of units it comprises. Thus, these commentaries are named as 6,000, 9,000, 12,000, 24,000, 36,000 etc. It is also believed that these commentaries correspond in terms of units, to Sanskrit works such as the *Viṣṇu Purāṇa, Śrī-bhāṣya, Bhāgavata, Rāmāyaṇa,* and *Śrutaprakāśika* respectively.

ten by Tirukkurukaipirān Piḷḷān (1068 A.D.), a direct disciple of Rāmānuja. It is believed that Piḷḷān was directed by Rāmānuja to write it. From the style and the extensive Sanskrit phraseology used in it which is almost similar to that of Rāmānuja, it is evident that Piḷḷān is faithfully following Rāmānuja's teachings.

The other commentaries on the *Tiruvāymoḻi* are:

1. Nañjīyar (1113 A.D.), a disciple of Bhattar—the commentary known as *Oṉpadināyirappaḍi* (9,000 *granthas).*
2. Periyavāccān Piḷḷai (1168 A.D.), a little more elaborate commentary titled as *Irupattunālāyirappāḍi* (24,000 *granthas).*
3. Vaḍakkutiruvīdi Piḷḷai (1167 A.D.), a much longer commentary known as *Īḍu Muppattiyārāyarappāḍi* (36,000 *granthas*).[1]
4. Vādikesari Aḻakiamaṇavāḷa Jīyar (1242 A.D.), with a shorter commentary named *Pannirāyirappāḍi* (12,000 *granthas).*
5. Raṅgarāmānuja (1650 A.D.) a brief commentary in Sanskrit known as *Oṉpadināyirappāḍi* (9,000 *granthas).*
6. Periya Parakālasvāmi (1676 A.D.), a fairly detailed commentary with the title of *Padinettāyirappaḍi* (18,000 *granthas*).
7. Vedānta Rāmānuja also known as Sākṣātsvāmi (1700 A.D.), a sub-commentary on Piḷḷān's *Ārāyirappāḍi* which is titled as *Iruppattunālāyirappāḍi* (24,000 *granthas*) and also *Śabdārtha,* explaining the meaning of the hymns.

It is said that Vedānta Deśika also wrote an elaborate commentary under the title *Nigama Parimaḷa,* but this work is not extant. What is now left are the two Sanskrit works in verses viz., *Dramiḍopaniṣat-sāra* and *Dramiḍopaniṣat-tātparya-ratnāvaḷī* which present the purport of the Tiruvāymoḻi. Alakiyamaṇavāḷaperumāl Nāyanār (13th century) has written a work in maṇipravāḷa under the title *Ācāryahṛdayam.* Though it is not a commentary as such on *Tiruvāymoḻi,* it is held in high esteem by the Teṅkalai sect of Vaiṣṇavas as it is claimed to present the purport and the inner meaning of the hymns of Nammāḻvār.

---

1. Some Śrī Vaiṣṇavas of Teṅkalai sect regard *Īḍu* as the commentary of Ṅampiḷḷai (*Nampiḷḷai Vyākhyānaṁ*) because it contains his oral discourses on *Tiruvāymoḻi* which were recorded in writing by his disciple, Vaḍakkutiruvīdi Piḷḷai.

Of all these, Piḷḷān's *Ārāyirappaḍi* is brief and precise. It brings out the philosophical implications of the hymns. At the beginning of each decad, it provides a brief introduction which explains the sequence of the different decads. It also reflects the thoughts of Rāmānuja as found in his works. That it is more authentic and reliable to know the mind of the Āḻvār is evident from the fact that Vedānta Deśika, Aḻakiyamaṇavāla Jīyar, Sākṣātsvāmi and Periya Parakālasvāmi closely follow Piḷḷān's views. The other commentators—Nañjīyar, Periyavāccān Piḷḷai and Vaḍakkutiruvīdi Piḷḷai—do not seem to lean heavily on Piḷḷān's comments and they have attempted to write an independent commentary on *Tiruvāymoḻi*. Nañjīyar, as a disciple of Parāśara Bhattar expresses mostly the views claimed to have been held by the latter. Periyavāccān Piḷḷai follows the same trend of thought as Nañjīyar. Vaḍakkutiruvīdi Piḷḷai elaborates the views of Periyavāccān Piḷḷai. His commentary which is popularly known as *Īḍu* contains details drawn from the *Rāmāyaṇa* and the Purāṇas by way of elucidating the theological and esoteric doctrines of Vaiṣṇavism along with several anecdotes preserved by tradition. Most of the theological details included in the *Īḍu* for interpreting the hymns are of later origin. In spite of this, it is an excellent theological treatise on the post-Rāmānuja Vaiṣṇavism.

It is beyond the scope of this book to attempt a comparative study of the commentaries on *Tiruvāymoḻi*. Our main interest is to expound the philosophical teachings of the Āḻvārs as contained in the original hymns. The theological details offered by way of interpretation of the hymns are, therefore, left out of our study. However, they have been made use of, wherever necessary, to bring out the true purport of the teachings of the Āḻvārs. The *Ārāyirappaḍi* of Piḷḷān and the *Dramiḍopaniṣat-tātparya-ratnāvaḷī* of Vedānta Deśika, supplemented with the commentaries of Periya Parakālasvāmi and Sākṣātsvāmi provide a better insight into the philosophical teachings of the Āḻvārs. These have been extensively made use of in presenting the philosophy of the Āḻvārs.

CHAPTER 2

THE DOCTRINE OF ULTIMATE REALITY

I. *The Philosophical Theory of Paratattva*

The theory of Ultimate Reality (*paratattva*), which is an important subject of Vedānta has received considerable attention of the Āḻvārs in general and Nammāḻvār in particular. The *Vedānta-sūtra* which is primarily concerned with an enquiry into the nature of Brahman, as is evident from the opening aphorism, attempts to determine the nature of the Ultimate Reality by specifying the criteria of Reality without mentioning the name of any cult God, though some commentators on the *Sūtras* equate the term Brahman with a specific deity. Nammāḻvār adopts the same kind of philosophic approach in dealing with the theory of Reality. In the first ten hymns of his classical *Tiruvāymoḻi*, which contains the quintessence of the Vedānta, he presents the theory of Ultimate Reality without stating the name of any deity. He portrays the nature of Reality in unambiguous terms and in conformity with the Upaniṣadic teachings. To clear the suspicion of dogmaticism he states categorically that his teachings about the Reality have the support of the authoritative scriptural texts.[1]

According to Nammāḻvār, the Ultimate Reality is the Supreme Personal Being. At the very outset Nammāḻvār defines it as the one who is endowed with infinite auspicious attributes *par excellence*. In his own words, He who posseses infinite

---

1. TVM I.1.7 *śuḍar-miku śuritiyuḷ uḷaṉ*.

unsurpassable bliss is the Reality.[1] He is essentially of the nature of spiritual knowledge and bliss.[2] He is distinct from the material objects which are cognized by the sense organs and also from the sentient souls which can be comprehended by the mind cleansed of all impurities through yogic practice.[3] He exists at all times and in all places.[4] There is none who is either higher than Him or equal to Him.[5]

All the sentient beings and the non-sentient entities in the universe derive their existence (*sattā*) from that one Supreme Person.[6] Their sustenance (*sthiti*) also is dependent on Him.[7] All their activities are controlled by His will (*saṅkalpa*).[8] He abides in all that exists in the universe as their *antarātmā* and controls them from within.[9] He pervades every particle of water in the ocean, every minute particle of ether and earth and all the subtle individual souls.[10] Though He is in every object and in every place, He is invisible.[11] He is the one who creates the universe and dissolves it.[12] The universe is organically related to the Supreme Being in the same way as the physical body is related to the soul within.[13] All these facts are well-established by the unquestionable scriptural texts.

The above description of the nature of the Ultimate Reality, as summed up succintly in the opening ten hymns of the *Tiruvāymoli*, settles the major controversial issue in Vedānta as to whether Brahman is *nirviśeṣa*, undifferentiated or *saviśeṣa*,

---

1. TVM I.1.1 *uyarvaṟa uyarnalam uḍaiyavaṉ yavaṉ avaṉ*.
   The word *uyarnalam* in this hymn literally means *ānanda, par excellence*, as described in the Ānandavalli of of *Taittirīya Upaniṣad*. But it is interpreted by the commentators as *ananta kalyāṇa-guṇa*, infinite auspicious attributes. See Piḷḷān, AP I.1.1 *ānandādi asaṅkhyeya kalyāṇa-guṇa-mahodadhi*.
2. TVM I.1.2 *uṇar muḻu nalam*.
3. TVM I.1.2.
4. TVM I.1.3 *oḻivilaṉ paranda annālam uḍaiyoruvan*.
5. TVM I.1.2 *edir nikaḻ kaḻiviṉum iṉaṉilaṅ mihunarai iḷaṉ*.
6. TVM I.1.4 See DTR 11, *svāyatta aśeṣa sattā*.
7. TVM I.1.5 See Piḷḷān, AP *jagad-rakṣaṇaṁ tadadhīnam*.
8. TVM I.1.6 See Piḷḷān, AP *samasta pravṛtti nivṛttihaḷum paramapuruṣa saṅkalpādhīnam*.
9. TVM I.1.7.
10. *Ibid*. I.1.10.
11. *Ibid*. *karandu eṅgum paranduḷaṉ*.
12. TVM I.1.8 *viṇmudal muḻuvaduṁ varaṉmudalāy,*
    avai muḻudu uṇḍa paraparaṉ.
13. TVM I.1.7 *uḍalmiśai uyireṇa karandu eṅguṁ paranduḷaṉ*.

differentiated. Nammāḻvār as well as other Āḻvārs uphold the *Saviśeṣa Brahma-vāda*, which obviously appears to have been in vogue long before Śaṁkara. The teachings of the Āḻvārs, therefore, lend greater support to Rāmānuja than to Śaṁkara.

It is worth noting the detailed exposition of the nature of Ultimate Reality as expressed in the hymns scattered all over the *Divyaprabhandham*. The most striking feature of the Reality as portayed prominently by the Āḻvārs is that the Supreme Being of Vedānta is personal God in the name of *Nārāyaṇa* who possesses not only infinite auspicious attributes but also a spiritual body bedecked with weapons and ornaments. Such a view of Reality has undoubtedly a theological complexion of the God of Religion, affirming the supremacy of one particular deity as against others. We shall deal with this aspect of Reality separately. At present we may take note of the philosophical view of Reality.

In reply to the question 'What is Brahman?', the *Tattirīya Upaniṣad* says:

> "That from which all beings are born, that by which when born they live and that unto which, when departing, they enter."[1]

On the basis of this statement, the *Vedānta-sūtra* defines Brahman as that from which proceed the creation, sustenance and dissolution of the universe.[2] Accordingly Brahman, the Ultimate Reality of metaphysics, should be the primary cause of creation, sustenance and dissolution of the universe. In conformity with this Vedānta theory, the Āḻvārs repeatedly point out that the Supreme Being is the one who creates the universe, proctects it and also dissolves it.[3] They also mention additional cosmic

1. TUp III.1 *yato vā imāni bhūtāni jāyante;*
   yena jātāni jīvanti;
   yat prayanty-abhisaṁviśanti;
   tad vijijñāsasva;
   tad brahmeti.
2. VS I.1.2 *janmādyasya yataḥ.*
3. TVM I.9.1 *evaiyum yavarum taṉṉuḷḷē āhiyum ākkiyum kākkum avaiyuḷ taṉimudal.*
   See also TVM X.5.3 *tānē ulahellām, tānē paḍaittiḍandu, tānē uṇḍu umiḻidu tānē āḻvānē.*
   See also TVM IX.3.2, IV.10.3, VII.1.3, X.7.9, VIII.1.5.
   See also PTM III.1.10 *mūvalahu uṇḍu umiḻndu alanda.*
   MTi 2. *nī paḍaittu iḍandu uṇḍu umiḻnda pār.*
   ITI 47. *jñālaṁ aḻandiḍandu uṇḍu umiḻinda aṇṇal.*

functions referred to in the Vedas and Purāṇas viz., pervasion of the entire universe by three strides, retention of it in the body during deluge and the restoration of the universe hidden in the ocean. They describe these functions in the metaphorical terms of 'swallowing the universe' (*uṇḍu*) implying the dissolution, 'retention of it in the stomach' indicating the protection during the period of deluge and 'spitting it out' (*umiḻndu*) signifying the act of creation. The fuller implications of these metaphors will be explained in a later chapter.[1]

The Upaniṣadic passage relating to the cosmic creation states that in the beginning (prior to creation) only (*sat*), which is also known as Brahman and Ātman, existed and the same *one* Reality without a second willed to become *many*.[2] These passages emphasise the fact that *sat* or Brahman is the source of the universe. As explained in the *Vedānta-sūtra,* it is the material cause (*upādāna-kāraṇa*) of the universe.[3] It creates the universe by its will (*īkṣaṇa* or *saṅkalpa*) without the aid of any other accessories. These teachings of the Upaniṣads are manifestly brought out in several hymns by Nammāḻvār. Thus he says:

> At that time (prior to creation) when there was nothing-neither the celestial beings (*devas*) nor the cosmic universe, nor the living beings nor other entities—the *Ādippirāṉ* (primordial Deity) created along with the four-faced Brahmā, the devas and the universe with the living beings.[4]

Another hymn states more specifically that the Supreme Being is one only without a second (*tāṉ ōruruvē taṉivittāy).*[5] This cryptic statement is a reiteration of the *Chāndogya Upaniṣadic* text viz., *sadeva saumya idam agra āsīt ekameva advitīyam.* The implication of this statement, as interpreted by Rāmānuja, is that Brahman is both the material (*upādāna*) and instrumental cause (*nimitta*) and that it is not in need of any accessories (*sahakārī*) for the purpose of creation of the universe. The three words in the

1. See Chapter 3.
2. See ChUp VI.2.1 AiUp I.1, BrUp III.4.10.
3. See VS I.4.23 *prakṛtiśca....*
4. TVM IV.10.1 *oṉrum tēvum ulahum uyirum maṟṟrum*
   yādumillā aṉṟu nāṉmukaṉ taṉṉoḍu
   tēvar ulahōḍu uyir paḍaittāṉ..... Cp. *Mahopaniṣad, eko ha vai nārāyaṇa āsīt na brahmā neśāna na dyāvā pṛthivī.*
5. TVM I.5.4.

Tamil hymn—*tāṉē, ōr, taṉī*—signify the absence of *upādānāntara, sahakāryantara* and *nimittāntara* respectively.[1] In other words, the Supreme Person, according to Nammāḻvār is the threefold cause (*trividha-kāraṇa*). That is, He is the sole material cause, He Himself is the instrumental cause and He Himself (His *saṅkalpa*) serves as the accessory cause. Tirumaṅgai Āḻvār describes the Supreme Being as *ādikkuṁ ādi*, meaning that it is the primary source of the universe.[2] Even though He is the material cause, He is not subject to any modification but remains unchanged.[3]

The Supreme Being is a transcendental Reality. It is also immanent in the universe. Both these aspects of Reality are brought out clearly in the hymns. The repeated references to the all-pervasive character of *Paramātman* in several hymns reveal beyond any doubt His immanence or *antarātmatva*. The simple statement made in the very first decad of the *Tiruvāymoḻi* that the Supreme Being pervades everywhere at all times supports this view. The *Antaryāmī Brāhmaṇa* of *Bṛhadāraṇyaka Upaniṣad* states that *Paramātman* (Brahman) abides in all entities in the universe—the five physical elements, the sun, space, moon, stars, ether, all beings (*sarva-bhūta*), the five sense organs including *manas* and the individual self (*vijñāna* or *ātman*); though none of these entities knows His presence, He controls it from within. This Upaniṣad further asserts that *Paramātman* dwelling inside every entity including the soul is its *ātman, antaryāmī* and *amṛta* (*eṣa ta ātmā antaryāmī-amṛtaḥ*).[4] While acknowledging all these facts Nammāḻvār goes a step further to emphasise the immanent character of *Paramātman.* In a very characteristic way he says:

> The Supreme Being abides in every particle of water of the wide-spread cool ocean, in the same way as it pervades the gross physical elements of the cosmic universe; it also abides in the infinitesimal souls and in every minute particle of earth.[5]

In other words, He exists both within and outside the sentient beings and non-sentient entities of the universe, though His pres-

---

1. See *Īḍu* I.5.4, See also ŚS I.5.4.
2. PTM IX.7.1.
3. TVM I.5.2 *ninainda ellā poruḷhaḷkum vittāy mudalil śidaiyāmē.*
4. BrUp V.7.7.
5. TVM I.1.10, See also TVM X.10.8 *muṟṟa karandu oḷittāy.*

ence is not comprehensible. Nammāḻvār uses two significant words to express this truth: *karandu eṅguṁ-parandulaṉ. Karandu* which literally means hidden (*antarhita*) implies that the presence of the Supreme Being inside an object is not known by it (*adṛśya*). The word *enguṁ-parandulaṉ* means that He abides in every place (*sarvatra*) by His pervasion. The fuller implication of it is that *Paramātman* abides in all that exists in the universe, both within and without, by virtue of His all-pervasive character, as stated in the Taittirīya Nārāyaṇa Upaniṣad.[1] Nammāḻvār expressly states in another hymn that the Supreme Being creates the universe and pervades inside every entity (*uḷḷāy*) and also outside it (*purattāy*).[2] This indicates that the immanence of *Paramātman* is full and complete. Keeping this in mind, Vedānta Deśika uses the expression, *sarvatattveṣu pūrtiḥ*[3] which means *Paramātman* pervades fully in all entities by His *svarūpa*. This signifies that the soul which is monadic in nature (*aṇu*) devoid of any form or physical structure, unlike the particle of earth, has in it the *Paramātma-svarūpa*. Similarly, the *vibhu-dravya* such as *kāla* (time) which has no outer space is associated with *paramātma-svarūpa*.[4] It is in this sense that Nammāḻvār describes the *svarūpa* of *paratattva*.

Though the Supreme Lord is immanent in all that exists in the universe—both the sentient beings as well as non-sentient things—He remains unaffected by the changes in them such as growth, decay and other modifications. Thus says Nammāḻvār:

> The Lord is the very sentient beings and non-sentient things; but He is not touched by their defects; He is also beyond the comprehension of the five sense organs; He is constituted of spiritual knowledge; the *jīvātaman* (soul) inside the body is not affected (by the defects of the body); if this is possible the same principle holds good in respect of *Paramātman*.[5]

1. TNUp, 94 *antaḥ bahiśca tat sarvaṁ vyāpya nārāyaṇaḥ sthitaḥ.*
2. TVM VII.8.8 *muṉṉiya mūvulahum avaiyāy avaṟṟai paḍittu*
   piṉṉum uḷḷāy purattāy.
   The word *uḷḷāy* means one who abides inside an entity; *purattāy* means one who abides outside it.
3. DTR 11.
4. See PPS I.1.10.
5. See TVM III.4.10 *yavaiyum yavarum tāṉāy avaravar śamayam tōṟum*
   tōyvilaṉ pulaṉaiṉdukkum śolappaḍān uṇarviṉ mūrtti
   āviśēr ūyiriṉuḷḷāl ādumōr paṟṟilāda
   pāvaṉai adaṉaik-kūḍil avaṉaiyum kūḍalāmē.

The implication of this hymn, as elucidated by the commentators is to reveal the transcendental spiritual character of the Supreme Being who is untouched by defects (*doṣair-aduṣṭam*).[1] The *Vedānta-sūtra*, as interpreted by Rāmānuja, points out that Brahman is free from defects even though it abides in all things, because all the Scriptural and Smṛti texts declare that by its very nature it is free from all imperfections and is also endowed with auspicious attributes.[2] The *Chāndogya Upaniṣad* says: This Supreme Being is free from evil, free from old age, free from death, free from grief, free from hunger and thirst.[3] The *Viṣṇu Purāṇa* states that *Viṣṇu-svarūpa* is free from all defects.[4] On the strength of these authoritative texts, Rāmānuja describes Brahman as *samasta-heya-pratyanīka* or the one who is opposed to all defilements. This is one of the essential characteristics of the Supreme Being.[5] To illustrate this point the *Vedānta-sūtra* offers two analogies of sun and its reflection in the waves and the all-pervasive space (*ākāśa*) as conditioned by several pots.[6] When the sun is reflected in the waves of water, the distortions in the image caused by the waves do not affect the sun. In the case of the all-pervasive sky, it becomes conditioned in several pots of varying sizes but the differences in the dimension of the receptacles do not apply to the space. In the same way, Brahman though immanent in the objects of the universe, remains unaffected by the defects or changes taking place in the latter.

In conformity with the teachings of the Vedānta, Nammāḻvār also states that the Supreme Lord abides in all sentient beings and non-sentient entities but He remains unaffected by their defects. The description of the Lord as the very personification of knowledge (*uṇarviṉ-mūrtti*) is presumably intended to convey the fact that as a transcendental Spiritual Being the defects found in the sentient beings and the material objects do not apply to Him. He uses the analogy of the soul and body to support this theory.[7] The soul abides in the physical body but the defects of

1. DTR 37.
2. VS III-2-II *na sthānato'pi parasya ubhayaliṅgam.*
3. ChUp VIII.1.5.
4. VP I.23.53 *samasta heyarahitaṁ viṣṇvākhyaṁ paramaṁ padaṁ.*
5. RB III.3.33 *heya-pratyanīkohyānandādi brahmaṇaḥ asādhāraṇa-rūpam.*
6. VS III.2.18 and III.2.20.
7. TVM III.4.10, See fn 5 on p. 48.

the body such as growth, decay, the experience of pain and pleasure etc., do not in any way touch the *svarūpa* of *jīvātman*. In the same way, the defects found in the universe do not apply to *Paramātman*. To emphasise the defectless character of *Īśvara*, Nammāḻvār describes Him as *amalaṉ* (free from defects). He also uses other phrases such as *tīrttaṉ, pavittiraṉ, tūyaṉ* which all imply His spiritual purity. After describing God in terms of contradictory objects and qualities, he states that He is the threefold universe but He is also not the universe.[1] In another verse he expresses with wonder how the Lord who is immanent in the entire universe remains unaffected with his transcendental character.[2] Tiruppāṇālvār describes the *Ādipirāṉ* (Reality) as *amalaṉ, vimalaṉ, nimalaṉ* and *ninmalaṉ*, all implying the purity *par excellence*.[3] Tirumaṅgai Āḻvār openly says that God is free from birth, death and old age.[4]

The Upaniṣads describe Brahman as *paraṁ-jyotis*, the Supreme Light in the sense that it is a transcendental spiritual entity constituted of eternal knowledge (*jñāna*) and not subject to any modification. The implication of such a description is that the Ultimate Reality, though it is immanent in all the entities in the universe, is not touched by any defects. Nammāḻvār as well as other Āḻvārs often use this expression in describing the Supreme Being. In one of the hymns he addresses the Supreme Deity as *paraṁ-śōdi* (The Tamil for *paraṁ-jyotis*) and states that He is the highest of all other luminaries (luminous entities in the universe) and that there is nothing comparable to it.[5] He also describes the Supreme Person as *paraṁ-śuḍar* and *paraṁ-śuḍar-jyotis* or as one possessing a lustrous divine form. Tirumaṅgai Āḻvār addresses God as *Nandā-viḷakku* meaning the unchanging eternal Light. All these terms imply that the Supreme Being is the very personification of spiritual knowledge. What is essentially spiritual in nature cannot be defiled by the defects found in the material entities. In the same sense the *Antaryāmī Brāhmaṇa* speaking of the immanence of Brahman in all entities uses the word *amṛta* along with the term *antaryāmin* to reveal the fact that

1. TVM VI.3.6 *mūvulahaṅgaḷumāy allaṉāy*.
2. TVM VII.8.1.
3. *Amalanādipirāṉ*, verse 1.
4. PTM IV.3.2 *pirappoḍu mūppu oṉṟu illavaṉ....*
5. TVM III.1.2.

Paramātman as a transcendental Reality remains unaffected by the defects of the universe even though He is hidden in all objects as *antaryāmin. Nammāḻvār* upholds the same philosophic truth as is evident in the third hymn of the opening decad of the *Tiruvāymoḻi.* Thus he says:

> It cannot be conceived that He possesses this (quality) and that He does not have that (quality); He is in the earth (and all the regions below it); He is in the sky (and all the regions above it); He pervades all non-sentient entities having a physical form and also all sentient beings devoid of any physical form; He is associated with all objects grasped by sense organs but He is beyond their grasp. Such is the Supreme Person who is everywhere and at all times and who is endowed with auspicious attributes.[1]

The fact that *Paramātman* though abiding in all entities in the universe is free from defects and also endowed with auspicious attributes reveal the twofold characteristic of Brahman known as *ubhaya-liṅgatva,* as pointed out by the *Vedānta-sūtra* and strongly upheld by the Viśiṣṭādvaita Vedānta. The theory is fully reflected in the hymns of Nammāḻvār.

The significant feature of the philosophical theory of Reality is the presentation of the concept of the organic relationship of body and soul. The Supreme Being which is equated with the universe is conceived as the Universal Soul (*Ātman*) and all that exists in the universe as its body (*śarīra*). This concept of body-soul relation (*śarīrātma-bhāva*) constitutes the unique doctrine of Viśiṣṭādvaita Vedānta (*pradhāna-pratitantra*) as expounded by Rāmānuja. Though this concept is found in the *Antaryāmī Brāhmaṇa of the Bṛhadāraṇyaka Upaniṣad* and briefly referred to in the *Rāmāyaṇa* and *Viṣṇu Purāna,* it is for the first time that it finds a clearer exposition in the *Tiruvāymoḻi.* Among the Vaiṣṇava saints, Nammāḻvār has the credit of presenting this philosophical theory more explicitly than others to explain the equation of the Supreme Being with the universe. Though he has not developed this concept into a doctrine in the manner

---

1. TVM I.1.3 *ilaṉadu uḍaiyaṉidu eṉa niṉaivu ariyavaṉ,*
nilaṉiḍai viśumbiḍai uruviṉaṉ aruviṉaṉ,
pulaṉoḍu pulaṉalaṉ oḻivilaṉ paranda,
annalaṉ, uḍaiyoruvanai aṇuhinaṁ nāmē.

Rāmānuja has done with all the philosophical implications, we can find in the *Tiruvāymoḻi* sufficient number of hymns upholding the theory. Without going into the details of the doctrine, he states in clear terms that the Supreme Being abides in everything as invisible in the same way as the soul is in the body.[1] Though he does not advance any arguments in support of the theory, he states that this fact is well-established in the self-revealed scriptural texts which should be taken as a sufficient proof or *pramāṇa* for the doctrine. He does not refer to any particular scriptural texts but Piḷḷān, who is the first authoritative commentator on the *Tiruvāymoḻi*, quotes comprehensively all the texts found in the Upaniṣads, the Itihāsas and Purāṇas as an elucidation of the pithy statement of Nammāḻvār. In the absence of any direct reference to the *Tiruvāymoḻi* by Rāmānuja, it may be difficult to say conclusively that Rāmānuja was directly influenced by this teaching of Nammāḻvār in formulating the doctrine of organic relationship. The main source for this doctrine is the *Antaryāmī Brāhmaṇa* of the *Bṛhadāraṇyaka Upaniṣad*. However, it would not be wrong to assume that Rāmānuja who was acquainted with the *Tiruvāymoḻi* would have found an additional support in the teachings of Nammāḻvār for developing this doctrine. The important point we should take note of is that the central doctrine of Viśiṣṭādvaita is clearly voiced in the *Tiruvāymoḻi*.

It is worth noting how Nammāḻvār has expounded this doctrine. The *Puruṣasūkta* of *Ṛg-Veda* states: "All this is *Puruṣa*". The *Chāndogya Upaniṣad* says: "All this is Brahman" (*sarvaṁ khalvidaṁ brahma*). Another Uapniṣadic text points out that all this is *Ātman* (*ātmāvā idaṁ sarvaṁ*). The *Viṣṇu Purāṇa* equates Viṣṇu with the universe (*jagacca saḥ*). In the same strain Nammāḻvar speaks that the Supreme Being is all that exists in the universe. Thus, he says:

> You are water, you are earth, you are fire, you are air, you are the sky. You have become the two shining sun and moon, you are Śiva and Brahmā....[2]

In another place he says with a sense of wonder:

1. TVM I.1.7 *uḍalmiśai uyireṉa karandeṅgum paranduḷaṉ.*
2. TVM VI.9.1 *nīrāy nilaṉāy tīyāy kālāy neḍuvāṉāy,*
   śirār śuḍarhaḷ iraṇḍāy śivaṉāy ayaṉāṉāy.

> God is fire, water, earth, sky and air; He is the father, mother and the children, all their relatives and all other individuals in the universe.[1]
>
> He is the luminous moon and sun, the bright numerous stars as well as the darkness; He is the torrential rain; He is the fame and infamy; He is also the cruel God of Death.[2]

Not only Nammāḻvār equates God with the variety of objects in the universe including the physical body and the soul but he also speaks of God in terms of objects which are contradictory in nature. Thus he says:

> God is poverty and wealth, heaven and hell, enmity and friendship, poison and nectar.[3]
>
> He is the happiness and suffering, the mental conflict and clear thinking, the anger and favourable disposition, heat and cold.[4]

The Āḻvār goes on describing God as a town and village, knowledge and ignorance, the brightest light and the pitch darkness. He is also the merit and sin, the good and bad results arising from them, the remembrance and forgetfulness, existence and non-existence. God is also spoken in terms of incompatible qualities such a straight-forwardness and conceitedness, black and white, truth and falsehood, youth and old age, new and old.[5]

We come across similar statements in the hymns of other Āḻvārs equating the Supreme Being with the universe. The three earliest Āḻvārs—Poyagai, Pūdattār and Pey—equate the Supreme Lord with the five elements.[6] Tirumaṅgai Āḻvār addressing the Supreme Lord says:

> You are the transcendental universe (*nitya-vibhūti*) and the physical universe; so also the variety of living beings existing there.[7]

---

1. TVM VII.8.1.
2. TVM VIII.8.2.
3. TVM VI.3.1 *nalkuravum śelvum narakum śuvargamumāy,*
   velpahaiyum naṭpum viḍamum amudamumāy....
4. TVM VI.3.2.
5. TVM VI.3.3-5.
6. MTi 22; ITi 24; MuTi 29.
7. PTM IV.1.3 *vānāḍum maṇṇādum maṟṟuḷḷa palluyiruṁ tānāya emperumāṉ.*

> You have become all the sentient beings and all the non-sentient entities.[1]

In one of the hymns, he speaks the very physical elements such as fire, water, earth etc., as God.[2] He also equates God with qualities which are of contradictory nature such as truth and falsehood, good and evil, happiness and suffering, heaven and hell, anger and calmness.[3]

What is the implication of such an equation of God with the universe? As the nature of the two entities—Brahman and universe—is different, they cannot be identical. How then is their equation to be understood? There are two possible explanations as offered by the Vedāntins. According to one explanation, of the two entities only one is absolutely real, while the other is to be taken as an illusory manifestation of what is real. This is the theory adopted by the Advaita Vedānta while interpreting the crucial Upaniṣadic texts such as "Thou art that" and "All this is Brahman". Such an explanation is plausible if the doctrine of *Māyā* which is admitted to account for the cosmic illusion is acceptable. The other explanation is that the two entities are real and distinct but they are one in the sense of a substance as qualified by the attributes. This is the view maintained by the Viśiṣṭādvaita Vedānta in explaining the statements where the terms are found in apposition (*samānādhikaraṇavākya*). It presupposes that there is an inherent or organic relationship between the two entities, as in the case of the body and soul (*śarīra-śarīrī*). In the case of Brahman and universe, Brahman as organically related to the universe is one.

This is not the place to go into the details of these two theories and their relative merits. Our main concern here is to find out the views of the Āḻvārs on this subject. All the commentators, without an exception, have explained these hymns speaking about God as universe by adopting the concept of body-soul relation. Does Nammāḻvār also subscribe to the same view? We shall try to answer this question objectively on the basis of his hymns.

As already observed, Nammāḻvār at the very outset of the *Tiruvāymoḻi* refers to the concept of 'body-soul' as follows:

1. PTM IV.1.2 *yāvarumāy yāvaiyumāy. . .*
2. *Ibid.* IV.9.5 *tī emperumān nīr emperumāṉ.*
3. *Ibid.* IV.5.8 and 9.

> The Supreme Being who dissolved this universe is manifest as the sky, fire, air, water and earth as also all other things made out of these (five) elements; like the soul inside the body, He (abides) in all those things as invisible and by pervading everywhere; this is well-established by the authoritative Revealed Scripture.[1]

The purpose of using the analogy of body and soul, as is evident in this hymn, read along with the three earlier hymns and the one following it later is to explain the immanence of the Supreme Being (*Īśvara*) as the inner controller of the entities, both sentient as well as the non-sentient in the universe. As explained earlier, the word used in these hymns, *karandu* (which means hidden inside) and *eṅgum parandu* (which means pervading everywhere), signify that the Supreme Being abides in all the entities as invisible and pervades everywhere both within and without. The analogy of the soul and body is cited to explain this fact. Though the fuller implications of the body-soul relation as explained by Rāmānuja are not mentioned by Nammāḻvār, these can be drawn from the other hymns, without unduly imposing the views developed later by the Vaiṣṇava Ācāryas. The soul is considered to be distinct from body. The soul which is present in the body sustains it and also controls it from within. On the basis of this analogy, Nammāḻvār upholds that *Īśvara* is the ground or supporter (*ādhāra*) of all that exists in the universe and that He also controls them from within as *antarātmā*. In a characteristic way he says:

> We the masculine beings present here and those that are near, far and inbetween, the feminine beings that are present here, near, far and inbetween, the neuter things referred to as that, this and the other (situated in a similar manner), the perishable as well as non-perishable entities, along with their good and defective qualities and all that existed in the past and what will come in the future—everything subsist in that Supreme Being.[2]

---

1. TVM I.1.7 *tiḍa viśumbu erivaḷi nīr nilam ivaimiśai,*
   paḍar poruḷ muḻuvatum āy avai avaitoṟum,
   uḍal miśai uyir eṉa karandu eṅgum paranduḷaṉ,
   śuḍar miku surutiyuḷ ivai uṇḍa śuraṉē.
2. TVM I.1.4 *nām avaṉ ivaṉ uvaṉ avaḷ ivaḷ uvaḷ evaḷ,*
   tām avar ivar uvar adu idu udu edu,
   vīm avai ivai uvai avai nalaṁ tīṅgu avai,
   ām avai āyavai āyniṉṟa avarē.

This hymn, as interpreted by all the commentators, reveals that *Īśvara* is the ground (*ādhāra*) of the universe comprising sentient and non-sentient entities and the latter derives its existence (*sattā*) from the former. The relationship that exists between *Īśvara* and universe is of the nature of *ādhāra-ādheya*. That is, *Īśvara* is *ādhāra*, the supporter and universe is *ādheya*, the supported, as in the case of *jīva* and body.

In another hymn Nammāḻvār states in a striking way that the Supreme Lord who sustains all the entities in the universe—both sentient and non-sentient, controls their activities in the form of action and cessation from action. Thus he says:

> Those who stand, sit, lie, move and those who do not stand, sit, lie and move (the different activities and cessation from activities) are controlled by that one Supreme Lord who Himself is not subject to any change and whose nature is also beyond any comprehension.[1]

Taking the analogy of the soul and physical body, *Paramātman* controls by His will all the activities and also cessation from activities of all beings in the universe. This brings out the relationship that holds good between *Īśvara* and the universe in terms of *niyāmaka* (controller) and *niyāmya* (that which is controlled).

These views are upheld on the authority of the Revealed Scripture, as is stated by Nammāḻvār. Though he does not quote the relevant Scriptural texts, it is obvious from the commentary of Piḷḷān and others that he has in mind the *Antaryāmī Brāhmaṇa* and other Scriptural texts. The Upaniṣadic passage states specifically that *Īśvara* abides in all the entities—the five physical elements, the psychical entities, the individual self etc., and none of them is aware of His presence but as the *antaryāmī*, He controls them.[2] Another Scriptural text says explicitly that *Īśvara* is the ruler of all individuals as abiding inside them.[3] The same

1. TVM I.1.6 *niṉṟanar irundaṉar kiḍandaṉar tirindaṉar,*
niṉṟilar irundilar kiḍandilar tirindilar,
eṉṟum ōr iyalviṉar eṉa niṉaivu aṟiyavar,
eṉṟum ōr iyalvoḍu niṉṟa em tiḍarē.
2. BrUp V.7.7.
3. *Taittirīya Āraṇyaka* III.11.10 *antaḥ praviṣṭaḥ śāstā janānāṁ sarvātmā.*

truth is reiterated in the *Bhagavadgītā*.[1]

The concept of body and soul used in the Upaniṣadic passage and the same being referred to by Nammāḻvār acknowledges the difference (*bheda*) that exists between *Īśvara* and the universe of *cit* and *acit*. The cosmic universe constituted of five elements and the transcendental realm (*nitya-vibhūti*) made of pure, unalloyed *sattva* are regarded as the glorious property (*vibhūti*) of the Supreme Lord. The cosmic universe though subjected to modification is *nitya* (eternal). Even during dissolution, it is not totally destroyed but remains in an unmanifest form. The transcendental universe which is constituted of spiritual substance (*śuddha-sattva*) is imperishable. There are several hymns which speak of the eternal character of the universe, while describing the glory of God. In the same way, the individual souls which are distinct from *Iśvara* are regarded as eternal and spiritual in character. Nammāḻvār openly condemns the theory of identity of the *Paramātman* and the *jīvātman*. The two are regarded as of different nature like two contradictory entities and their becoming one is out of question. He therefore states categorically that *jīvātman* is only *jīvātman* (*adu aduvē*).[2] The implication of this statement as explained by Piḷḷān, is that *jīvātman* and *Paramātman* cannot become one in the sense of absolute identity (*aikya*) just as *bhāva* and *abhāva*, two contradictory qualities, cannot become one.[3]

The admission of absolute difference between *Īśvara* and the universe and also their reality rules out the possibility of interpreting the hymns of Nammāḻvār referring to the equation of the Supreme Being with the universe, as oneness or identity in the manner understood by the Advaita Vedānta, viz., Brahman alone is real and the universe is phenomenal in character. The only other alternative is to interpret such hymns speaking of equation as oneness in the sense of Brahman as the *antarātmā* of all that exists in the universe is one, while the universe of sentient beings and non-sentient entities is His body (*śarīra*) in the technical sense that it is always sustained and controlled by the Supreme Lord.

---

1. BG XVIII.61 *Īśvaraḥ sarvabhūtānāṁ hṛddeśe arjuna tiṣṭati,*
bhrāmayan sarvabhūtāni yantrārūḍhāni māyayā.
2. TVM VIII.8.9 *kudiṟṟāhil nallururaippu kūḍāmaiyai kūḍināl.....adu aduvē.*
3. See Piḷḷān, AP VIII.8.9.

This doctrine of *śarīra-śarīrī-bhāva* was adopted by Rāmānuja for reconciling the *bheda-śrutis* and *abheda-śrutis* on the basis of *Antaryāmī Brāhmaṇa*. The credit of developing the doctrine fully on logical ground no doubt goes to him. However, Nammāḻvār was the forerunner among the Vaiṣṇava saints to present this important theory. Apart from the reference to this analogy of soul and body, Nammāḻvār explicitly states in several hymns that God dwells inside the body of an individual and also in all entities. In a direct way Nammāḻvār says:

> The *paraṁ-paraṉ* (the Supreme Being) is the one who dwells in all the entities of the cosmic universe (*aṇḍattahattān*) and in all the entities outside (*purattuḷḷān*); He also resides inside my body (*uḍal uḷḷān*) and stays in the mind of this humble servant (*aḍiyen uḷḷān*).[1]

All the Āḻvārs state that *Pramātman* abides in the heart.[2] In conformity with the Upaniṣadic teaching Nammāḻvār points out that the *Paramātman* enters into the three worlds which are comparable to the impenetrable forest cave and pervades the entire place.[3] He uses the word *pukku* which means 'enter into', thereby reflecting the statement of *Taittirīya Upaniṣad* speaking of the *anupraveśa* (entry) of Brahman into all the created objects.[4] As immanent in all entities, Brahman becomes the *antaryāmī* or the Inner contoller. This is the philosophic basis for admitting the theory of organic relationship between the Supreme Being and the universe (*śarīrātma-bhāva sambandha*), which constitutes the distinctive doctrine of the Viśiṣṭādvaita Vedānta. Nammāḻvār, who lived long before Śaṁkara and Rāmānuja, has upheld this important theory.

II. *Paratattva as Nārāyaṇa*

The dominant feature of the theory of Reality as presented in the *Tiruvāymoḻi* and other *prabandhams* is the identification of the

1. TVM VIII.8.2 *aḍiyenuḷḷāṉ uḍaluḷḷāṉ aṇḍatthattāṉ purattuḷḷāṉ....paraṁ-paraṉ*
2. MTi 99 *uḷḷattil uḷḷāṉ...*
   ITi 28 *manattuḷḷāṉ.....*
   MuTi 3 *manattuḷḷāṉ....*
   NanTi 86 *uḷḷuvār uḷḷattu uḷaṉkaṇḍāy...*
3. TVM X.10.8 *muṟṟa immūvulahum perundūrāy tūṟṟil pukku muṟṟakkarandu oḷittāy....*
4. TUp *tat sṛṣṭvā tadevānuprāviśat.*

para-tattva or the Brahman of the Upaniṣads with the God of Religion. At the very outset Nammāḻvār states:

> "*That person* (*yavaṉ*) who is endowed with infinite auspicious attributes *par excellence* is *He* (*avaṉ*)."

This implies, as the *Taittirīya Upaniṣad* says,[1] that the one Reality is *parama-puruṣa*, the Supreme Person. To make it more specific, he equates the Supreme Person with Nārāyaṇa. The other Āḻvārs have also acknowledged the Supreme Being as Nārāyaṇa.

The use of the term Nārāyaṇa for the *para-tattva* has far deeper significance than adopting it as merely the name of a cult God, as commonly believed. In the first place, it is a term employed by the Upaniṣads as synonymous with the terms such as *Sat*, *Ātman* and *Brahman*, all denoting the *para-tattva*. The *Taittirīya Nārāyaṇa Upaniṣad* specifically states that Nārayaṇa is *para-Brahma*; Nārāyaṇa is *para-tattva*; Nārāyaṇa is *paraṁ-jyotis* and Nārāyaṇa is *Paramātmā*.[2] The Upaniṣads have employed the term Nārāyaṇa because it connotes all the essential characteristics of the Ultimate Reality. As Nammāḻvār himself explains, the word Nārāyaṇa means the Lord (*Nāthan*) of the entire universe.[3] The Lordship implies that He is the controller (*Niyantā*) of the universe by virtue of His all-pervasiveness, both within and without. In another hymn he defines the term as one who is the abode (*āśraya*) of countless souls possessing the characteristics such as knowledge and bliss and who is also endowed with infinite number of auspicious attributes.[4]

Tirumaṅgai Āḻvār devotes the entire opening decad of *Periya Tirumoḻi* to emphasise the theological significance of this term Nārāyaṇa included in the eight-syllabled *Nārāyaṇa mantra* which was imparted to him by God, as is evident from his own hymns.

---

1. TUp *sa yaścāyaṁ puruṣe; yaścāsau āditye; saekaḥ.*
2. TNUp 93 *nārāyaṇa paraṁ brahma tattvaṁ nārāyaṇah paraḥ*
   nārāyaṇa paro jyotir-ātmā nārāyaṇaḥ paraḥ.
   See also *Mahopaniṣad* I.1 *eko ha vai nārāyaṇa āsīt....*
   In this passage dealing with the causation of the universe, the term Nārāyaṇa is used in place of *Sat*, *Ātman* and *Brahman* in the *Chāndogya*, *Aitareya* and *Bṛhadāraṇyaka Upaniṣads* respectively in the same context. Nārāyaṇa is therefore regarded the same as Brahman.
   See for details *Vaiṣṇavism*, pp. 53-54.
3. TVM II.7.2 *muḻuēḻ ulahukkuṁ nāthaṉ.*
4. TVM I.2.10 *eṉperukku annalattu oṉporuḷ īṟila vaṇpuhaḻ nāraṇaṉ.*

To the Āḻvārs this word is of such a spiritual significance that the chanting of it would pave the way for liberation from bondage. Periyāḻvār goes to the extent of saying that a mother who names her child as Nārāyaṇa would never go to hell.[1]

As revealed in several hymns, Nammāḻvār regards Nārāyaṇa as *para-tattva* because He is *Sarveśvara*. The word *Sarveśvara* means the Lord of all. It implies that He is the Lord of all other deities including the *caturmukha-Brahmā* and *Rudra*, the two important Vedic deities popularly acknowledged as higher Gods. In other words, Nārāyaṇa is higher than Brahmā and Rudra. In this sense Nammāḻvār describes Him as *paraṁ-paraṉ*.[2] Against the background of the Paurāṇic concept of trinity of Gods viz., Brahmā, Viṣṇu and Śiva, Nammāḻvar asserts that Nārāyaṇa (who is the same as Viṣṇu) is a higher deity who alone enjoys the status of the Supreme Being. He upholds this view not as a dogma but on the basis of justifiable arguments. To show his openmindedness in this regard he appeals to the folks in a general way to study intensely the Sacred texts, to reflect over what is read repeatedly, discuss often what is taught in them and then arrive at a proper conclusion regarding the relative status of Viṣṇu, Brahmā and Rudra.[3] In a more specific way he says:

> If one dispassionately ponders over the issue whether the three deities together constitute one Reality or they are different with equal status, it becomes obvious to one's mind, taking into consideration the characteristic features of the three deities as enunciated in the Sacred texts, that Nārāyaṇa is the highest deity.[4]

These general statements are elucidated by a reference to the teachings contained in the Upaniṣads, Epics and Purāṇas. The *Śvetāśvatara Upaniṣad* states that the Supreme Being first created Brahmā.[5] The *Nārāyaṇa Upaniṣad* explicitly points out that Brahmā was brought into existence by Nārāyaṇa and that from Nārāyaṇa

1. PeriTM IV.6 *Nāraṇaṉ taṁ annai ṅarakam puhāḷ....*
2. The words *paraṁ-paraṉ* and also *paraparaṉ* used in the opening decad of TVM literally mean higher than the high (*parasmāt paraḥ*). The high deity represents caturmukha-Brahmā and higher than him is Nārāyaṇa. The term *paraṁ-paraṉ* is employed by Nammāḻvār for *Brahman* of the Upaniṣad.
3. TVM I.3.6.
4. TVM I.3.7.
5. ŚvUp VI.18 *yo brahmāṇaṁ vidadhāti pūrvam.*

was born Rudra etc.[1] In the same way Nammāḻvār says:

> He (the Supreme Being) who created the illustrious Nāṉmukaṉ (the four-faced Brahmā) bade him to create the exalted celestial beings, sages and several other living beings.[2]

In another hymn he writes:

> The Supreme Lord who is one only without a second created the first three (Brahmā, Rudra and Indra) the numerous celestial beings, sages, the living beings and all others.[3]

In one of the decads which is exclusively devoted to establish the supremacy of Nārāyaṇa, Nammāḻvār speaks explicitly:

> At the time (prior to creation) when there was nothing—neither the celestial beings (devas), nor the cosmic universe, nor the living beings, nor other entities—the primordial deity (*ādippirān*) created along with the four-faced Brahmā, the devas, the living beings and the universe.[4]

This hymn is the reiteration of the statement in the *Mahopaniṣad* relating to the primary cause of the universe. The Upaniṣad says:

> (In the beginning) only Nārāyaṇa existed, neither Brahmā, nor Īśāna (Rudra) nor the heaven, nor the earth, nor the stars, nor the water and fire, nor the moon and sun.[5]

All the Vaiṣṇava Ācāryas extoll this hymn of Nammāḻvār since it teaches in a clear way that Nārāyaṇa is *para-tattva*. While commenting on the hymn, Piḷḷān quotes exhaustively all the

---

1. NUp *nārāyaṇāt brahmā jāyate; nārāyaṇāt rudro jāyate....*
2. TVM I.5.3 *māyonihaḷāy naḍaikaṟṟa vānōrpalarum munivarum,*
   nī yōnihaḷai paḍaiyeṉṟu niraināṉmuhaṉai paḍaitta avaṉ.
3. TVM I.5.4 *tāṉ ōruruvē taṉivittāy taṉṉil mūvar mudalāya.*
   The word *mūvar* is interpreted to refer to Brahmā, Rudra and Indra (since Viṣṇu of the trinity is an incarnation of Nārāyaṇa). Even if we take this word to refer to Brahmā, Viṣṇu and Rudra, Nārāyaṇa is the primary cause of Brahmā and Rudra, as there are several statements to this effect, while Viṣṇu is a manifestation (*prādurbhāva)* of Nārāyaṇa as a *devatā* along with other deities.
4. TVM IV.10.1 *oṉṟum tēvum ulahum uyirum maṟṟum yātum illā aṉṟu,*
   nāṉmukaṉ taṉṉoḍu tēvar ulahōḍu uyir paḍaittāṉ...
5. *Mahopaniṣad eko ha vai nārāyaṇa āsīt na brahmā*
   neśāno nāpo nāgniṣomau neme dyāvā-pṛthivī
   na nakṣatrāṇi na sūryo na candramāḥ.

available *Śruti* and *Smṛti* texts to substantiate the claim of Nammāḻvār.

Tirumaḻiśai Āḻvār states explicitly that Nārāyaṇa created the four-faced Brahmā and that the latter himself created Śaṁkara.[1] All the other Āḻvārs have acknowledged this fact.

Besides the scriptural authority in support of this theory, the Āḻvārs also refer to several mythological episodes drawn from the Itihāsas and Purāṇas to prove the subordinate status of Brahmā and Rudra. The Purāṇas narrate that during the great deluge Viṣṇu was floating on the water; a lotus stalk sprang from His naval at the time He willed to create the universe and then Brahmā was born from the divine lotus. Viṣṇu taught him the Vedas and after imparting the spiritual knowledge, He commanded him to create the universe. Thereafter, Brahmā created Rudra, the other devatās, the human and all other living beings and entities. The Purāṇas also state that Brahmā, who is the repository of Vedic knowledge, lost the Vedas as a result of its being stolen by the demon and the same was restored to him by Nārāyaṇa. The legend related to Rudra points out that he was cursed by Brahmā due to an offence committed to the latter and this curse was removed only by Viṣṇu. One other episode narrates the terrific war encountered by Rudra with the powerful demon Tripura and that the former was enabled to kill the latter with the assistance of Viṣṇu. Whatever may be the credibility of these mythological episodes, the Āḻvārs refer to them quite often to prove the fact that deities other than Nārāyaṇa are subject to origin and affliction and that they cannot therefore, be taken as the Supreme Being. They all seek His protection and they all worship Nārāyaṇa. In this connection, it may be noted that in none of their references to Brahmā and Rudra, the Āḻvārs exhibit any sectarian bias, unlike the followers of Śaivism and Vaiṣṇavism of later period. Nammāḻvār speaks the glory of these two deities in such venerable terms as he would use in respect of His own beloved consort, Lakṣmī. All the three—Lakṣmī, Brahmā and Rudra—are mentioned together as if they stand on the same footing in respect of their greatness. All of them are stated to have an abode in the body of Nārāyaṇa.[2] Lakṣmī resides

1. NanTi 1 *nāṉmukaṉai nārāyaṇaṉ paḍaittāṉ nāṉmukaṉuṁ*
tāṉ mukamāy śaṁkaraṉai tāṉ paḍaittāṉ....
2. TVM II.8.3, See also TVM IV.8.1.

in His chest, whereas Brahmā is accommodated in His naval and Rudra on the right side of His body. Brahmā and Rudra are held in high esteem as the propagator of Vedic knowledge and the spiritual preceptor of the devatās respectively. The hymns provide a clear evidence that at the time of Nammāḻvār Viṣṇu was acknowledged as the Supreme Deity and that there was no apathy towards Śaivism.

Is not Viṣṇu included in the trinity subject to origin? How can He be regarded as a Supreme Deity? In one of the hymns, Nammāḻvār describes the Supreme Being as the Lord of the three deities (*oru mūvarāhia mūrtti*).[1] In another place, He says that He is the primary cause of the three deities (*mudal mūvarkkum mudalvaṉ*).[2] A few other hymns mention that the primordial Lord took the form of Viṣṇu, Śiva and Brahmā (*tāṉum śivaṉum piramaṉumāhi paṇaitta taṉimudal*).[3] We come across a similar statement both in the *Atharvaśikha Upaniṣad* and *Viṣṇu Purāna*.[4] If these statements are interpreted with reference to a larger number of other hymns which repeatedly emphasise that only Brahmā and Rudra are brought into existence, it follows that Viṣṇu referred to in the trinity is an incarnation (*avatāra*) of the Supreme Being as a *devatā* in the name of Viṣṇu for the purpose of performing the task of protection (*rakṣaṇa*) of the universe, while Brahmā and Rudra are created as two deities for performing the functions of creation and dissolution of the universe respectively. A similar interpretation is offered by Rāmānuja on the Upaniṣadic text and the verse of Viṣṇu Purāṇa referred to above. The hymns of Āḻvār lend support to this interpretation. In the very opening decad devoted to define the nature of *paratattva*, Nammāḻvār says:

> The Supreme Lord is beyond the comprehension of even Brahmā and other divine beings; He is the primary cause of the cosmic matter, the five elements and all that exists; He also protects them by retaining the same in His body during the period of deluge; He is the one who (functioning

1. TVM III.6.1.
2. TVM III.6.2.
3. TVM VIII.8.4, VIII.4.6, VIII.4.9, IX.3.2.
4. *Atharvaśikha* Up II.15 *brahma viṣṇu rudrendrāḥ te sarve samprasūyante.*
VP I.2.66 *sṛṣṭi-sthityanta-karaṇīṁ brahmaviṣṇuśivātmikāṁ;*
sa saṁjñām yāti bhagavān eka eva janārdanaḥ.

> through the media of Rudra) destroyed three citadels; He is the propagator of spiritual knowledge to the celestial beings through Brahmā; He creates the world and dissolves it through *Ayaṉ* (Brahmā) and *Araṉ* (Śiva) as their indwelling self (*antarātmā*).[1]

In the later part of the *Tiruvāymoḻi*, he states more explicitly:

> The Lord is the one, who controls the creation, sustenance and dissolution and who as their inner controller directs Brahmā and Śiva and who by manifesting Himself along with them protects the universe.[2]

The implication of this hymn is that the Supreme Being is the primary cause of the three important cosmic functions as stated in the *Vedānta-sūtra*[3] but the functions of creation and dissolution are carried out by the two deities created by Him, while the function of sustenance or protection is done by Himself as an incarnation in the name of Viṣṇu. Incarnation does not amount to birth or origin in the ordinary sense but a mere manifestation (*āvirbhāva*). Hence Viṣṇu is not a deity brought into existence by any Higher Deity as in the case of Brahmā and Rudra. Nammāḻvār asserts that what he says is not a laudatory statement but it is the real truth (*puhalvu illai*).[4] In another place he expresses a regret that he is called upon to prove this, while it is a well-established fact.[5]

If Nārāyaṇa alone is the Supreme Deity, who is to be worshipped for attaining the highest spiritual goal, why do people worship other deities? This is an important question and Nammāḻvār himself raises it and provides an explanation.[6] He points out that it is a fact that there are numerous other deities referred to in the hymns of *Ṛg-Veda* and these Gods are wor-

1. TVM I.1.8.
2. TVM VIII.4.9 *paḍaippoḍu keḍuppuk kāppavaṉ pirama paraṁ-paraṉ, śivappirāṉ avaṉē; iḍaippukku ōr uruvum oḻivu illai avaṉē...*
   See Pillan, AP *brahma-rudra-rūpeṇa, svena rūpeṇa ca nikhila jagat-sṛṣṭi-sthiti-saṁhārahetubhūtanāy.*
3. VS I.1.2.
4. TVM VIII.4.9.
   See Piḷḷān, AP *ivvarthattil stuti illai.*
   See also RRB *ayam arthaḥ paramārtha iti bhāvaḥ.*
5. TVM II.2.2 *ēpāvam paramē...*
6. TVM IV.10.6.

shipped by other religious cults for securing the desired goals. It is also true that these Gods sought for by others for boons such as wealth, happiness, heavenly bliss do confer them to their devotees. While acknowledging these facts, he states that all these deities have been brought into existence by the Supreme Being, Nārāyaṇa, who as their *antarātmā* or the Inner controller grants them the power to confer the desired fruits.[1] Thus, the worship offered to these deities ultimately goes to the Supreme Being who is actually the giver of the boons sought for. This fact is revealed by the Scriptural texts.[2] In view of these explanations, Nammāḻvār advocates the exclusive worship of Nārāyaṇa.

There is yet another reason for upholding the exclusive worship of Nārāyaṇa. According to Vedānta, the supreme goal of life (*parama-puruṣārtha*) is *mokṣa* or the liberation of the soul from bondage. The Sacred texts point out that Janārdana (Nārāyaṇa) is the giver of *mokṣa* (*mokṣa-prada*).[3] Based on this authority, Nammāḻvār also teaches that the Supreme Being alone confers *mokṣa* (*vīḍu-mudalām*).[4] As explained in another hymn, the implication of it is that other deities who are worshipped by the devotees cannot grant final liberation from the cycle of births and deaths. In a characteristic way Nammāḻvār says:

> By passing through several births, you have worshipped several other deities by singing their glory, dancing with joy before them, offering salutation to them and serving them in many other prescribed ways and you have seen the result of it.[5]

The implication of the hymn is that the worship of other deities has not yielded the cherished *mokṣa,* but on the contrary,

---

1. TVM I.1.5 *avaravar vidhivaḻi aḍaiya ninṟāṉarē.*
2. Piḷḷān, while commenting on the hymn (I.1.5) quotes the following Scriptural and *Smṛti* texts in support of this view.
   Taittirīya Āraṇyaka, iṣṭāpūrtaṁ bahudhā jātaṁ jāyamānaṁ viśvaṁ bibharti bhuvanasya nābhiḥ...
   BG VII 21 & 22 *yo yo yāṁ yāṁ tanuṁbhaktaḥ śraddhayā arcitum-icchati.* Also IX.24 *aham hi sarva yajñānāṁ bhoktā ca prabhurevaca.*
3. See *Matsya Purāṇa, mokṣam-icchet janārdanāt.*
4. TVM II.8.1 *iṇaivaṉām epporuḷkum vīḍumudalām.*
   See also I.5.10 *vīḍu tiruttuvāṉ.*
5. TVM IV.10.7 *ōḍiyōḍi palapirappuṁ pirandu maṟṟōr daivaṁ pāḍiyāḍi paṇindu palapaḍikāl vaḻiyēri kaṇḍīr....*

it has only lead to rebirth. Nammāḻvār, therefore, exhorts the devotees to seek the feet of Lord Tirunārāyaṇa, who as the Supreme Deity, is the sole refuge.[1]

III. *Paratattva as Śriyaḥ-pati*

We have examined how the Ultimate Reality of the Upaniṣads is equated with Nārāyaṇa as the Supreme Deity (*para-devatā*). This Deity, according to Nammāḻvār, is not a mere Nārāyaṇa but *Tiru-nārāyaṇa,* that is, Nārāyaṇa as associated with Goddess *Śrī* or Lakṣmī (the word *Tiru* in Tamil stands for *Śrī* in Sanskrit). In other words, the Supreme Being is *Śriyaḥ-pati,* a concept which is generally used in Vaiṣṇava treatises. Though the word *Śriyaḥ-pati* is not found in the hymns, the Āḻvārs use other Tamil words such as *Tirumāl, Maṇavāḷaṉ, Śrīdharaṇ* which bear the same meaning as *Śriyaḥ-pati.* These terms signify, as Nammāḻvār states, that the Supreme Lord is the distinctive consort of Goddess Śrī (*Tirumagaḷār taṉikkēḷvaṉ*).[2] God is often described as *Mādhava, Tirumārpaṉ,* because He is ever enjoying the presence of *Lakṣmī* residing in His chest.[3] Though Goddess *Śrī* is acknowledged as the beloved consort of Nārāyaṇa in accordance with the Scriptural teachings, it is important to know whether she is inseparably related to Him enjoying equal ontological status. In post-Rāmānuja period, the doctrine of Goddess has given room for a few controversial issues and it is, therefore, worth taking note of the views of Nammāḻvār on this subject as found in his hymns.

The first point to be taken note of is that Goddess Lakṣmī is accorded an esteemed place in the divinity. The *Viṣṇu Purāṇa,* the oldest and the most authoritative Purāṇa points out that *Śrī,* as the divine mother of the universe is eternal (*nitya*), inseparable from Viṣṇu (*anapāyanī*) and all-pervasive (*sarvagataḥ*).[4] It also says that She is posited in the chest of Viṣṇu.[5] In conformity with these teachings, the Āḻvārs refer to Lakṣmī in several hymns

1. TVM IV.1.1 *tirunāraṇaṉ tāḷ kālampera cintittu yuminō.*
2. TVM I.6.9.
   See also PTM V.1.10 *tāmaraiyāḷ tan kēḷvaṉ.*
3. TVM I.5.5 *maḍavāḷai mārpil koṇḍa mādhavā.*
   See also TVM III.7.8.
4. VP I.8.17 *nityaiveṣā jaganmātā viṣṇoḥ śrī-ranapāyini;*
   yathā sarvagato viṣṇuḥ tathaiveyam devijottama.
5. VP 1.9.117 *viṣṇuvakṣasthala-sthitām.*

as one who is inalienable from Viṣṇu and posited for ever in His chest.[1] In one of the hymns, Nammāḻvār graphically describes Goddess as inseparably poised in the chest of the Lord ever saying that She shall not be apart from Him even for a moment.[2] All these hymns reveal the inseparable relationship between the God and Goddess.

The second important point stressed by Nammāḻvār is that the divine couple together serve as the *upāya* or means for attaining *mokṣa* and also the *upēya* or supreme goal in the sense of divine service (*kaiṅkarya*) in the *paramapada*. Thus, he exhorts to the devotees to meditate (*cintana*) on Tirunārāyaṇa (*Śriyaḥpati*).[3] The purpose of meditation on God is to attain the highest spiritual goal by overcoming the obstacles in the form of past *karma* standing in the way of God-realization. This point is manifestly brought out in another hymn. It says: "The majestic Lord, along with His beloved consort, removes the two fold *karma* (*karma* in the form of good and bad deeds) and confers the highest goal to be achieved by spiritual discipline."[4] The implication of this verse, as explained lucidly by Piḷḷān, is that the Supreme Lord grants *mokṣa* by way of removing the obstacles and while conferring such highest goal, he does it in the company of His beloved spouse.[5] In another hymn, Nammāḻvār explicitly states that Goddess removes the sins standing as obstacles for attaining God.[6] He himself admits that after seeing the majesty of the

---

1. TVM I.5.5 *maḍavāḷai mārpil koṇḍāy mādhavā.*
   I.10.3 *kombarāvu nuṇṇēriḍai mārpaṉ.*
   III.1.6 *pūvinmēl māduvāḻ marpiṉāy.*
   III.7.8 *tirumārpaṉai.*
   VI.10.1 *alarmēlmaṅgai uraimārpā.*
   IX.4.1 *tirumārvinil śērtirumālē.*
   PTM III.1.2 *tirumārvaṉ.*
   PeTi I.1.2 *valamārpiṉil vāḻhiṉṟa maṅgai.*
   ITi 52 *malarāḷ-mārvaṉ.*
2. TVM VI.10.10 *ahalahillēṉ iraiyum eṉṟu alarmēlmaṅgai uraimārpā.*
3. TVM IV.1.1 *tirunāraṇaṉtāḷ kālaṁpera cintittu uyminō.*
4. TVM I.6.9 *tarumavarum payanāya, tirumahaḷār taṉikkēḷvaṉ,*
   perumai uḍaiya pirāṉār, irumai viṉai kaḍivārē.
5. See Piḷḷān, AP I.6.9 *anda perudarkaridāna sampattai tandu, aruḷum iḍattil pirāṭṭiyōḍe*
   kūḍa niṉṟu tandu aruḷum eṉhirār.
6. TVM IV.5.11 *vērimārāda pūmēl iruppāḷ viṉai tīrkkumē.*
   See also *Īḍu* IV.5.11 *ittiruvāymoḻi kaṟṟarai periya-pirāṭṭiyār,*
   tamakkē bharamāhak-koṇḍu samasta
   duḥkaṅgaḷaiyum pōkkuvār eṅgirār.

Lord in the glorious company of *Tirumakaḷ* (Lakṣmī) that he was able to renounce the worldly pleasures caused by the sense organs and then attain His feet.[1]

Nammāḻvār also seeks the grace of both the Lord and His consort for rendering divine service. While addressing the presiding deity of Tiruppuḷiṅguḍi (a pilgrim centre near Āḻvār's birth place), he pleads:

> Oh Lord, reposing in Tiruppuḷiṅguḍi, shower your grace on us (devotees) who have been rendering appropriate services at your temple generation after generation with the grace of yourself and also that of the lotus-born Goddess.[2]

In the same context he appeals to the deity:

> May you shower your grace on the devotees who are dedicated to divine service; may you and your lotus-born spouse get up (from your reclining position) and remain seated to be worshipped by the three worlds.[3]

All these hymns reveal that the divine couple is not only the *prāpya* or the supreme goal to be attained for rendering the ever lasting divine service (*nitya-kaiṅkarya*) but also they together serve as the *upāya* for *mokṣa*. This view is further strengthened by the fact that Nammāḻvār performs *śaraṇāgati* at the feet of the presiding deity of Tirumalai, Lord Śrīnivāsa in whose chest Goddess Lakṣmī dwells for ever. The prayer in the form of actual self-surrender for *mokṣa* is addressed to the Lord as inseparably associated with Goddess.[4] Some commentators on this particular hymn have taken the view that the prayer seeking refuge is mainly addressed to God, whereas the Goddess, though associated inseparably with the Lord, is intended to act as a mediator (*puruṣakāra*) to secure the desired goal. The concept of *puruṣakāratva*, as explained in the Vaiṣṇava treatises of post-Rāmānuja period, is not mentioned explicitly in the hymns of

---

1. TVM IV.9.10 *oṇḍoḍiyāḷ tirumagaḷuṁ nīyumē nilā niṟpa,*
   kaṇḍa śatir kaṇḍu oḻindēn aḍaindēn uṉ tiruvaḍiyē.
2. TVM IX.2.1 *paṇḍaināḷāle nin tiruvaruḷuṁ paṅgayattāḷ tiruvaruḷum koṇḍu....*
3. TVM IX.2.3 *toṇḍarōrku aruḷi, taḍaṅgoḷ tāmaraikkaṉ*
   viḻittu nī eḻundu uṉ untāmaraimaṅgaiyum nīyuṁ
   iḍangoḷ mūvulahum toḻa irundu aruḷāy.
4. TVM VI.10.10.

the Āḻvārs. On the other hand, the hymns of Nammāḻvār refer to the capacity of Goddess Lakṣmī to remove the sins and also confer *mokṣa*. In view of these facts, the role of Goddess is not restricted only to *puruṣakāratva*, but she can also serve as *upāya* for *mokṣa*. However, the followers of Teṅkalai sect interpret these hymns in favour of *puruṣakāratva* only.

The ontological status of Goddess *Śrī* is another important point that requires clarification. There is no mention in the hymns whether Goddess is *sarvagata* or all-pervasive as *Viṣṇu Purāṇa* says. Nor is there any indication that She is *aṇu* or monadic, as the *jīvātman* is. In the absence of these facts, there is room for the controversy that has arisen in the post-Rāmānuja period viz., whether Goddess is on a par with Viṣṇu enjoying the status of *Īśvaratva* (supreme sovereignty) or whether She is a subordinate deity, like other *cetanas*, though of higher order. These doubts have been generated by the Vaiṣṇava Ācāryas of later period presumably out of sectarian bias. Going by the teachings of Scriptural and Smṛti texts and in particular the *Viṣṇu Purāṇa* as well as Pāñcarātra-Āgamas, Lakṣmī is on a par with Viṣṇu in all respects and the divine couple constitute one Reality.[1] If the other Vaiṣṇava doctrines taught by Nammāḻvār strictly conform to the Vedas, Itihāsas and Purāṇas, we can assume that the theory regarding the ontological status of Goddess *Śrī* as stated above is also acceptable to him. Āḷavandār, Rāmānuja and his immediate successors and also the older commentators on *Tiruvāymoḻi* maintain the same view. They have not ascribed a subordinate position to Goddess. The clear-cut statement of the Vaḍakkutiruvīdi Piḷḷāi, the author of the famous *Īḍu* (commentary on the *Tiruvāymoḻi*) on this issue in his Introduction is worth noting. He states:

> Both at the time of approaching (the Divine Being for self-surrender) and also at the time of enjoyment (when rendering Divine service in *mokṣa*), the divine couple alone is the goal without any distinction.[2]

1. See Srinivasa Chari, *Vaiṣṇavism—Its Philosophy, Theology and Religious Discipline*. Chapter 8, pp. 167-175
2. See *Īḍu*, Introduction (*Mudal Śriyaḥpati*)—*āśrayaṇavēḷaiyōḍu bhogavēḷaiyoḍu vāśiyara ōru mithunamē uddēśyam*. Even this statement is interpreted by the followers of Teṅkalai Sect in favour of Goddess *Śrī* being a *puruṣakāra* at the time of seeking self-surrender and not as an *upāya* for *mokṣa*.

Piḷḷān, who is the earliest commentator on *Tiruvāymoḻi* and who is claimed to express the thoughts of Rāmānuja, holds the same view. Besides, the hymns themselves though not explicitly, but by implication, indicate a status for Lakṣmī as equal to that of Īśvara. As pointed out earlier, Nammāḻvār speaks of Godhead as inseparably associated with Lakṣmī. In several hymns, he addresses God as the beloved consort of *Tirumāmakaḷ* (Lakṣmī).[1] As already observed, the divine couple is the object of worship both at the time of performing self-surrender (*prapatti*) and during the time of offering continuous divine service (*nitya-kaiṅkarya*). Presumably based on these views of Nammāḻvār, Rāmānuja in the *Śaraṇāgati-gadya* states that Goddess *Śrī*, who is *anapāyanī* (inseparable from Bhagavān) possesses all the characteristics of God viz., *svarūpa, rūpa, guṇa, vibhava, aiśvarya* etc., as appropriate to His status (*anurūpa*) and also as liked by Him (*svābhimata*).

Nammāḻvār conceives God as associated not only with *Śrī* but also with *Bhū-devī* and *Nīlā-devī*. There are several hymns referring to all the three feminine deities as consorts of the Supreme Lord. Lakṣmī or *Śrī* is known as *Tiru-makaḷ* or *Periya-pirāṭṭi, Bhū* as *Maṇ-makaḷ* or *Bhūmi-pirāṭṭi* and *Nīlā* as *Āyarmaḍa-makaḷ* or *Nappiṉṉai-pirāṭṭi*. All the three are regarded as consorts of Viṣṇu.[2] Though all the three deities are spoken as beloved spouses of the Lord, each one has distinctive glory of Her own. Lakṣmī, who is the dearest to God, is the personification of compassion (*dayā*) and enhances the glory of God by her permanent presence in the chest of the Lord. Bhū-devī is equally dear to the Lord and She is the very personification of *kṣamā* (forgiveness). Nīlā is described as one possessing an enchanting beauty and She is the object of enjoyment for the Lord (*anubhava-sukhaṁ*).

Regarding their relative ontological status, Rāmānuja and his immediate successors have regarded Lakṣmī as an integral part of Reality, while the other two deities are accorded a lower

1. TVM VI.10.4 *tirumāmakaḷ-kēḷvaṉ*.
   Also VII.7.9 *eṉ tirumakaḷśer mārpaṉ*.
   VI.8.10 *eṉ tirumārvarku*.
   VI.10.10 *ahalahillēn iraiyum eṉṟu alarmēlmaṅgai uraimārpā*.
2. TVM I.9.4 *uḍaṉamar kātal makaḷīr tirumakaḷ maṇmakaḷ āyar maḍamakaḷ, eṉṟivar mūvar*.
   See also V.6.11.

status. This view is supported by the *Viśvaksena Saṁhitā*, a Pāñcarātra treatise belonging to the period earlier than Nammāḻvār. This *Saṁhitā* points out that Lakṣmī, as the principal consort, is *vibhu* by virtue of Her *svarūpa*, whereas *Bhū* and *Nīlā* are omnipresent by virtue of their infinite knowledge. The former has a higher status and forms part of divinity, whereas the latter though permanent consorts of Viṣṇu, have a relatively lower status.[1] Though Nammāḻvār does not mention these facts explicitly in his hymns, he seems to be in favour of the view held by the *Pāñcarātra Saṁhitā*. This is evident from the implications of the hymns describing the origin of these feminine deities and the functions they perform. Lakṣmī manifested herself (*prādurbhāva*) and not born in the ordinary sense, during the time of churning the mythological milky ocean (*kṣīrābdhi*) for obtaining nectar (*amṛta*). She is, therefore, designated as *kṣīrodbhava*. Soon after her advent she chose as her abode the chest of Viṣṇu. This episode is narrated in the *Viṣṇu Purāṇa* and also in other Purāṇas. Nammāḻvār as well as other Āḻvārs refer to this event in several hymns in the context of speaking her glory. She has been accorded a respectable place and also respectable status as the most dearest consort of Viṣṇu and as one who enhances the glory of the Lord by Her permanent association with Him. Tirumaṅgai Āḻvār speaks of God as *Tiruvukkum Tiru*. Such descriptions are not forthcoming in respect of *Bhū* and *Nīlā*.

Bhū-devī, who is a permanent consort of Viṣṇu (*Viṣṇupatnī*), is the presiding deity of earth (*bhūmi*). During the great deluge She was taken away by the demons and hidden in the bottom of the ocean. Out of compassion Viṣṇu in the form of *Varāha* (boar) rescued her.[2] There are Vedic hymns and several anecdotes in the Purāṇas narrating this event. The Āḻvārs are very fond of referring to this frequently. She is described as the personification of forgiveness (*kṣamā*). Being possessed of this virtue, She is prompted to play the role of preventing Her Lord

1. See *Viśvaksena Saṁhitā* (quoted in *Śrīsūkta Bhāṣya*)
yathā mayā jagad-vyāptaṁ svarūpeṇa svabhāvataḥ;
tathā vyāptaṁ idaṁ sarvaṁ niyantrī ca tathā iśvarī
tathā bhūmiśca nīlā ca śeṣabhūte mate mama;
svarupatastu na tayoḥ guṇato vyāptiriṣyate.
2. TVM IV.2.6.

from inflicting punishment for the sins committed by the devotees.

Nīlā who is an incarnation of *Bhū-devī* is presented as a maiden of a *gopa* (cowherd) in Bṛndāvan possessing an enchanting beauty. God-incarnate Kṛṣṇa was attracted by her charm and he wed her after killing seven powerful bulls, which was a deal set up by her father to exhibit the valour of a person wanting to marry her.[1] The Āḻvārs refer to this episode in several hymns. She is described as the very personification of physical beauty which captures the Lord to such an extent as it would prevent Him from looking at the sinners.

As pointed out earlier Nammāḻvār describes the three consorts in the following words: *Tirumakaḷ, Maṇmakaḷ* and *Āyar-maḍamakaḷ.* Each word has a specific significance as explained by the author of the *Īḍu.*[2] The word *Tirumakaḷ* implies that Lakṣmī is the principal consort (*pradhāna-mahiṣī*). She alone has a place in the chest of the Lord, never desiring to be separated from Him even for a moment (*ahalahillēṉ*). She alone has the right of being the queen (*paṭṭattukku uriyāḷ*) and the Sovereign of the universe, as the *Śrī-sūkta* of *Ṛg-Veda* states (*Īśvarīṁ sarva bhūtānāṁ*). She is the very personification of compassion (*karuṇāmiva-rūpiṇī*)[3] and as such She can effectively play the role of a mediator.

The word *maṇmakaḷ* means *bhū-devī* or the presiding deity of earth (*viśvadhāriṇī*). She is figured as the personification of *kṣamā* or forgiveness. According to Hindu tradition, *kṣamā* is an essential characteristic of *bhūmi* or earth, because it ungrudgingly supports all the living beings.[4] As representing *kṣamā*, She plays the important role of pleading God on behalf of the devotees not to take cognizance of their sins.

The word *Āyar-maḍamakaḷ* indicates that Nīlā is the daughter of a *gopa* (*āyar*). She is described as the personification of enjoyment.[5] As an object of enjoyment, the Lord is captured by her to such an extent that He would not take cognizance of the sins

1. TVM IV.3.1; also II.5.7, III.5.4, and IV.2.5.
2. *Īḍu* I.9.4.
3. See VD. *Dayaśatakam,* verse 6.
   Samasta jananīṁ vande caitanya-stanya-dāyinīm;
   śreyasīṁ Śrīnivāsasya kāruṇāmiva rupiṇīm.
4. See *Rāmāyaṇa* II.2 *kṣamayā pṛthivīsamaḥ.*
5. *Īḍu* I.9.4 *anubhava-sukham tāṉāy.*

of the devotees. Expressed metaphorically, Tirumakaḷ stands for the glory of Lord (*avan aiśvaryam*); *maṇmakal* represents the land where it grows (*adu viḷaiyum bhūmi*) and *maḍamakaḷ* is the one who is the enjoyer of that glory (*attai bhujikkira bhoktavānavaṉ*).[1]

The above interpretation of the hymn related to the three consorts reveals that Nammāḻvār has in mind a degree of difference in the relative status and the role of the three feminine deities. Presumably, based on the teaching of Nammāḻvār, Rāmānuja in his *Śaraṇāgati Gadya* acknowledges a degree of difference in the status of the three consorts of Viṣṇu. He uses two separate words as *Śrī-vallabha* and *evam-bhūta bhūmi-nīlā-nāyaka* to indicate the difference in their ontological status.[2] Thus, it may be seen that the doctrine of Goddess which is a distinctive tenet of Vaiṣṇavism has its basis in the teaching of the Āḻvārs.

1. *Īḍu* I.9.4. *anubhava-sukham tāṉāy*.
2. See VD's *Gadya-bhāṣya*.

CHAPTER 3

THE DOCTRINE OF GOD

We have presented in the previous chapter the philosophical view of the Ultimate Reality (*Paratattva*) as stated in the hymns of the Āḻvārs. We have seen how this Reality is equated with Nārāyaṇa, the Supreme Deity who is inseparably associated with the Goddess *Śrī*. According to the Āḻvārs, the Brahman of the Upaniṣads is the *Śriyaḥpati* (*Tirumāl* in Tamil) of Vaiṣṇava religion. He is essentially of the nature of *ānanda* or bliss, *jñāna* or knowledge and *amala* or purity *par excellence*. He is infinite (*ananta*) and abides in every thing in the universe, both the sentient and non-sentient, as its inner controller (*antaryāmin*). He is the primary cause of the creation, sustenance and dissolution of the universe.

Besides the philosophical view of Reality which is well in conformity with the Upaniṣadic statements, the Āḻvārs also present a comprehensive doctrine of God, rich in its theological significance. For the first time in the history of Vaiṣṇavism we come across a description of Godhead in all its glorious aspects. It enjoys credibility since the Āḻvārs, as mystic saints gifted with spiritual knowledge are claimed to have intuited God and spoken from depth of their experience.

The concept of Godhead as a Supreme Person (*Puruṣottama*) has several aspects. It covers God's essential nature (*svarūpa*), the divine attributes (*guṇa*), the divine personality (*divyamaṅgaḷa vigraha*), the divine incarnations (*divyāvatāra*) and the divine activities (*divya-līlās*). The Upaniṣads have accorded greater importance to the essential nature of God as the Supreme Being. The Āgama treatises have paid more attention to the visual aspects of the divine personality. The Itihāsas and Purāṇas, on the other hand, have emphasised the divine attributes and divine functions. The religious texts have devoted their attention to such selected divine attributes as are of emotional appeal to the devotees. The Āḻvārs, on the other hand, have dwelt on all these aspects of the divinity. The uniqueness of the *Divyaprabandham* lies in presenting a grand description of the Divine Being full of emotional appeal to the devotees. The doctrine of God as conceived by the Āḻvārs therefore deserves separate consideration. We shall deal with it in the present chapter under the following headings:

I. Divine Attributes
II. Divine Personality
III. Divine Incarnations
IV. Divine Activities.

I. *Divine Attributes*

In the Viśiṣṭādvaita Vedānta, a distinction is drawn between the *svarūpa* or the essential nature of an entitiy and the *dharma* or the attribute it possesses. Rāmānuja uses the term *svabhāva* for the latter. Every entity in the universe, both metaphysical and physical, comprises two aspects viz., *dharma* or the attribute and *dharmī* or the substrate in which the former inheres. A quality by itself does not exist and it is inherently related to the substrate. Similarly, a pure substrate devoid of a quality is inconceivable. This epistemological principle applies even to God who in this system is a spiritual entity (*ajaḍa dravya*). The Upaniṣads describe the essential nature of Brahman in terms of *satya, jñāna* and *ananta*. Similarly, it speaks of Brahman as one who possesses infinite knowledge and bliss (*ānanda*).

The Āḻvārs also have acknowledged the distinction between the *svarūpa* of God and His *guṇas* or attributes. Intuitively they have perceived what God is in respect of His essential nature and what He possesses as attributes. Thus, Nammāḻvār states at the outset of his *Tiruvāymoḻi* that the Supreme Being is He who is endowed with *ānanda par excellence*.[1] In this hymn he refers to the attributes of God. In the subsequent hymns he

1. TVM I.1.1 *uyarnalam uḍaiyavaṉ yavaṉ avaṉ*.

speaks of the *svarūpa* of God, where he describes Him as one who is different from the sentient souls and non-sentient entities and that He abides in every entity in the universe within and without, as its *antarātmā*.[1] Whenever the Āḻvārs describe the transcendental and immanent character of the Supreme Being, they refer to His *svarūpa*. When they sing the greatness of God in terms, such as *aruḷāḷaṉ* or the compassionate, *eḷiyavaṉ* or the one who is easily accessible and *neḍumāl* or as the one deeply attached to the devotees, they refer to His attributes. As a classic example of these two aspects of God, Tirumaṅgai Āḻvār devotes an entire decad[2] to portray the *paratva* and *saulabhya* of God in the form of a dialogue between two cowherd maids, one upholding the former, while the other extols the latter.

Before we outline the select divine attributes individually, we may take note of a few general points. In the Viśiṣṭādvaita Vedānta, the attributes are classified under two categories: (a) essential and (b) secondary. The essential attributes are those which determine the nature of Brahman or God. These are known as *svarūpa-nirūpaka dharma*. The secondary ones are those which belong to the object but they become known only after the *svarūpa* of the object is determined. These are known as *nirūpita-svarūpa viśeṣaṇa*. According to the Upaniṣads, *satyatva, jñānatva, anantatva, ānandatva* and *amalatva* are the essential attributes of God. All the other qualitites of God come under the secondary category. We have already discussed the essential attributes in the earlier chapter and we are concerned here only with the secondary attributes.

The term *ananta* used by the Upaniṣad to define Brahman, implies that Brahman, as a *saviśeṣa* entity is infinite not only in respect of its essential nature (*svarūpa*), but also with regard to its attributes. *Viṣṇu Purāṇa* states explicitly, God is endowed with infinite number of auspicious attributes.[3] Following this teaching, the Āḻvārs too maintain the same view.[4] They repeatedly emphasise that God's *svarūpa* and *guṇas* are beyond the

---

1. TVM I.1.2 and I.1.10.
2. PTM XI.5.
3. VP VI.5 84 *samasta-kalayāṇaguṇātmako asau.*
4. TVM II.5.9. *ellaiyil śīr.*
   III.3.3 *eṇṇil tolpukaḻ.*
   V.7.7 *andamil pukaḻ.*

comprehension of the human intellect.[1] Not even the celestial deities such as Brahmā, Rudra and Indra, who are gifted with spiritual knowledge, are in a position to speak fully of the glory of the Supreme Being.[2] His greatness is immeasurable. The Poygai Āḻvār exclaims with wonder: "Who can comprehend and speak the Lord's glory."[3]

Even though the divine attributes are countless and beyond human comprehension, the Āḻvārs have enumerated a large number of them. In fact, each hymn mentions more than one *guṇa.* The *Tiruvāymoḻi* of Nammāḻvār and the *Periya Tirumoḻi* of *Tirumaṅgai* are abundant with *bhagavad-guṇās.* Vedānta Deśika has taken special note of these divine qualities. In his *Dramiḍopaniṣat-tātparya-ratnāvaḷī,* he enumerates 1,001 attributes by selecting one from each of the thousand hymns of the *Tiruvāymoḻi.* Often the Āḻvārs dwell on the same *guṇas* in several of their hymns though in different contexts. Many times they do not directly mention the attributes by name but refer to a mythological episode that would imply a divine quality. In fact, a large number of divine deeds to which the hymns make repeated references are inṭended primarily to highlight the divine attributes with illustrations drawn from the Epics and Purāṇās. Thus for instance, there are several references to the episode of Vāmana (the incarnation of Viṣṇu as a dwarf) who measured the entire universe with three strides. The mention of this event is primarily intended to demonstrate the virtue of the loving disposition of God to protect His devotees.

Though the divine attributes referred to in the *Divyaprabandham* are far too many, they may be classified under the following headings for the purpose of our study:

(1) *Guṇas* related to God as Supreme Being (*Śarveśvara*).
(2) *Guṇas* related to the divine personality (*divya-maṅgaḷa-vigraha*).
(3) *Guṇas* exhibited during the manifestations of God (*avatāras*) and through His divine activities (*līlās*).

1. TVM I.9.6 *yavarkkum cintaikkum gocaramallaṉ,*
See also TVM II.2.1 *eṇṇiṉ- mīdiyaṉ emperumāṉ.*
2. TVM I.9.2 *viṇṇavarkku eṇṇalariyāṉ.*
3. MTi 68 *uṇarvār ār uṉperumai.*

We shall discuss the first one in the present section and the other two in sections II, III and IV.

Divine Attributes as Related to Sarveśvara

The most important attribute of God as *Śarveśvara* is *jagat-kāraṇatva,* that is, God as the primary cause of the creation, protection and dissolution of the universe. Following the teaching of the *Taittirīya Upaniṣad* the *Vedānta-sūtra* has adopted it as an important criteria for determining an ontological entity as *Īśvara.* The Āḻvārs have duly acknowledged it and have, therefore, given added emphasis to these cosmic functions of God. We have already discussed this matter in an earlier chapter.

Allied to the concept of *jagat-kāraṇatva,* the Upaniṣads conceive three fundamental attributes of Brahman or God. In Viśiṣṭādvaita terminology these are known as *ādhāratva* or being the supporter of the universe, *niyantṛtva* or being the controller of the universe and *śeṣitva* or being the Lord of the universe. Nammāḻvār refers to these characteristics in the opening decad of the *Tiruvāymoḻi.* The Supreme Being is the *ādhāra* of the entire universe since all that exists in the universe derives its *sattā* or existence from Him. As the indwelling soul (*antaryāmī*) He controls the activities of all the sentient beings and the non-sentient entities. As the Sovereign of the universe, He is the *śeṣin.*[1]

God as *Śarveśvara* is the ruler of not only the physical universe but also the transcendental realm known in the Viśiṣṭādvaita as *nityavibhūti* including the *paramapada,* the eternal abode of Viṣṇu referred to in the *Ṛg-Veda.* The latter appears to be of greater importance to the Āḻvārs, since they often extol God as *Viṇṇōrkōṉ, Vāṉōrnāyakaṉ* and *Vaikuṇṭhaṉ.* He is also described as *Daivyanāyaka, Devādideva* which imply that He is the Lord of all celestial deities. The opening hymns of the *Tiruvāymoḻi* intended to define the nature of the Ultimate Reality specifically mentions that the Supreme Being is that person who is the ruler of the *nitya-sūris,* who are eternally free from bondage. In another context Nammāḻvār also openly states that Nārāyaṇa is the only deity, who can confer *mokṣa,* the supreme spiritual goal.[2] These

1. See Chapter 2, pp. 43-44.
2. TVM I.5.10 *vīḍu tiruttuvāṉ...*
   See also TVM II.2.1 *vīḍumuḍal muḻudumāy...*
   See also p. 68.

descriptions of God indicate two important attributes of God viz., *ubhayavibhūti-nāthatva* or the Lordship of the transcendental and physical universe and *mokṣa-pradatva* or the capacity to confer *mokṣa*.

The attributes so far outlined are important both for philosophy and theology. Philosophically, they establish the Supremacy of Nārāyaṇa as the *paratattva*. For the theologian they reveal the glory of God. The Āḻvārs have, therefore, highlighted these attributes in their hymns.

There is another group of divine attributes which are regarded as important both by the Pāñcarātra Āgamas and the *Viṣṇu Purāṇa*. These are: *jñāna* or omniscience, *śakti* or omnipotence, *bala* or strength, *aiśvarya* or Lordship, *vīrya* or energy and *tejas* or splendour. These six known as *ṣaḍguṇas* constitute the essential characteristics of the Supreme Lord. *Viṣṇu Purāṇa* defines *Bhagavān* (a name synonymous with Viṣṇu) as one who possesses these six attributes.[1] The Upaniṣads also refer to these *guṇas*.[2] A sound concept of God should necessarily include these attributes. The Āḻvārs who were influenced by the Pāñcarātra Āgamas have, therefore, acknowledged these. We may see how the Āḻvārs have conceived each one of these divine qualities.

Jñāna

The term *jñāna* is used in two senses in the Viśiṣṭādvaita Vedānta. Firstly, it refers to the very *svarūpa* of Brahman and in that context it means that Brahman or God is essentially of the nature of knowledge. It is in this sense that the definition of Brahman as *jñāna* is understood. The *Bṛhadāraṇyaka Upaniṣad* also describes Brahman as *vijñānaghana* or the personification of pure knowledge. Secondly, the term *jñāna* refers to an attribute (*guṇa*) and it then means that Brahman or God possesses knowledge (*jñāna-guṇaka*). In this sense the Upaniṣad describes *Īśvara* as *Sarvajña* or omniscient. The term *jñāna* included in the six *guṇas* referred to by the Pāñcarātra Āgamas, is understood in the sense of an

1. VP VI.5.79 *jñāna-śakti-balaiśvarya vīrya tejāmsy-aśeṣataḥ;*
bhagavat-śabda vācyāni vinā heyair-guṇādibhiḥ.
See also *Ahirbudhnya Saṁhitā* II.5.3.
ṣāḍguṇyam tat paraṁ brahma sarvakāraṇa-kāraṇaṁ.
2. MuUp I.1.10 *yassarvajñas-sarvavit.*
ŚvUp VI.8 *parāsya śaktiḥ vividhaiva śrūyate svābhāvikī jñāna-bala-kriyāca.*

attribute. It implies that the Lord is *sarvajña* or omniscient. The fuller meaning of *sarvajña,* as explained by Nāthamuni, is that God directly knows everything simultaneously as it is.[1] That is, he can perceive directly through the attributive knowledge without the aid of the sense organs.

The Āḻvārs use this term in both the senses. Whenever they describe God as *jñāna-mūrtti* or the personification of knowledge, they uphold the view that the Supreme Being is essentially of the nature of knowledge. Nammāḻvār speaks of the *para-tattva* as *muḻu-uṇar*[2] and in this context he means that it is wholly constituted of knowledge. Following the Upaniṣadic teaching, the Āḻvārs also frequently address God as *paraṁ-jyoti, śuḍar-jyoti* etc. In all such references, *jñāna* is applicable to the *svarūpa* of God. That is, God is the embodiment of pure infinite knowledge or spiritual *light.* Whenever the Āḻvārs describe God as omniscient or as the one who possesses infinite knowledge, they refer to the attributive aspect of knowledge. Nammāḻvār uses the expression *uṇarvin-mūrtti,* which implies that knowledge is a *guṇa* or an essential attribute of God. In addition to the acceptance of *jñāna* as *svarūpa* of God, it is necessary also to admit it as an essential attribute of *Paramātman* because it is only through His knowledge that God performs the important functions such as creation of the universe by *saṅkalpa* (will), showering of grace (*anugraha*), dispensing punishment to the sinners (*nigraha*), conferring of *mokṣa* etc. The Pāñcarātra texts have, therefore, included *jñāna* in the sense of an essential attribute among the six *guṇas.* Realizing this fact, the Āḻvārs have duly acknowledged this divine attribute as is evident from the hymns.

Śakti

Śakti in a general sense means power but in the context of God it refers to the extraordinary power that God possesses in performing the various divine feats. It is an important attribute and the Āḻvārs have taken cognizance of it in more than one way. They visualise the display of Lord's *śakti* in the creation of the variegated universe without any aid by a mere wish or *saṅkalpa.*

---

1. See *Nyāyatattva* (Quoted by VD in *Gadya-bhāṣya*) *yo vetti yugapat sarvaṁ pratyakṣeṇa sadā svataḥ.*
2. TVM I.1.2.

They see the *śakti* of the Supreme Being in the performance of divine deeds which are impossible for others (*aghaṭitaghaṭana sāmarthya*). In order to illustrate the extraordinary divine power, the Āḻvārs speak with wonder the manifestation of God as an infant reposing on a tiny banyan leaf containing within Himself the entire universe in a potential form during the great deluge. The lifting of the *govardhana* hill by Lord Kṛṣṇa to protect the cowherds and cows from the torrential rain caused by the wrath of Indra is seen by the Āḻvārs as a demonstration of divine power.

Bala

Bala means strength. The Āḻvārs experience this divine quality in the capacity displayed by God in holding up the created entities such as the heaven, the planets, the physical universe in their respective positions without any strain. The deeds performed by God-incarnate Rāma, Kṛṣṇa, Paraśurāma, Narasiṁha in killing the powerful demons without any strong weapons or assistance of others is viewed by the Āḻvārs as an exhibition of Lord's *bala*. Nammāḻvār expresses his dismay at the power demonstrated by Lord Kṛṣṇa in killing the ferocious *Bāṇāsura*, who according to mythology possessed thousand hands with weapons and who was also assisted by Rudra.

Tejas

Tejas literally means lustre and the Āḻvārs use this word in this sense. The lustre is generally attributed to the divine body. Thus, they describe God as *śuḍar-mūrtti* or *śuḍaroḷi-mūrtti*, meaning thereby that God possesses a spiritual body which is shining with extraordinary brilliance. To illustrate its lustrous character, the Āḻvārs compare it to the luminosity radiated by thousands of suns. They also compare it to the shining colour disseminated by the thousands of freshly blossomed lotus flowers.

Following the Upaniṣadic teaching, *tejas* is also understood in the sense of *paraṁ-jyotis* or Supreme Light which stands for the very Brahman.[1] Brahman is the light of the lights (*jyotiṣāṁ jyotiḥ*) in the sense that it is the supreme spiritual light from which all the luminous entities such as sun, moon, stars, light-

1. See ChUP VIII.11.2 *paraṁ-jyotir-upasampadya svena rūpeṇa abhiniṣpadyate.* See also BrUp VI.4.16 *taṁ devāḥ jyotiṣāṁ jyotiḥ....*

ning etc., derive their light, as the *Kaṭha Upaniṣad* points out.[1] The Āḻvārs have also conceived God in this philosophic sense. Nammāḻvār often addresses God as *paraṁ-jyotis*. Tirumaṅgai Āḻvār, addresses Him as *nandā-viḷakku*. In both instances, they mean by this term the very Supreme Being who is transcendental spiritual light.

Vīrya

Vīrya means energy and in the context of God, it refers to the special power possessed by God to remain unchanged in spite of His being the material cause of the universe. Nammāḻvār acknowledges this divine quality when he says that despite the performance of many gigantic feats, His greatness is not affected a bit.[2]

Aiśvarya

Aiśvarya means Lordship or Sovereignty. It signifies the quality of rulership of the entire universe by His unchecked freedom. By virtue of God's rulership, the Upaniṣads describe Brahman as *sarvasya-vaśī*, the controller of all and *sarvādhipatiḥ* or the Lord of all.[3] The Āḻvārs have been greatly attracted by this divine aspect and repeatedly sing His glory in terms of His being the Lord of the transcendental realm and the physical universe.

There is yet another group of important divine attributes which have been prominently portrayed in the *Divyaprabandham*. As these are of special theological significance and are of greater emotional appeal, the God-intoxicated Āḻvārs refer to them quite repeatedly in their songs using the mythological episodes as illustrations. The important attributes are:

Saulabhya or easy accessibility
Sauśīlya or gracious condescension
Vātsalya or loving disposition
Kṛpā or compassion

---

1. KaUp II.11.15 *tameva bhāntam-anubhāti sarvaṁ tasya bhāṣā sarvamidaṁ vibhāti.*
2. TVM I.5.2 *ninainda ellāporuḷkalkun vittāy, mudalil śidaiyāmē. . .*
   uṉperumai māśūṇādō māyōṉē.
   See RRB I.5.2 *vicitra āścarya śakti-śālinī.*
   See also TVM I.3.3 *yāvaiyuṁ yāvaruṁ tāṉāṁ, amaivuḍai nāraṇaṉ māyaiyai aṟipavar yārē—'māya'* here means wondrous *śakti.*
3. BrUp VI.4.22.

Audārya or generosity
Bandhutva or friendly relationship.

Saulabhya

As a divine attribute it implies that God who is the Supreme Transcendental Being (*para*) also makes Himself easily accessible to the devotees by His willingness to manifest Himself in different forms either as incarnations (*vibhava-avatāras*) or as *arcā* deities. It is because of this quality possessed by God that it is possible for the humble human beings to approach Him for redemption. The mystic saints are so greatly attracted by this divine quality that they repeatedly extol it in their hymns. The importance attached to this attribute may be seen from the fact that it is the first and foremost *guṇa* that finds a mention in the *Tiruvāymoḻi*. Nammāḻvār, soon after teaching the nature of *para-tattva* and the means of attainment in the first two decads, commences the third decad with the praise of God's *saulabhya*. The hymn states:

> For those who are devoted to God, He is easily accessible, but for others (who despise Him), He distances Himself.

In this connection, the Āḻvār refers to the episode in which the child Kṛṣṇa as God-incarnate was tied with a rope to a mortar by his mother when she caught him stealing the butter. The episode signifies to the Āḻvār how the Supreme Lord of the universe submits Himself to such a trifle punishment at the hands of a human being, thereby displaying His *saulabhya*. Tradition has it that the Āḻvār was emotionally moved by the contemplation of this event that he fell into a trance.

There are several such incidents to which the Tirumaṅgai and other Āḻvārs refer in order to reveal this *saulabhya guṇa*. In the opinion of the Āḻvārs, the very incarnation of the Supreme Being in the form of human and other living beings irrespective of the status and place of descent is a clear demonstration of His *saulabhya*.

Sauśīlya

This term signifies the gracious condescension of the Supreme Being to come down to the level of ordinary human beings and mix with them freely without any inhibition. The classic example of this divine quality can be seen in the manner in which the God-incarnate Rāma fondly embraced Guha, a hunter in the forest. This quality is of special appeal to the Āḻvārs who have mentioned it several times in their songs. In one of the decads[1] Nammāḻvār elucidates it in an interesting way. He addresses Lord Kṛṣṇa as *kaḷva* or thief who stole the butter. But he condemns himself for having defiled the Lord because as the lowest humble human being he is unfit to speak about the greatest Lord of the universe. Even though the Āḻvār addressed God contemptuously, the latter graciously responds to him, as explained by the commentators.[2] This is taken as an indication of His *sauśīlya.*

There are other ways in which the Āḻvār enjoys this divine quality. Considering the status of God, the various kinds of worship offered to Him even by the exalted celestial beings are insignificant. But, yet the Lord accepts them with delight and gratitude, thereby showing his great virtue.[3]

In a characteristic way, the Āḻvār enjoys the Lord's *sauśīlya* by pointing out that the Lord assumed the human form as a Gopāla, the head of the cowherds in order to mix with them freely. He ate the butter, as if he needed it as an antidote to the remnant of the earth swallowed at the time of dissolution. But actually it was done to display his fondness to the articles considered dear by His devotees (*bhakta-vastu-prasatteḥ*).[4]

More important than these events, the Āḻvār sees this divine quality in the fact that God chose him, who is an humble individual of lowest rank, to sing His glory.

Tirumaṅgai Āḻvār glorifies the Lord as one who truly offers Himself to those who are devoted to Him (*aḍiyavarkku meyyaṉ*).[5]

Vātsalya

Vātsalya refers to the loving disposition of God to devotees. It is the special affection that God shows towards the devotees unmindful of their sins and defects, as in the case of a mother's love to the child. The classic example cited to illustrate this quality is the cow which licks the newly born calf unmindful of

1. TVM I.5.
2. DTR I.6 *kṣudrāhvānābhimukhyāt....prāha nāthaṁ suśīlaṁ.*
3. TVM I.5.2.
4. DTR 16.
5. PTM III.1.3 *aḍiyavarkku meyyaṉākiya deyvanāyakaṉ.*

the dirt on its body. Some of the later Vaiṣṇava Ācāryas have exaggerated the theological significance of this attribute. The Āḻvārs have conceived *vātsalya* in terms of *āśrita-vātsalya*, deep affection towards those who seek God, *āśritya-vyāmoha*, a special attachment towards them, *āśrita-pakṣapāta*, a partiality towards them as against others, *āśrita-virodhi-hartā*, as one ready to destroy the obstructive forces standing in the way of the devotees and *āśrita-saṁrakṣaṇa-tatpara* or as one who is dedicated to protect those seeking refuge in Him. Though all these terms as such do not figure in the hymns, the ideas underlying them are conveyed through the Paurāṇic episodes cited by the Āḻvārs. The various deeds of God in His incarnations reveal the quality of loving disposition towards His devotees. Nammāḻvār glorifies this attribute by repeatedly praising God for blessing him with divine knowledge, for residing inside him unmindful of his past sins and specially chosing him to sing the glory of God. Apparently Rāmānuja would have taken note of the ideas of Āḻvār when he describes God in his favourite phraseology viz., *āśrita-vātsalyaika-mahodadhi*[1] or the ocean of the unique affection towards devotees.

Kṛpā

Kṛpā or *kāruṇya* means compassion. The Tamil word for it, which is frequently mentioned by the Āḻvārs is *aruḷ*. The concept of grace is based on it. This is an outstanding quality of God because it serves as the impelling force for undertaking the cosmic functions of creation, for incarnating Himself as the human and other living beings and for showering His grace on the devotees. The Āḻvārs have extolled this divine virtue in different ways. At the very outset of the *Tiruvāymoḻi*, Nammāḻvār refers to the *kṛpā* of the Supreme Lord in blessing him with spiritual knowledge leading to devotional love even without any demand and the observance of requisite spiritual discipline on his part. If God chose him to act as a media to sing His glory, when he himself has no capacity to do it, it is again His *kṛpā*. It is the divine *kṛpā* that eventually helps an aspirant for *mokṣa* to attain God, more than the prescribed *sādhana*, either (*bhakti-yoga*) or the act of self-

1. Yāmuna also uses this phrase.
See *Stotraratna*, verse 58 *niravadhika-vātsalya-jaladheḥ*.

surrender. It is out of *kṛpā,* Lord Kṛṣṇa lifted the Govardhana hill to save the cowherds and cows from the torrential rain. There are several such episodes which are cited in the *Divyaprabandham* to illustrate the greatness of *kṛpā.*

The Vaiṣṇava theology of post-Rāmānuja period draws a distinction between *nirhetuka-kṛpā* and *sahetuka-kṛpā*. The former refers to the spontaneous flow of God's *kṛpā* towards the devotee, not being linked to a known cause (*hetu*) such as human effort. The latter is applicable to the grace which is showered on a devotee in response to a good deed done by him. There is considerable controversy on this subject between the two sects of Vaiṣṇavas—Teṅkalai and Vaḍakali. We need not go into these details. Our concern here is to see how the Āḻvārs have viewed this issue. The hymns of Āḻvārs, taken as they are, convey the idea of both *nirhetuka-kṛpā* and *saketuka-kṛpā*. Thus, for instance, the opening hymn of Nammāḻvār which states that God blessed the Āḻvār with knowledge leading to *bhakti* (*mati-nalaṁ*), it does not indicate that such a gift was granted to him in response to a specific prayer or some good deed performed by the Āḻvār. In another instance, he says explicitly that God shows His grace without a reason and He does so to those whom He choses to bless (*veṟidē aruḷ śeyvar śeyvārhaḷku uhandu*).[1] In both these cases, the *aruḷ* or grace is not attributed to a cause (*nirhetuka*). On the other hand, the Āḻvār says in one of the hymns that he uttered falsely (without sincere devotion) the name of God as *kaiyār-cakkarattu* or the one holding the disc in hand and in response to it he was truly blessed.[2] In another hymn he states that he uttered unintentionally the word *Tirumālirumśolai* (the hill where God dwells) but God entered into his mind.[3] These two instances reveal that God showers His grace in response to some act of an individual, however trifle it might be. This is a case of *kṛpā* linked to a *hetu* (*sahetuka*). More importantly Nammāḻvār says that he does not have the capacity to perform either *jñāna-yoga* or *bhakti-yoga* but he would expect God to grant to him the desired goal. Here again, the Āḻvār does not tell that the fruit

1. TVM VIII.7.8 *aṟiyēṉ maṟṟu aruḷ eṉṉaiyāḷum pirāṉār*
veṟidē aruḷ śeyvar seyvārhaḷku uhandu.
See also *Īḍu* VIII.7.8.
2. TVM V.1.1.
3. TVM X.8.1.

aspired for is to be linked with an effort on his part. The Āḻvārs as gifted saints deeply devoted to God express their humility as a subordinate individual to God, almost like a tool in His hand and without showing an ego, they expect the spontaneous flow of the divine grace. But at the same time they advocate either the practice of *bhakti-yoga* or the performance of the act of self-surrender or the observance of other modes of worship such as singing His glory, offering of flowers etc. The idea behind these exhortations is apparently to emphasise the need of performing some good deed in order to merit the *kṛpā* of God. This is exactly the concept of *sahetuka-kṛpā*. Thus, the Āḻvārs speak of both kinds of *kṛpā* without implying a conflict between the two. The controversy on the subject appears to have arisen at a later period by way of interpreting the hymns of the Āḻvārs.[1]

Audārya

Audārya means generosity. As a divine quality it implies that God is bountiful. That is, God confers on His devotees boons generously, much more than what is sought. The more significant aspect of *udāratva* extolled by Nammāḻvār is that the Sovereign of the universe showers on His devotee such spiritual gifts as divine knowledge, divine vision, divine service (*kaiṅkarya*) even when this is not sought. In one of the hymns, he characteristically says that He is an inexhaustible watershed from which one can draw all that is wanted (*koḷḷa kuraivilaṉ*). Realizing this truth, he pleads before God that He should not expect him to perform some good deed or observe spiritual discipline to deserve a boon but He should yet confer it on him. While singing the glory of an *arcā* deity, the Āḻvārs express the view that God has chosen to manifest Himself as an image of worship for the purpose of enabling them to worship Him and offer divine service. All these statements exemplify the generosity of God.

Bandhutva

Bandhu in common parlance means a relative. The father, mother, brother, sister, etc., are treated as relative of a person. This relationship is based on blood affinity and the benefits that one

1. See *Śrīvacanabhūṣaṇa*, aphorisms, pp. 393-397.

derives from the other. This benefit lasts only for a limited time. It is, therefore, regarded as *sopādhika-bandhutva* or relationship conditioned by external factors. In the case of God, the *bandhutva* is *nirupādhika* or unconditioned. That is, God is a *bandhu,* a relative of all celestial and living human beings and also other living beings irrespective of their status in life.[1] He is father, mother, brother and a friend for all and at all times to everybody. It is a bond which is permanent and unalienable. The Āḻvārs have conceived such a concept of *bandhutva* in respect of God. They often address God as *attā,* meaning father. He is called *āptatbandhu* and *āpatsakha,* benefactor and friend for one in distress. In one of the decads,[2] Nammāḻvār speaks contemptuously of the manner in which the human beings cling blindly to their relatives on the basis of a relationship which is ephemeral. He therefore, exhorts that wise people should seek refuge in God who is the only real *bandhu.*[3]

We have dwelt with selected divine attributes that are found mentioned in the *Divyaprabandham.* There are besides, several other attributes which are mentioned in the hymns. In fact, every epithet used to praise God is interpreted by the commentators as an attribute. In the Viśiṣṭādvaita epistemology, the *dharma* or attribute is distinct from the *dharmī* or *svarūpa,* though the two are inherently related. Bearing this explanation in mind, we have presented the attributes of God, insofar as they are related to God as *Sarveśvara.* We shall consider the other attributes related to divine body in the subsequent section.

II. *Divine Personality*

The concept of *saviśeṣa* Brahman or Brahman as qualified implies not only the possession of numerous attributes (*ananta-kalyāṇa-guṇa*) but also spiritual divine body (*divyamaṅgala-vigraha*). In other words, God who is identical with Brahman of the Upaniṣad is *Puruṣottama,* a Supreme Person, as stated in the *Chāndogya Upaniṣad* and the *Bhagavadgītā.*[4] The description of Viṣṇu in the

1. CP *Jitante stotra, surāṇāṁ asurāṇām ca sāmānyam adhidaivataṁ.*
2. TVM IX.1.
3. TVM IX.1.1.
   See also *Mumukṣuppaḍi,* aphorism 39.
4. Ch Up VIII.12 *sa uttamaḥ puruṣaḥ.*
   BG XV 1.7 *uttamaḥ puruṣastu anyaḥ paramātmetyudāhṛtaḥ*
   CP RB I.1.1 *brahmaśabdeṇa....puruṣottamo abhidhīyate.*

Ṛg-Veda as one who measured the universe with three strides, the reference to Brahman in the *Chāndogya Upaniṣad* as *hiraṇmayaḥ puruṣaḥ* and many such statements in the Itihāsas, Purāṇas and Āgamas, show beyond any doubt that the metaphysical Ultimate Reality is a God with a divine personality. This fact is fully supported by the direct experience of God by the Āḻvārs. Nammāḻvār in the very opening hymn of the *Tiruvāymoḻi* describes the Reality as that person who is endowed with *ānanda par excellence* (*uyar nalam uḍaiyavan*). Theologically, the concept of God devoid of bodily form is not of significance as it does not serve the purpose of the devotees desirous of worshipping Him and longing for His direct vision. We may now examine how the divine personality is conceived by the Āḻvārs.

The Vaiṣṇava theology uses the term *divyamaṅgala-vigraha* for the divine body. The implication of the term is that the body assumed by God is not a material stuff constituted of the five physical elements like the human body but constituted of pure spiritual substance known as *śuddha-sattva* which is admitted in the Viśiṣṭādvaita Vedānta on the authority of Scriptural texts.[1] The *Viṣṇu Purāṇa* points out that the body of God is immutable (*avikāra*); pure (*śuddha*) and eternal (*nitya*) and always remains in the same form (*sadaikarūpa*).[2] Such a body is assumed by His own will for the sake of the devotees (*bhaktānugrahakāmyayā*).[3]

The Āḻvārs uphold the same theory. Nammāḻvār describes the divine body as spiritual in character shining with lustre like the bright rays of the sun (*kadirin śuḍar uḍambu*).[4] The *Chāndogya Upaniṣad* says that the divine body is of gold complexion from the toe to the head. In the same way, the Āḻvār also states that the body is lustrous like the pure gold. Such statements are found in large number in the *prabandhams* of other Āḻvārs. These are not mere imaginary descriptions because the mystic saints actually perceived God in this form. Peyāḻvār at the very first glimpse of God expresses his joy of the vision in the words: "I

1. See *Puruṣa Sūkta* (*Yajurveda* recension) 16 *ādityavarṇaṁ tamasastupāre*.
   See also RV VII.100.5 *kṣayantamasya rajasaḥ parāke*.
   TNUp 2 *tadakṣare parame vyoman*.
2. VP I.2.1.
3. See p. 90 fn 1.
4. TVM III.1.5.

beheld Goddess Lakṣmī, I beheld the gold coloured body."[1] In the same way, Tirumaṅgai expresses with dismay that the body of the deity (in this case the Lord Soundararājan, the *arcā* idol in Tirunāgai) is shining like gold.[2] The description of the divine body in terms of lustrous, golden colour is intended to emphasise its spiritual or non-material character which is not only eternal, self-luminous but it is also not subject to any modification.

Quite often the Āḻvārs describe God in terms of the colour of the dark blue cloud. The Purāṇas also present the same idea. A few Āḻvārs mention different complexion for God in different *yugas* or the epochs. It is stated that God manifests Himself with white complexion (*pāl*) in Kṛtayuga, in reddish gold colour (*poṉ*) in Tretāyuga, green colour (*paśambu*) in Dvāpara and blue black (*kārvaṇṇam*) in Kaliyuga.[3] The most commonly accepted view is that the divine body is comparable to the dark blue complexion of the clouds. Nammāḻvār refers to Him as *Meghavaṇṇa* or one who is of the colour of clouds. The comparison to the clouds implies the generosity of God (*udāra svabhāva*). Just as the clouds voluntarily shower on earth cool fresh water, likewise God showers boons to devotees generously.

The Āḻvārs are also very fond of comparing God with the freshly blossomed red *lotus.* We come across several hymns in which the Āḻvārs revel in equating the divine body with the beauty of the red lotus. To cite one of the hymns of Nammāḻvār:

> His eyes are red like lotus ponds; His lips and feet also like red lotus; lustrous is His body like red gold.[4]

Such descriptions of the divine body comparing it to the best attractive and colourful objects of nature are offered to convey to the human minds the aesthetic beauty of the Divine Being.

Besides the visual portrayal of God, the Āḻvārs delight even more by comparing Him to sweet nectar (*amṛta*). They describe Him with such terms as *ārāvamuda,* non-satiating nectar. They also address God as *amuda* or nectar, *tēṉ* or honey, *kaṉṉal* or sugarcandy and sometime a combination of all the sweetest

---

1. MuTi 1 *Tirukkaṇḍēṉ Poṉmēni kaṇḍēṉ ..*
2. PTM IX.2.1 *Poṉṉivar mēṉi ....*
3. See NanTi 24.
4. TVM II.5.1.

objects in the universe.[1] The Upaniṣads speak of Brahman as *ānanda* and *rasa*. These terms imply that Brahman is the very bliss *par excellence* and it is also blissful. Nammāḻvār refers to both these aspects. God is possessed of bliss (*nalam uḍaiyavaṉ*) and He is also wholly constituted of bliss (*muḻu-nalam*). But from an aesthetic standpoint this description seems inadequate to the Āḻvārs. They therefore conceive God as *Ārāvamuda* or nectar that brings no satiation. In other words, God is perennial source of nectar (*amuda*) and however much one enjoys Him, one never feels satisfied. The presiding deity at the temple in Kumbakonam (South India) is named as *Ārāvamudan* and several Āḻvārs including Nammāḻvār have sung the glory of this deity. Tradition has that this term had a magical spell on Nāthamuni who on hearing the single decad of *Tiruvāymoḻi* devoted to Ārāvamuda, went in search of finding out the entire *Tiruvāymoḻi*.

In one of the hymns, Nammāḻvār explains that God's bodily form remains unchanged for all the time. Everytime it is seen, it looks new like the freshly blossomed lotus.[2] The *Ṛg-Veda* refers to Viṣṇu as *yuvā*, which means that He is ever young like a twenty-five year old person. The Purāṇas describe Him as *manmatha-manmatha*. Manmatha is the God of love and physical beauty and God is greater than him in respect of the captivating beauty. In other words, He is the personification of the beauty *par excellence*.

There are other qualities which are attributed to the divine body. These are broadly grouped under the category of *vigraha-guṇas*. Rāmānuja uses the word *rūpa-guṇa* as distinct from *divyātma-guṇas*. The latter are the general attributes of God as *Sarveśvara* and we have discussed them in the earlier section. The former refers to the attributes related to the divine body. The important ones, which the Āḻvārs have experienced and spoken in their hymns are *aujvalya* or lustrous, *saundarya* or beautiful, *yauvana* or youthful and *lāvaṇya* or handsome.

Besides the beauty of the divine body as a whole (*avayava-samudāya*), each part of the body from head to toe is seen as bewitching. Tiruppāṇāḻvār in his *Amalanādipirāṉ*, breaks into

---

1. TVM II.3.1 *tēṉum-pālum neyyum kaṉṉalum amudum ottē*.
   See also DTR 25 *citrāsvādānubhūtiṁ*...
2. TVM II.5.4.

ecstacy at the beauty of each part of the divine body. The feet is compared to radiant lotus; the apparel worn by Him is seen as reddish; the garment on the waist is compared to the twilight with ruddy glow; the lips are matched with coral; eyes are like a lotus petal. Being enraptured by the beauty of the divine form of the deity at Tirumāliruṁśolai, Nammāḻvār asks the Lord Himself to explain His charm:

> May you clarify, O Tirumāl, if your facial lustre has spread itself into your shining crown? Whether the dazzling feet is reflecting in the lotus on which you are standing? Are the jewels and the shining silken garments the reflection of the glow of your waist?[1]

Tirumaṅgai Āḻvār, who had visited a large number of shrines, describes the beauty of the *divyamaṅgala-vigraha* of each deity in a mystic language which is unmatched for its intensity of devotion. When this Āḻvār sees for the first time the image of Soundararāja at Tirunāgai, he feels overwhelmed at the sight of the bewitching beauty of the deity:

> His body is made of gold. It is glowing like the hillock of emerald; the ornaments worn on the body (necklace) is shining like the lightning; the lips appear animated as though they are the ones reciting the Vedas; what a wonder that He possess such a beauty.[2]

In another hymn he says:

> I do not know whether (this deity) is the same as the Lord who resides in the inner recess of the lotus-like heart or is He the one who is found in the orb of the sun which causes lotus buds to bloom. The moment I see Him, I bow down involuntarily in adoration. Why is my mind captivated by the sight of Him? He must be my Lord. His eyes are beautiful like the lotus petals. His palms resemble the lotus flower. His body resembles the dark clouds. How wonderful![3]

Imagining himself as mother Yaśodā, Periyāḻvār in his mystic

1. TVM III.1.1.
2. PTM IX.2.1.
3. PTM IX.2.7.

trance enjoys the infant Kṛṣṇa and not being able to contain his joy, calls everyone to come and enjoy the sight of the beautiful child:

> Come and look at the soft feet which the infant is trying to insert into its mouth with both hands. The ten fingers are like the precious stones being strung together; the anklets decorated with silver ornament are shining.[1]

The physical beauty of the divine body is visually enhanced by the ornaments and weapons worn by God. Among the weapons the most important ones are the *śaṅkha* (conch) and *cakra* (discus). Without any exception all the Āḻvārs refer to these two weapons. In fact, the *śaṅkha* and *cakra* are the identity marks of Viṣṇu like the presence of Goddess Lakṣmī in His chest since these are not possessed by any other deity. When the Āḻvārs address God, they call Him *āḻiyāṉ*, as one possessing *cakra*. The *cakra* is praised repeatedly as a personified deity who is ready to destroy the wicked forces. The other important weapons of Viṣṇu are: *gadā* (club), *śāraṅga* (bow), *khaḍga* (sword). Most of the Āḻvārs refer to all these weapons. Tirumaṅgai Āḻvār speaks of eight weapons in respect of the deity known as Aṣṭabhuja, the Deity with eight hands at Kāñchi.[2]

The divine ornaments (*divyābharaṇa*) with which God is bedecked are many. Nammāḻvār says that the ornaments are numerous, so also the names are many.[3] But the important ones which are mentioned in the hymns are: the crown on the head (*kirīṭa*), the earrings (*makara kuṇḍala*), the necklace (*hāra*), the waist band (*mekhala*), the ornaments on the shoulders and wrist (*valaya*), the *kaustubha* on the chest, the anklets and the sandals covering the feet. The crown is regarded as the symbol of the sovereignty of the Lord. God is often addressed as '*muḍiyāṉē*' the one wearing the crown. The feet is extolled by all the Āḻvārs since these represent the very divine body. When Nammāḻvār at the opening hymn advocates to offer salutation to the lustrous feet (*śuḍaraḍi*), he means the divine body. The other Āḻvārs too

1. PeriTM I-3.
2. PTM II.8.3.
3. TVM II.5.6 *palapalavē ābharaṇam pērum palapalavē.*

exhort the devotees to serve the feet of the Lord in the same sense.

The *tulasī* (basil leaf) as a decorative feature of Viṣṇu finds a special mention in all the *prabandhams.* The reason for this is that the *tulasī* is considered holy and dearest to Viṣṇu. The Āḻvārs in their praise of their deity do not fail to notice the crown and the chest of the idol decorated with *tulasī.* In one of the decads depicting the dejected mood of Nammāḻvār, the Āḻvār yearns fondly for the *tulasī* with which the Lord was worshipped during His incarnations as Vāmana, Rāma, Kṛṣṇa etc.[1]

The description of God with such weapons and ornaments is in conformity with the *Viṣṇu Purāṇa* which describes God as possessing divine weapons and beautiful ornaments.[2] The Itihāsas, the Epics and the Āgama treatise present the same picture. The *astras* or weapons stand for the evolutes of *prakṛti,* according to the *Viṣṇu Purāṇa.* Each weapon of Viṣṇu and the ornament He wears represent the *nityasūris,* who adorn or serve God in these forms. They are not to be taken as objects made of material substance. On the contrary, they are regarded as spiritual entities made of *śuddhasatva* or immaculate substance. Each one of them is an aspect of divinity. It is, therefore, considered as a personified and visualisable deity. The *cakra,* for instance, is a weapon of God but it is also venerated as a deity. *Adiśeṣa,* the mythic serpent is a *nitya-sūri,* who is the symbol of total dedication of a soul to the service of God (*śeṣa-vṛtti*) and as such he serves as a bed, a couch and an umbrella to God.[3] Similarly, *Garuḍa* is not an ordinary bird, but represents a *nityasūri* serving as His mount. *Viśvaksena,* the heavenly angel is another *nitya-sūri,* who serves God as the commander of the celestial deities. All these facts are also evidenced by the Scriptural and Smṛti texts. The Āḻvārs have taken note of them and voiced the same in their hymns. The statements of the Āḻvārs, which are based on direct intuition, strengthen the teachings of these religious treatises. The *Divyaprabandham* has in turn influenced the Vaiṣṇava Ācāryas as can be noticed in Ālavandār's *Stotra-ratna*

1. See Chapter 8.
2. VP I.22.76 *astra-bhūṣaṇa-saṁsthāna-svarūpam.*
3. See MTi 53 *śeṉṟāl kuḍaiyām irundāl śiṅgāsanamām,*
niṉṟāl maravaḍiyām nīlkaḍaluḷ eṉṟum puṇaiyām.

and *Catuḥ-ślokī* and also in the *Gadyas* of Rāmānuja.

Another justification for the manifestation of God in human form is provided by a significant verse of *Jitanta-stotram,* which is regarded by some as a *khilasūkta* of *Ṛg-Veda.* The relevant verse says:

> You do not have any physical qualities such as white or black (rūpa); you do not possess any physical organs such as head or legs (*ākāra*); nor are there any weapons or ornaments on you (*āyudha*); nor do you have an abode (*āspada*); nevertheless out of your infinite compassion towards devotees, you manifest yourself with a lustrous bodily form bedecked with ornaments and weapons in an abode of yours.[1]

The implication of this verse is that the Supreme Being in His transcendental form does not possess a body nor carries weapons and ornaments; but He assumes all these out of His own free will for the sake of the devotees who need to worship Him in a personified form.

It is in this light that the Āḻvārs have tried to experience the glorious image of God. An undifferentiated Reality or a concept of God as an absolutely impersonal being or an abstract principle has little significance for a theistic philosophy. The *Divyaprabandham* which is claimed as a treatise on *Bhagavad-viṣaya* provides a deeper insight into all aspects of Godhead. Vaiṣṇavism as developed into a monotheistic system by Rāmānuja and his followers owes a great deal to the teachings of the Āḻvārs.

III. *Divine Incarnations*

The Āḻvārs have made a distinctive contribution to the understanding of the doctrine of *avatāra* which is a distinctive feature of Vaiṣṇavism. The concept of *avatāra* can be traced to the *Ṛg-*

---

1. See *Jitanta Stotram na te rūpam na cākāro nā-yudhāni na cāspadam;*
tathāpi puruṣākāro bhaktānām tvam prakāśase.

See also *Sāttvata Saṁhitā* II.69-70.
śāntaḥ samvit-svarūpastu bhaktānugrahakāmyayā;
anaupamyena vapuṣāhy-amūrto mūrtatām gatah.
The Ultimate Reality is devoid of a form (*amūrta*) but it assumes a limited form (*mūrtatā*) for the sake of devotees and this limited form is incomparable (*anupama*).

Veda. The *Puruṣa-sūkta* states that the *Puruṣa* (God) though unborn takes birth in many forms.[1] This statement implies that God who is eternal has no origin or birth but yet He manifests Himself in different forms. Such a manifestation is termed as *prādurbhāva* which means that which already exists reveals itself in different forms, as distinct from the term *utpatti* or birth. Another Ṛgvedic passage describes Viṣṇu as descending from His heavenly abode when He is invoked through Vedic *mantras* to be present in a sacrificial pillar (*yūpa*).[2] This Vedic statement conveys the idea of the *avatāra* or *avataraṇa* which means 'descent'. There are several Vedic passages which speak of a few *avatāras*, such as *Matsya, Kūrma, Varāha, Trivikrama* or *Vāmana*.

The Itihāsas and Purāṇas have presented prominently the various *avatāras* of God with descriptive details. The *Bhagavadgītā* explains briefly the philosophy underlying the nature of divine descent, the purpose, the timing and its significance. Both the Pāñcarātra and Vaikhānsa Āgamas have accorded greater importance to this doctrine and in particular to the incarnation of God in the form of icon to be worshipped (*arcā*) along with the details of modes of worship and the rituals with which the icons are consecrated. The Āgamas also enunciate clearly the five forms of *avatāra* viz., *para, vyūha, vibhava, arcā* and *antaryāmī*. The doctrine of *vyūha* is developed in greater detail in the Pāñcarātra Āgamas.

The Āḻvārs were influenced by all these ideas. Though they have not explicitly discussed the doctrine, they have referred to all types of *avatāras* extensively in their hymns providing a deeper insight into their significance. This has in turn influenced the later Vaiṣṇava Ācāryas who have offered a rational justification for the theory in general and in particular for the worship of God in the form of icon at temples. A study of the views of the Āḻvārs on this subject is, therefore, of special importance.

The Pāñcarātra treatises refer to five kinds of *avatāra* namely *para, vyūha, vibhava, arcā* and *antaryāmī*. The *para* is the existence of the Supreme Being in the eternal abode known as *paramapada* as a deity in the name of *Para Vāsudeva* assuming a spiritual body bedecked with the divine weapons and ornaments and

---

1. *Puruṣasūkta* (*Yajurveda* Recension) II.2 *ajāyamāno bahudhā vijāyate.*
2. ṚV III.8.4 *yuvā suvāsāḥ parivīta āgāt*
   sa u śreyān bhavati jāyamānaḥ.

seated on the *Ādiśeṣa* (the divine serpent) along with His consorts and surrounded by the divine attendants. The *vyūha avatāra* is the manifestation of the same *para-vāsudeva* in four forms known as Vāsudeva, Saṅkarṣaṇa, Pradyumna and Aniruddha for the purpose of performing specific cosmic functions such as creation, sustenance, dissolution of the universe. The *vibhava avatāra* refers to the manifestation of God in the form of celestial, human or other living beings for the purpose of protection of the devotees and destruction of evil. The *arcā* is the manifestation of God in the form of icon either on His own or in response to the prayers of human beings to provide an opportunity to them to offer divine worship. The *antaryāmī* is the presence of God in the heart of devotees to enable them to do meditation.

We shall presently point out how the Āḻvārs have viewed each one of these forms. The noteworthy point of their teaching is that it is the same one Supreme Person who manifests Himself in these five forms. That is, the Āḻvārs do not make any distinction between the transcendental form of God known as *para-tattva* in Vedānta and the *para-vāsudeva* in the Pāñcarātra, the *vyūha-vāsudeva* lying in the milky ocean, the *vibhava* forms such as Vāmana, Rāma and Kṛṣṇa, the *arcā* deities or icons in the temples and the *antaryāmī,* the indwelling God. Philosophically, this is the correct theory because if the one Supreme Being assumes, out of His will, different manifestations, similar to the same one person appearing on the stage in different roles, there should be no distinction between one form and the other. But such view is not so clearly manifest in the Pāñcarātra treatises, though it may be implicit. These works give the impression that there are degrees of difference between the various manifestations, some higher and other lower. Some texts accord greater importance to the *para* forms; others consider the *vyūha* manifestation as important. Most of the texts emphasise the importance of *arcā* deities. The *vibhavas* are presented in these texts with varying degrees of importance, while the *antaryāmī* form finds only a casual mention. One cannot fail to notice the gradation in importance of the five forms of *avatāra* in the Āgamas.

Unlike the Pāñcarātra Āgamas, the Āḻvārs speak with one voice that all the five forms represent the one and only Supreme Being. Thus says Nammāḻvār:

> The Supreme Being resides in the transcendental realm (*para*); He resides in the Tirumalai hills (*arcā*); He is lying in the milky ocean (*vyūha*); He moves on earth with different roles (*vibhava*); He is immanent in all the entities in the universe (*antarātmā*) and also inside one's heart (*antaryāmī*).[1]

There are serveral verses of this kind which speak of the identity of one form of manifestation with the other. While addressing a particular deity at the temple in the form of icon, the Āl̲vār states that He is no other than Kṛṣṇa of Bṛndāvan. When speaking of Kṛṣṇa, he mentions in the same breath that He is the one lying in the milky ocean (*vūyha*). When singing the glory of the Supreme Being in the *para-rūpa* in the transcendental abode, he expresses with joy that the same Lord has chosen the heart of the devotee as His abode (*antaryāmī*). In one of the decads, Nammāl̲vār mentions the twelve names of *Viṣṇu*—Keśava, Nārāyaṇa, Mādhava, Govinda, Viṣṇu, Madhusūdana, Trivikrama, Vāmana, Śrīdhara, Hṛiṣīkeśa, Padmanābha and Dāmodara.[2] According to the Pāñcarātra Āgama, these twelve names represent twelve sub-*vyūhas* but the commentators take them as twelve names of Viṣṇu. These names though sound differently, do not make any difference to the Āl̲vār. He uses them as synonyms in the twelve hymns starting with *Keśava* and ending with Dāmodara. In his opinion, these names, even if they are applicable to the sub-*vyūhas* do not imply any distinction between them in respect of their ontological status.

In the same way, the various *arcā* deities are known by different names such as Ādipirān̲, Śrīnivāsa, Raṅganātha, Ārāvamuda, Soundararāja but the Āl̲vārs do not see any difference between the one deity and the other, as common folks believe. While singing the glory of the deity at Tirumālirumśolai, who is known as Al̲agar, he speaks in the name of the Lord at Tirumalai. The deity at Tirunāvāy (a religious centre in Kerala) is described as the very Vāmana, the *vibhava avatāra* of Viṣṇu. There are numerous hymns in the *Tiruvāymol̲i* in which the Āl̲vār

1. TVM VI.9.5 *viṇmīdu iruppāy malaimēl nir̲pāy kaḍal śērppāy*
maṇmīdu ul̲avāy evar̲r̲uḷ eṅgum mar̲aindu ur̲aivāy
eṇmīdu iyan̲r̲a puravaṇḍattāy enadāvi
uḷmītu āḍi urukkaṭṭādē oḷippāyō.

2. TVM II.7.

equates one deity with another and one form of manifestation with another.

This characteristic feautre of *avatāra* can be noticed very conspiciously in the *prabandhams* of Tirumaṅgai Āḻvār. The *Periya Tirumoḻi* is full of songs in praise of several *arcā* deities found in the various Vaiṣṇava shrines right from Badari in the Himalayas to Tirukkuruṅguḍi in the extreme south. Decad after decad, the hymns present the same description of the *arcā* deity except for the change of the name of the presiding deity at these religious centres and their surrounding landscape. The glory of each deity is sung with the epithets that refer to the greatness of Lord Kṛṣṇa and His *līlās* or the valour or Rāma who destroyed the wicked Rāvaṇa, or the majestic form of Narasiṁha who killed Hiraṇyākaśyapa and the marvellous feat of Vāmana who measured the universe with three strides. The *arcā* deities for Tirumaṅgai Āḻvār are the same as the Supreme Being who incarnated Himself in different manifestation.[1] The theological implications of the *arcā* deities will be discussed later in detail. For the present it may be noted that the Āḻvārs have revealed without any shadow of doubt the central philosophy of *avatāra* viz., that the one Supreme Being, the Ultimate Reality of Metaphysics assumes different forms and names for making Himself easily accessible to the devotees. Existentially, He remains the same Reality.

We may now examine how each kind of *avatāra* is viewed by the Āḻvārs. The Pāñcarātra literature describes *parāvatāra* as a manifestation of the Supreme Being with a divine body in the name of *para-vāsudeva,* who eternally resides in *paramapada,* the transcendental abode of Viṣṇu. The Āḻvārs do not use the word *para-vāsudeva*. They describe Him as Vaikuṇṭhanātha, which means the Lord of Vaikuṇṭha. They also repeatedly use the expressions *Viṇṇōrnāyaka, Amararkōn, Amararkaḷ-adhipati* etc., which mean the Ruler of the *nitya-sūris* who according to *Ṛg-Veda* exist in the *paramapada*.[2] The God in this realm is spoken as one who is worshipped at all times by the *nitya-sūris* and the released souls. He is also described as one who is seated on Ādiśeṣa, the

1. See PTM I.2, II.4, VIII.8.
2. ṚV I.22.20 *tadviṣṇoḥ paramaṁ padaṁ sadā paśyanti sūrayaḥ.*

divine serpent along with His three consorts, *Śrī, Bhū* and *Nīlā* and other divine attendants.[1]

Such a God existing in the *paramapada* who manifests Himself with His full glory is regarded by the Āḻvār as *para-rūpa.* This is evident from the fact that Nammāḻvār yearns for a full vision of this resplendent, Supreme Being to whom He wishes to render continuous eternal service. Obviously, this is the state of *mokṣa* in which only liberated souls (*muktātmā*) and eternally free souls (*nityas*) are able to enjoy the full glory of God.

The theory of *vyūha* as expounded in Pāñcarātra literature does not figure in the *Divyaprabandham.* It is difficult to guess the reason for its omission. However, we find numerous references to the manifestation of God as one lying in the sleeping posture on *Ādiśeṣa,* the multi-hooded divine serpent. The theological significance attached to this form of Viṣṇu, as explained by the commentators is that it symbolises God in the state of *yoga-nidrā,* contemplating over the ways to protect the universe. According to the Pāñcarātra Āgamas, the task of protection of the universe is assigned to Aniruddha, one of the four *vyūhas.* In Vaiṣṇava theology, Aniruddha is equated with Vāsudeva who in the guise of *Viṣṇu* is responsible for *pālana* or protection. Brahmā and Rudra, the other two deities of the Hindu trinity are brought into existence by Vāsudeva through whom as their *antarātmā,* the tasks of creation and dissolution of the universe are carried out. If this explanation provided by Vaiṣṇava theology on the basis of some Pāñcarātra texts is acceptable, the manifestation of God as *Kṣīrābdhiśāyi* or the one reposing in the milky ocean can be regarded as *Vyūha Aniruddha.* The hymns of the Āḻvārs, however, do not say anything in this regard.[2]

The *vibhava avatāras* figure prominently in the *Divyaprabandham.* The Pāñcarātra treatises enumerate thirty-nine such *avatāras.* Of these the following ten are considered to be important on the basis of the extra special function performed by each: Matsya,

1. TVM VIII.1.1 *tēvimārāvār tirumakaḷ pūmi eva, maṟṟu amarar āḷśeyvār.....* CP *Laiṅga Purāṇa, vaikuṇṭhe tu pareloke śriyāsārdham jagatpatiḥ; āste viṣṇuḥ....*
2. Tirumaḻiśai Āḻvār in his *Tiruccanda-viruttam* refers to *nālumūrtti* (four forms) which is interpreted by some commentators in favour of four *vyūhas.* In the absence of the mention of the actual names of *vyūhas,* it is doubtful if this word means four *vyūhas.* For the same reason, the term *mūvarāhiya mūrtti* used by Nammāḻvār (III.6.1) cannot be taken as a reference to three *vyūhas.*

Kūrma, Varāha, Narasiṁha, Vāmana, Paraśurāma, Rāma, Kṛṣṇa, Balarāma, Kalki. Most of the Āḻvārs have acknowledged these principle *avatāras* with the exception of Kalki which is yet to take place. But Nammāḻvār, Tirumaṅgai and Periyāḻvār mention Kalki too. Among the other *avatāras*, which have been mentioned by a few Āḻvārs are: Hayagrīva, Haṁsa, Nara-Nārāyaṇa, Nyagrodhaśāyi, Kṣīrābdhiśāyi.

The *avatāra* of Viṣṇu as an infant child reposing on Nyagrodha (banyan) leaf during the great deluge is of special attraction to the Āḻvārs as it is repeatedly mentioned in their hymns. The reason for its frequent reference is that the Āḻvārs see in this *avatāra* the two great attributes of God viz., the *nirhetuka kṛpā* or the unconditioned compassion and *rakṣakatva* or the concern for providing protection for the universe.

Of the ten principal *avatāras*, Vāmana is of special attraction to the Āḻvārs. All of them speak with admiration the manner in which Viṣṇu as a dwarf tricked Mahābali by begging space measuring three footsteps and took possession of the entire universe.

The *avatāra* of Kṛṣṇa has equally engaged the attention of all the Āḻvārs. The *līlās* of Kṛṣṇa as a child, as a youth and as a man constitute the pet theme of the mystic outpourings. Periyāḻvār imagines himself as Yaśodā and pours out his emotional feelings towards Kṛṣṇa as mother Yaśodā would do to her infant child. Tirumaṅgai Āḻvār also in the guise of a cowherd maid speaks the glory of Kṛṣṇa *līlās*. Āṇḍāḷ as a bride of Bṛndāvan craves for a reunion with Kṛṣṇa. Nammāḻvār devotes entire decad to the deeds of Kṛṣṇa, from his birth onwards to his last day of departure from the cosmic universe. The reason for an extensive coverage of *Kṛṣṇāvatāra* is the display of God's *saulabhya* or easy accessibility in the exploits of Kṛṣṇa to which the Āḻvārs were attracted.

The next two *avatāras* of importance to the Āḻvārs are Narasiṁha and Rāma. In Narasiṁha, the Āḻvārs see the protective power or the readiness to protect the pious devotees through the destruction of evil forces. In the case of Rāma, the Āḻvārs perceive the noble quality of *āśrita-rakṣaṇa* or protection of a devotee dedicated to God.

The *avatāra* as Varāha, boar, who uplifted the earth submerged in the bottom of the ocean is also of great appeal to the Āḻvārs.

In this *avatāra*, they see the divine virtue of special concern of the Supreme Being to protect the universe and His special affection to *Bhū-devī*, the presiding deity of earth.

In this connection, it may be observed that the Āḻvārs were not so much interested in the narration of the various *vibava avatāras* in all their detail, as we normally find in the Purāṇas. If they have mentioned only a few *avatāras*, it was because they felt absorbed in the contemplation of the attributes that were manifest in these superhuman deeds. For instance, the repeated reference in the hymns to the deed of Kṛṣṇa in holding aloft the Govardhana hill from the deluge of rain unleashed by Indra, just to protect men and innocent animals is to recall the divine quality of the *nirhetuka kṛpā*. The hymns do not bear the complexion of mythology even though they include the legendary episodes. Their main focus is to reveal the God's glory through His deeds.

The *arcā avatāra* or the manifestation of God in the form of *icons* has engaged the special attention of the Āḻvārs. In fact, the major part of the Tamil *prabandhams*, particularly those of Tirumaṅgai Āḻvār, Nammāḻvār and the first four Āḻvārs, is devoted to the singing of the glory of *arcā* deities that existed during their period in the Vaiṣṇava shrines spread all over India. The *Divyaprabandham* covers in all 106 religious centres, majority of which are located in South India. The important centres in the North referred to by a few Āḻvārs are: Badarinath, Devaprayag, Saligrama in the Himalaya mountain, Dwaraka in the west coast, Mathura, Brindavan, Ayodhya and Naimiśāraṇya in the North. With the exception of Nammāḻvār, all the Āḻvārs are believed to have visited these centres and expressed in words the grandeur of the deity and places as witnessed by them. As mystic saints gifted with spiritual knowledge and deep devotion to God, they have visualised a grandeur of unique type in the icons which ordinary human beings fail to see. In the case of Nammāḻvār, it is claimed that he was in Yogic meditation for 16 years and hence he did not visit any of the religious centres but visualised the deities at selected shrines through Yogic perception and sang in praise of their glory.

It is interesting to note that most of the hymns with the exception of a few do not actually describe the beauty of the image of worship. On the other hand, they praise the particular deity in the background of the glorious *avatāras*, the wondrous deeds performed by them during the incarnation and the divine attributes. The verses contain a rich poetic imagery of the surrounding landscapes of the centre. The style of the poetic language adopted in the hymns and the kind of description of the divine glory look alike. The poems addressed to the different deities are however infused with devotional fervour and thirst for communion with God. Though the hymns are addressed primarily to particular deities, they are filled with philosophical and theological ideas.

What is the main objective of the Āḻvārs in devoting greater attention to the *arcā* deities? Are these hymns intended to promote *bhakti* among common people? Are they aimed to give importance to the *arcā avatāra* and thereby justify image worship? Are they meant to disseminate spiritual knowledge and promote religious way of life through worship of deities at temples? These are relevant questions and an answer to them will reveal the significance attached to the *arcāvatāra*.

According to the traditional account, the Āḻvārs were inspired by God to sing His glory. To be more specific, the deities at particular temples granted a vision of the image as in the case of Nammāḻvār and in respect of others, the particular deities motivated them to speak about the divine glory. The *Viṣṇu-sahasranāma* describes God as *stavyaḥ*, to be praised and *stava-priyaḥ*, as one fond of praise. It is, therefore, justified that the pious saints were inspired to sing in praise of God.

That the hymns are intended to promote *bhakti* movement, as is commonly believed, is a superficial explanation for the advent of *Divyaprabandham*, although it may incidentally serve this purpose in a historical context. The significance of the hymns addressed to *arcā* deities is something different. The first and foremost objective is to establish that the incarnation of God as *arcā* or iconic form is real. As we have explained earlier, the philosophy of *avatāra* is based on the theory that God descends on earth from His eternal abode assuming a human form to fulfil twofold function viz., protection of the pious individuals devoted to God (*sādhu-paritrāṇa*) and the destruction of evil force (*duṣkṛt-vināśa*). More importantly, in the context of *arcāvatāra*, He graciously condescends to make Himself available in an iconic form to enable the devotees to offer Him worship and to meditate on Him. This point is emphatically brought out in several hymns of the Āḻvārs. Every time they address a deity at a temple, they say that the Supreme Being, out of His compassion towards the suffering humanity has chosen to be present Himself at a particular place in the form of an icon (*vigraha*) purely for providing an opportunity to the devotees to worship Him. Thus, Nammāḻvār, while exhorting the worship of the presiding deity of Tirumālirumśoli (an important holy hill in South India), describes the centre as *māyōṉ maruviya kōyil*, that is, the place which the Supreme Being has chosen as a permanent residence.[1] He adds: "It is the place where the Lord resides for the purpose of offering Himself (His grace) to the devotees."[2] It is the centre where the glory of God is exhibited (*pīḍurai kōyil*) and by worshipping Him one can overcome the bondage. In the same strain, the Āḻvār speaks of the Tirumalai, a very famous holy hill in South India:

> That Benevolent Lord who saved the (cows and cowherds) from the torrential rain by uplifting the Govardhana hill, who in the past measured (with His three strides) the entire universe, has come down from His eternal abode to reside in the Tiruveṅgaḍa (Tirumalai) hill.[3]

Tirumaṅgai Āḻvār also speaks in the same strain about the Divine presence in the holy centres. Thus, in one of the decads devoted to sing the glory of Badari (the holy centre in the Himalaya), he says:

> My Lord who in the past assumed the body of a boar (*Varāha*) and rescued the earth submerged in the ocean, who killed the wicked demon Rāvaṇa by using the bow and arrow, is stationed here in Badari on the bank of Ganga.[4]

The main emphasis in all such hymns is to reassure the people who have doubts in their mind about the presence of divinity in holy centres that the Supreme Lord Himself has chosen the place as a permanent residence (*nitya-vāsa*) for the benefit of the devotees.

These statements of the Āḻvārs point out that God can man-

---

1. TVM II.10.1.
2. *Ibid.* II.10.4.
3. *Ibid.* III.3.8.
4. PTM I.4.1.

ifest Himself in any form that is required to fulfil a specific purpose. According to the *Sāttvata Saṁhitā*, the oldest Pāñcarātra treatise, God on His own assumes the form of an idol and makes Himself available to devotees for worship. This kind of idol is known as *svayaṁ-vyakta* or self-manifested image. The deity at places such as Tirumalai, Śrīraṅgam, Vānamāmalai, Badari are believed to be of this category. There is another category of idols. God reveals Himself in a physical form to those sages, who have continuously done penance for obtaining direct vision of God. When God descends to fulfil the desire of the sages, He may out of His will and compassion stay on in that spot in the form of an icon for enabling others to offer worship. Such idols are known as *Saiddha* or what is got established by sages.

The devotees also can make an image of worship in a stone or metal or wood and invoke divinity into it by means of the prescribed rituals. Such images are known as *mānuṣa* or man-made. The *Viṣṇudharmottara* enjoins that devotees should make an attractive idol of Viṣṇu out of any metal or stone and offer worship to it, prostrate before it, perform religious rites for it and meditate on it; by doing so they become free from all sins.[1]

The idols seen by the Āḻvārs are mostly of the first and second category. The monumental architecture of the temples in which we see these deities enshrined now might have come up at a later time. The idols must have existed in simple structure serving as a sanctum sanctorum at the time they were visited by the Āḻvārs ages ago. It would not, therefore, be correct to determine the age of the Āḻvār on the basis of the present architecture. When the Āḻvārs sang their hymns at these temples, they did so with an unshakable faith in the divinity that inheres in them.

The idols made out of metal or stone acquire spiritual character (*aprākṛtatva*) after they are consecrated by the prescribed rituals. The *Sāttavata Saṁhitā* says: "God enters into the idol by assuming a body corresponding to the idol made by an individual and becomes indistinguishable like water in the milk."[2] Soon after the consecration, such an idol becomes spiritual in character with the presence of divinity. The consecrated idols are regarded as *śubhāśraya*. *Śubha* means auspicious because it

1. *Viṣṇudharmottara* 103.16.
2. *Sāttvata Saṁhitā* VI.22 *bimbākṛtyātmanā bimbe samāgatyāvatiṣṭhate;*
karoty-amūrtān akhilaṁ bhogaśaktim tu ca ātmasāt.

is spiritual in character and as such is capable of removing the sins of the worshippers. It is *āśraya* because it serves as a fit object for meditation.

The *Vigrahas* have the form of a human being. But on this basis it is not correct to consider them as anthropomorphic because God choses human form or whatever form a devotee desires. Thus says Poygai Āḻvār, the earliest Vaiṣṇava saint: "In whatever form the devotees desire, God assumes a body in that very form."[1] The same truth is conveyed by the *Bhagavadgītā*.[2]

The main purpose of focussing on the glory of *arcā* deities is to impress on the common people the importance of worship of God as the easiest means of attaining liberation from bondage. This is evident from the fact that most of the hymns devoted to the singing of the glory of a religious centre or the deity therein also contain philosophical ideas apart from mere description of a deity. We can notice this characteristic feature prominently in the *Periya Tirumoḻi*. Tirumaṅgai Āḻvār moves on from place to place and sings the glory of a deity, generally using the same phraseology. The main purpose of such an effort, as commentators point out, is to remove the doubts of the people regarding the value of worship, make them understand its significance so that they can strive for spiritual upliftment. This appears to be the Āḻvārs' life mission focussing their attention on the temples serving as centres of religious activities.

The fifth kind of *avatāra* as *antaryāmī* is also acknowledged by the Āḻvārs. The word *antaryāmī* is used in the Upaniṣad to refer to the Paramātman or Brahman as the inner controller (*antarātmā*) of all sentient beings and non-sentient entities in the universe.[3] According to the Upaniṣads, as interpreted by Rāmānuja, Brahman creates the universe by its *saṅkalpa* or divine will and thereafter enters into every created entity along with the soul and then gives it the name and form.[4] This concept of *antaryāmitva* is common to all living beings and also material objects. This is, however, different from the *Antaryāmī avatāra* of God. *Antaryāmitva* as an *avatāra* implies that God or Brahman dwells in the heart of human beings in a subtle form (*sūkṣma-rūpa*) to

1. MTi 44 *tamar uhandadu evvuruvaṁ avvuruvaṁ tānē.*
2. BG IV.11 *ye yathā māṁ prapadyante tāṁ tathaiva bhajāmyaham.*
3. See BrUp V.7.2.
4. TUp III, See also ChUp VI. 3.2.

enable them to meditate on Brahman.[1] Whether or not God with a spiritual body as in the case of other *avatāra,* enters into the human body is not clear in the Upaniṣadic statements. However, the Vaiṣṇava theology accepts the view that God as the *antaryāmī* possesses a subtle form in the human beings as otherwise He would not be an object of meditation for a *upāsaka.*

The Āḻvārs have acknowledged both the concepts of *antaryāmitva.* The statement of Nammāḻvār in the opening decad of the *Tiruvāymoḻi* that God abides in every entity in the universe though He is invisible is a reiteration of the teaching of *Antaryāmī Brāhmaṇa.* That God is *antarātmā* of all that exists in the universe is repeatedly emphasised throughout the *Tiruvāymoḻi.* In an explicit way, the Āḻvār says "He is inside, He is outside, He is everywhere."[2]

Regarding the other concept of *antaryāmī* as an *avatāra* Nammāḻvār says in more than one hymn that Supreme Being has chosen his (Āḻvār's) heart as an abode in the same way as He enjoys being in Vaikuṇṭha or in any other holy centre.[3] The word *kōyil koṇḍān* used in this hymn signifies that the heart of Āḻvār is like a temple or a desirable abode for God. Tirumaṅgai Āḻvār too describes the residence of God within one's heart.[4] Obviously, these statements refer to the manifestation of God in a subtle form inside the heart. The significant feature of this teaching of the Āḻvārs which is not so obvious in the Pāñcarātra texts is that God who as an *antaryāmī* (as an *avatāra*) is not different in essence from the one in the *paramapada* (as Supreme Being), the one who lies in the milky ocean (as *vyūha*), the one who incarnates as Kṛṣṇa and Rāma (as *vibhava*), the one who is also present in the temple as *arcā.* Pūtattāḻvār says:

> The Supreme Being resides in my heart; He is stationed in Tiruveṅgaḍam; He is lying in the milky ocean; He is reposing in the extensive centre of Śrīraṅga; He is being glorified as the Devādi-deva by countless celestial beings; once in the

---

1. See RTS Chapter V, See also *Nyāya-siddhañjana,* p. 237.
2. TVM VII.8.8 *muṉṉiya mūvulahum avaiyāy avaṟṟai*
   paḍaittu piṉṉum uḷḷāy purattāy.
   See also VIII.8.2.
3. TVM VIII.6.5 *kōyil koṇḍān, adanōḍum eṉṉeñjakam.*
4. *Tiruneḍuntāṇḍakam, pērādu eṉṉeñjinuḷḷāy.*

past He killed the demon posing as the horse.[1]

Thus, the theory of *avatāra* finds a clear exposition in the *Divyaprabandham* which reveals fully the glory of God and provides adequate material for a more extensive development of the doctrine by Rāmānuja and his successors.

IV. *Divine Activities*

We have considered one aspect of the glory of God as seen by the Āḻvārs through His various incarnations. We shall now consider the divine activities (*līlās*) which also exhibit His glory in a grand way. The *Divyaprabandham* is replete with *bhāgavat-līlās*, as these have made great appeal on the minds of the mystic saints. The main objective of the Āḻvārs in citing the *līlās* is to promote *bhakti* among the common people and enable them to contemplate on God. *Dhyāna* or contemplation, is an important stage of *bhakti-yoga* and this needs *bhakti* or loving devotion to God. *Bhakti* assumes different forms. The *Bhāgavata Purāṇa* mentions nine modes of worship[2] which include *smaraṇa* or contemplation on the glory of God. *Smaraṇa* helps to cleanse the mind of its impurities and secure stability to perform *dhyāna-yoga* leading to the vision of God. In one of the decads of the *Tiruvāymoḻi* depicting the anguish caused by the separation from God, Nammāḻvār resorts himself to contemplation of the deeds of God-incarnate Kṛṣṇa for mental solace.[3] We find several such instances in the hymns of Tirumaṅgai, Periyāḻvār, Kulaśekaran and Āṇḍāḷ.

The divine activities referred to by the Āḻvārs are also many and they are repeated in the same poem. Thus, for instance, the feat of Vāmana measuring the universe with His three strides is mentioned several times in the same poem and also by all the Āḻvārs. Among the pranks of Kṛṣṇa as a child, his penchant for stealing freshly churned butter is a pet theme with most of the Āḻvārs. The divine deeds can be grouped under three categories:

1. The cosmic functions such as creation, protection and dissolution of the universe.

---

1. ITi 28.
2. BP VII.5.23, See Chapter 5, p. 128.
3. See Chapter 7, p. 176.

2. The deeds performed for the protection of celestial deities.
3. The deeds performed during the *avatāras* to punish the evil-doers and protect the pious individuals.

Cosmic Functions

The three cosmic functions namely, creation, protection and dissolution of the universe are important both from the philosophical and theological point of view. Philosophically, the Ultimate Reality, though it is transcendental should have a positive relation to the universe. In view of this the *Vedānta-sūtra* on the basis of the *Taittirīya Upaniṣad* adopts the *jagat-kāraṇatva* or that which is the primary cause of creation as an important criteria for determining the nature of the Ultimate Reality. Theologically, God in a monotheistic system should be the creator and saviour of the universe.

It is interesting how the Āḻvārs have explained these cosmic functions in their hymns. While accepting the basic functions stated in the Vedānta, they have described in a symoblic language: God creates the universe (*paḍaittu*), swallows it (*uṇḍu*), spits it out (*umiḻndu*), retains it in His stomach in a subtle form (*aḍaittu*) and restores the earth submerged in the ocean (*iḍandu*). Several hymns in the *Divyaprabandham* refer to these functions.

The metaphors of 'swallowing' and 'spitting' are used by the Āḻvārs to explain the philosophic concept of dissolution and evolution of the universe. These ideas are not borrowed, as some modern scholars think, from the ancient Tamil poetry. The *Kaṭha Upaniṣad* speaks of the entire universe comprising sentient beings and non-sentient entities as food for Brahman.[1] Based on this Upaniṣadic statement, the *Vedānta-sūtra* describes Brahman as *attā* or eater.[2] The metaphor of 'eating' is employed to denote the dissolution of the universe, one of the cosmic functions of Brahman. Following this teaching, the Āḻvārs too use the expression *uṇḍu* (eating) and *umiḻndu* (spitting) to describe the cosmic functions of God.

The restoration of the earth submerged in the ocean is part of the function of the protection of the universe. According to

1. KaUp I.2.25 *yasya brahma ca kṣatram ca ubhe bhavata odanaḥ.*
2. VS I.2.9 *attā carācara grahaṇāt.*

the Purāṇas, the earth was stolen by a demon and hidden in the bottom of the ocean. Viṣṇu taking the form of a boar dived deep into the ocean and restored it to its original position. This deed is of special significance to the Āḻvārs, because the presiding deity of earth is *Bhū-devī*, one of the consorts of Viṣṇu and the restoration of it amounts to the rescuing of *Bhū-devī*, who is dear to Him. The theological significance of this deed, as explained by Piḷḷān and other commentators, is that God is so compassionate that he cannot tolerate the affliction caused to the living beings in general and to *Bhū-devī* in particular.

The retention of the universe in the stomach of God during deluge is also a sybmolic way of explaining the protection of the universe during the period of deluge. Following the mythological account, the Āḻvārs depict the picture of the Supreme Being as an infant reposing on *nyagrodha* (*banyan*) leaf floating on the ocean. According to the Pāñcarātra treatise, *Nyagrodhaśāyi* is one of the 39 *avatāras*. The theological significance of this imagery as conceived in the hymns is to illustrate the two divine attributes viz., the capacity of the God to perform what is impossible for others (*aghaṭitaghaṭana sāmarthya*) and the unconditioned compassion (*nirhetuka kṛpā*). The former is self-evident and needs no explanation because the attribute of *sarvaśaktitva* (omnipotence) should include the possibility of performing what is normally considered impossible for others. As regards the latter, even without any demand or prayer on the part of the human and celestial beings, God is concerned with protecting them during the great deluge so that they are reborn during the time of creation. According to the Viśiṣṭādvaita Vedānta, creation cannot take place from what is non-existent. What exists in an unmanifested form is brought into existence in a manifested form. The universe comprising living beings and non-sentient entities is not totally destroyed during *pralaya* but it is dissolved into a subtle form; at the time of creation, the same is evolved into the variegated universe. The creation and dissolution of the universe is a sport (*līlā*) for God. The philosophical explanation for creation of the universe is to provide an opportunity to the countless *jīvas* to strive again to overcome the beginningless bondage and attain liberation. The Āḻvārs view it as an act of *dayā* or compassion towards the living beings.

The deeds which are of benefit to the celestial deities are:

1. The removal of the curse inflicted on Rudra by Brahmā.
2. The restoration of the Vedas to Brāhmā who had lost it as a result of the theft by a demon.
3. The restoration and propagation of Vedic knowledge to the *devatas* by assuming the form of Hayagrīva (man-horse) and Haṁsa (swan).
4. The assistance offered to Rudra in destroying the unconquerable citadel of the powerful demon Tripura.
5. The assistance provided to Indra, the kind of the *devatas*, to get back his kingdom which was about to be usurped by Bali, the king of demons.
6. The churning of the milky ocean to obtain the nectar (*amṛtamathana*) in order to protect the devatās from being destroyed by the demons.

Here again the Āḻvārs do not mention the details of the legends as narrated in the Epics and Purāṇas. They merely refer to these events to prove the supremacy (*paratva*) of Viṣṇu or Nārāyaṇa. According to them, Nārāyaṇa is the Supreme Deity, the sole creator and saviour of the universe and other deities are subordinate to Him.

The following are the other divine deeds which are referred to in the hymns:

1. The destruction of the wicked demon, Hiraṇyakaśyapa for the sake of protecting the pious and devoted child Prahlāda.
2. The killing of the powerful demon-king Rāvaṇa to save the celestial beings and the sages from his oppression and to establish righteousness (*dharma*).
3. The killing of Vāli, the wicked monkey-God to help the friendly Sugrīva.
4. The destruction of Kaṁsa to establish *dharma*.
5. The killing of a powerful demon, Bāṇāsura for helping Aniruddha.
6. The destruction of the Kauravas for the protection of the Pāṇḍavas.
7. A series of destruction of evil forces performed by Kṛṣṇa by the killing of wicked demons such as Pūtanā, Śakaṭāsura, Yamuḷārjuna, Bakāsura, Kapittha, seven ferocious bulls and the powerful elephant kuvalayāpīḍa.
8. A series of playful deeds performed by Kṛṣṇa during

his younger days—stealing of the butter, cheating the cowherd maids, grazing the cows, captivating the cowherd maids with his enchanting beauty, the performance of *rāsakrīḍā* (a folk dance) with *gopis,* lifting the Govardhana hill to protect the *gopas* and cows from torrential rain, the restoration of the children of a pious Brahmin from the heaven.

The main objective of citing these Purāṇic episodes is to explain the twofold purpose of *avatāra* viz., protection of the pious individuals (*sādhuparitrāṇa*) and destruction of evil (*duṣkṛt-vināśa*). Besides, the Āḻvārs see in all these deeds the following divine qualities:

1. *Āśrita-virodha nirasana*—the destruction of obstacles standing in the way of a devotee seeking refuge in God.
2. *Āśrita-vātsalya*—a loving disposition towards His devotees.
3. *Āśrita-pakṣapāta*—a partiality towards the devotees.
4. *Āśrita-vyāmoha*—a special attachment towards the devotees.
5. *Sauśīlya*—gracious condescension to mix freely with devotees unmindful of their birth and status.
6. *Saulabhya*—easy accessibility.

The fuller meaning of these attributes have been explained in the earlier section. It may be noted here that these are the most important qualities of a Divine Being from the standpoint of an ardent devotee seeking refuge in Him. The God-intoxicated Āḻvārs who crave for the vision of God are naturally attracted by this aspect of the divine glory. They have included these episodes in their devotional songs for the purpose of promoting *bhakti* among the common folks and induce them to turn towards God and refrain from the indulgance in the sensual pleasures. The Vaiṣṇava Ācārya have taken special note of these and elaborated them in their commentaries. Piḷḷān, the earliest commentator on *Tiruvāymoḻi* and so also Vedānta Deśika have laid greater emphasis on the theological implications of the divine *līlās* than the legends. This supports the view that the hymns of the Āḻvārs are not merely intended to promote *bhakti* but more importantly to impart the philosophic knowledge to the common people through the media of vernacular.

CHAPTER 4

THE DOCTRINE OF INDIVIDUAL SELF

The theistic mysticism presupposes the existence of a soul (*jīvātman*) as distinct from God (*Paramātman*) who is the object of spiritual experience. Only an individual deeply devoted to God yearns ardently to obtain the direct vision of God. What is the nature of an individual soul? Is it the mind (*manas*), the internal sense organ through which experience of external object takes place? Or is it an empirical ego denoted by 'I' (*ahaṁkāra*)? Or is it an eternal spiritual entity constituted of knowledge and bliss (*jñānānandamaya*)? Further, if it be a real spiritual entity as distinct from *Paramātman*, what is the nature of the relationship between the two? These are the important philosophical issues and we may find out what the Āḻvārs have to say on the subject.

The Tamil *prabandhams* do not present a detailed discussion of the doctrine of *jīva*. But there are a large number of hymns containing adequate references to *jīva* in different contexts from which we can gather the views of the Āḻvārs. The Aḻvārs have laid greater emphasis on the human bondage caused by the *karma* or the deeds of the past lives, than the ontological status of *jīva*, due to the fact that it stands as the greatest obstacle to the realization of God. They repeatedly call themselves as sinners (*pāviyeṉ*) because they are deprived of the vision of God. Though the bondage of soul is the dominant feature of their teachings, they have thrown sufficient light on the true nature of *jīvātman* and its ontological relation to *Paramātman*.

I. *The Nature of Jīva*

The Āḻvārs employ frequently terms such as *manas, neñju, uḷḷam* which generally refer to the mind or the internal sense organ through which experience of objects takes place. This corresponds to the *citta* in *Sāṅkhya-yoga* and *antaḥ-karaṇa* or the empirical ego conditioned by consciousness in Advaita Vedānta. They do not consider this as the soul (*jīva*). They use the word *uyir,* for the living spirit or *jīva.*[1] In one place Nammāḻvār mentions the Sanskrit word *jīva* for the soul as distinct from the physical body.[2] He describes it as *aruviṉaṉ*[3] which means that it is devoid of any physical form. It is essentially of the nature of knowledge (*jñāna*) and bliss (*ānanda*). It can be realized by the mind after getting rid of the mental impurities.[4] In another hymn, he states that it is a self-luminous entity abiding in the body.[5] The true nature of the *jīvātman* as *svayaṁ-jyotis* or self-luminous can be visualized in the state of *kaivalya* when the soul is totally liberated from bondage.

The *jīvas* are infinite in number. While defining the term *Nārāyaṇa,* Nammāḻvār states that He is the Deity who is associated with countless, souls which are of the nature of *jñāna* and *ānanda* (*eṇ perukku annalattu*).[6] The word *eṇ-perukku,* which is the equivalent of Sanskrit word *ananta* indicates that the souls are infinite numerically and *annalattu* means that they are constituted of essential qualities such as knowledge and bliss.[7] In one of the hymns he addresses God as the one who caused thousands of *jīvas.*[8] In several hymns, the souls are referred collectively as sentient beings (*yavarum*) as distinct from non-sentient entities (*yavaiyum*). The former cover all *cetanas* or living souls and the latter all *acetanas,* the non-living entities. These two terms correspond to the two metaphysical categories viz., *cit* and *acit,*

---

1. TVM I.1.7 *uḍalmiśai uyirena.*
   See also I.2.1 *ummuyir vīḍuḍaiyāṉiḍai.*
   MTi 73 *uḍaluṁ uyiruṁ ēṟṟāṉ.*
2. TVM VII.8.5 *kāyamum śīvanumāy.*
3. TVM I.1.3 *nilaṉiḍai viśumbiḍai uruviṉaṉ aruviṉaṉ.*
4. TVM I.1.2 *maṉaṉaha malamaṟa malarmiśai eḻutarum.*
5. TVM I.1.10 *iḍantihaḻ poruḷtorum—iḍam* means body and *tihaḻ* means shining; the total meaning is the luminous entity in the body.
6. TVM I.2.10.
7. See Piḷḷān AP I.2.10 *asaṅkhyeyarāy jñānānanda-svabhāvarāy irunda ātmā.*
8. TVM III.2.6 *parapallāyiraṁ uyir-śeyda paramā.*

accepted in the Viśiṣṭādvaita Vedānta. In the absence of any reference to the Advaitin's theory of the souls as either reflections of one Brahman in the numerous *antaḥ-karaṇas* (empirical ego) or Brahman conditioned by several internal organs, the plurality of the souls is an accepted fact. They are eternal (*manṉuyir*).[1]

The Āḻvārs also acknowledge the three types of *jīvas—baddha* or bound, *mukta* or released and *nitya* or eternally free. The numerous references in the hymns to a category of individuals in the name of *amarar, viṇṇavar, vānōr* etc., indicate the existence of eternally free souls or *nitya-sūris*. The acceptance of the theory of *kaiṅkarya* or divine service to the Lord in an eternal abode (*paramapada*) by the individual souls after they attain *mokṣa* implies the existence of *muktas* or souls totally free from bondage. In one of the hymns speaking about the glory of God, Nammāḻvār makes a pointed reference to *muktātmā* which is described as *arūpa* or devoid of physical form, countless (*alahil polinda*) and possessing *jñāna* that pervades in all ten directions (*tiśai pattāy*).[2] The *baddhas* are the souls which are caught up in the form of continuous series of births and deaths.

II. *Jīva and Human Bondage*

The bondage is caused by the beginningless *karma* or the deeds, good as well as bad, of the past lives.[3] The souls which pass through several lives[4] experience the suffering of birth, death, disease and old age.[5] *Karma* is *anādi* and so also the bondage caused by it has no beginning. But it has an end which comes when the individual gets rid of it totally by the practice of the prescribed spiritual discipline.

---

1. TVM I.2.2.
   See also MTi 60 *manṉuyirhaḻku ellām araṇāya.*
2. TVM VI.9.7 *puṟa aṇdattu alahil polinda tiśai pattāy aruvēyō.* Piḷḷān interprets these words in favour of *muktātmā* which exists beyond the cosmic universe (*aṇḍāt-bahi*), which possesses all-pervasive knowledge (*asaṅkucita jñāna*) and which are also countless (*asaṅkhyeya*).
3. TVM III.2.2 *tol mā-valviṉai* (*anādi mahā-prabala pāpāni*).
   TVM V.1.6 *iruvalviṉaiyār kumaikkum.*
   TVM II.6.5 *eṉ ulappilāda vem tīviṉaikaḷ.*
4. TVM II.6.8 *māṟi māṟi palapiṟappum piṟandu.*
5. TVM IV.9.5 *āṅgu uyirhāḷ pirappu irappu piṇi mūppāl tahaṟpu uṇṇum.*

In one of the hymns, Nammāḻvār explains how the bondage is caused. It says:

> In the earlier lives (through which the soul passed), I did not perform any good deeds; nor I abstained from doing evil deeds. On the contrary, I indulged in the enjoyment of sensual pleasures of transitory character and thereby I was dragged away from you.[1]

Who causes the bondage? Is God responsible for it? Or is the individual soul in any way responsible for it? These are important ethical issues relating to the problem of evil and freedom of soul.

Nammāḻvār points out that at the time of the creation of the universe *Īśvara* provides a body and sense organs to the soul.[2] The implication of this statement is that *jīva* is not created. It exists even during the period of dissolution in a subtle form, devoid of a body and sense organs. *Īśvara* causes its birth in the sense of associating the *jīva* with a physical component. On the basis of the type of body provided to a *jīva*, it is classified as *deva* (celestial being), *manuṣya* (human being) or *paśu* (animal) etc. This association of a body with a *jīva* is itself the bondage for the soul. The *jīva* is also enabled to function with the mental faculties and physical power given to it by God and consequently, it indulges in both good and evil deeds. The indulgence of the *jīva* through sense organs in evil activities causes further bondage to it. Is God then responsible for the human bondage insofar as He provides a body and sense organs to it? In one of the hymns, Nammāḻvār specifically states that God has placed the soul inside a physical body, which though full of dirt within, is outwardly covered in a neat form with the skin and make it indulge in all kinds of evil activities, thereby causing bondage.[3] In another hymn, he complains to God for binding the soul with the five sense organs which drag it towards sensual pleasures and keep it away from the God-realization.[4] All these statements

1. TVM III.2.6 *kiṟpan killēṉ eṉṟu, ilan munanāḷāl*
   aṟpaśaraṅgaḷ avai suvaittu ahaṉṟolindeṉ. . .
   See also TVM III.2.7 *meyjñānaminṟi viṉaiyiyal pirappu aḻundi.*
2. TVM III.2.1 *annāḷ nī tanda ākkaiyiṉ vaḻi uḻalven.*
3. TVM V.1.5.
4. TVM VII.1.1 *uṇṇilāviya aivarāl kumai tīṟṟi*
   eṉṉai uṉ pādapaṅkayam naṇṇilā-vahaiyē nalivāṉ

give the impression that God is responsible for human bondage. But this is not so. Though *Īśvara* is the primary cause for the creation of the universe along with all variegated created entities including the human and divine beings, the soul is caused to be associated with a specific physical component in accordance with the *karma* or the *puṇya* and *pāpa* arising from the past deeds of an individual. That is, a soul assumes the body of a celestial (*deva*) or that of a human being or animal, in accordance with the will (*saṅkalpa*) of *Īśvara* based on the merit and demerit of an individual. This is the basic postulate of Hindu religion. Though Nammāḻvār does not mention this point explicitly, it is implied in his general statements describing God as the very deeds (*karma*) performed by individuals and the very fruit or results arising from such deeds.[1] The following two hymns sung in an ecstatic mood by Nammāḻvār identifying himself with God convey this idea:

> It is I who control all deeds performed in the present time, those done in the past and those to be done in the future; I am the one who enjoy the fruits of these deeds; I am the one who prompt the doers (the individuals) in the respective deeds.[2]
>
> I indeed am the heaven providing happiness, the hell causing suffering and the state of *mokṣa* of supreme bliss; I am the souls that assume variegated physical bodies (*kolam koḷ uyirhaḷum*); I am the very primordial matter which undergo variety of modification.[3]

The equation of God with the souls assuming variety of physical bodies, the human activities and even the goals to be achieved by human endeavour signifies, as explained elsewhere,[4]

---

1. TVM III.5.10 *karumamum karuma palaṉum āhiya kāraṇan taṉṉai.*
2. TVM V.6.4 *śeyhiṉra kitiyellām yāne eṉṉum*
   śeyvānīṉṟanahaḷum yāne eṉṉum...
   śeydu munirandavum yāne eṉṉum
   śeykaippayaṉ uṇpēṉum yāne eṉṉum...
3. TVM V.6.10 *kōlamkoḷ śuvarkamum yāne eṉṉum*
   kōlamil narakamum yāne eṉṉum
   kōlemtihaḻ mokkamum yāne eṉṉum
   kolamkoḷ uyirhaḷum yāne eṉṉum
   kolamkaḷ tanimudal yāne eṉṉum.
4. See Chapter 2.

that God is the inner controller of all these. The significant phrase in this hymn, which is relevant in the present context, is *kōlam koḷ uyirhaḷ*. *Uyirhaḷ* means the souls; *kōlam-koḷ* means to put on a costume or disguise. The fuller meaning of this combined word is that the souls (which by their intrinsic nature have no physical form or appearance) assume different physical forms like a person appearing on a stage with different costumes. In other words, the souls put on a body of either a celestial or human or other living being and accordingly they are designated with different names as a *deva* or *manuṣya*. The important point for consideration is, who causes such an association of the soul with different physical bodies? Obviously, it is God who as the creator of the entire universe, causes it on the basis of the *karma* or past deeds of individual selves. This point though not mentioned in the hymn in question, is implied, as is explained by Piḷḷān in his commentary. Thus he states: "The souls are caused by *Īśvara* to enter different kinds of bodies by (His will) in accordance with the *karma* of individuals."[1]

The association of the soul with a body and sense organs is itself bondage because the latter entangle the soul with activities good and bad and consequently, make it reap their benefits in the form of happiness or suffering. More than this, the body which is also known as *avidyā* or *māyā* functions as a *veil* and prevents an individual from securing the true knowledge of *jīvātman* and *Paramātman*. The senses are personified as five powerful wicked demons, because they drag the individuals to indulge in sensual pleasures and prevent them from the God-realization.[2] In view of this, Nammāḻvār as well as other Āḻvārs repeatedly refer to human bondage and emphasise the need to overcome it.

Now the question arises: who is to remove it? Is it done by human endeavour or by God Himself? The general tenor of the hymns relating to this subject is that God who is the primary cause of the bondage should also remove it. Nammāḻvār in all

1. See Piḷḷān, AP V.6.10 *karmānuguṇamāha devādi śarīrapraveśam paṇṇakkaḍava ātmākkaḷum.*
2. See TVM VII.1.1.
See fn. 4 on p. 131.

his prayers pleads before God to remove his *vinai* or *karma*. He even goes to the extent of stating that no one else other than compassionate Almighty can cause its destruction. If this position is accepted, then there would be no room for human endeavour. If the soul is absolutely dependent on God (*atyanta-paratantra*), there would be no scope for human freedom.

Prima facie, what is stated above appears to be the view of Nammāḻvār. But on closer examination of his hymns, this does not seem to be the correct position. Nammāḻvār at the very outset advocates the divine service as a means of attaining the spiritual goal. He commends the renouncement of all worldly attachments and the surrender of one's self to God in order to attain Him. He advises the devotees to adopt the path of *bhakti* or *bhakti-yoga* as a means of God-realization. In the case of those who do not have the capacity to follow the arduous *bhakti-yoga,* he advocates self-surrender to the feet of God as the sole refugee for attaining the spiritual goal. He also prescribes the simple modes of worship of God such as *nāma-saṅkīrtana* to get rid of the sins of the past and overcome the obstacles standing in the way of God-realization. He himself admits that he was able to root out the sins of the past by unceasing contemplation on the glory of God and by singing His glory.[1] All these statements which are also endorsed by other Āḻvārs would become meaningless, if the *jīva* was not an agent of action with the freedom to perform the prescribed religious deeds. As *Vedānta-sūtra* says, *jīva* is the *kartā* or the doer as otherwise the religious commands would have no significance.[2] The statements of Nammāḻvār, which speak of God as the one who should remove the sins of the past are only intended to emphasise the fact that human endeavour needs the grace of God for its success. God as the primary cause of creation has provided to every individual the faculty of intellect to think and the physical organs to function. This is done out of His unconditioned compassion (*nirhetuka-kṛpā*). In this respect, the *kartṛtva* or doership is a gift of God.[3] The capacity to think and act which is granted by God is to be

1. TVM II.6.6 *uṉṉai cintaiśeydu śeydu uṉ neḍu-mā-moḻiśai pāḍi āḍi,*
eṉ muṉṉait-tīvinaihaḷ muḻuvēr arindaṉaṉ yāṉ.
2. VS II.2.33 *kartā śāstrārthavattvāt.*
3. Cp VS II.3.40 *parāttu tat śruteḥ.*

utilized by an individual with the aid of the *śāstra* in the right direction for a purposeful goal. To this extent, he is a free agent of action. If it were not so, then all the scriptural injunctions in the form of a command to do the right thing and abstain from what is morally wrong would be rendered meaningless. The equation of God with all deeds as well as the results accruing from them (*kṛti* and *karma-phala*) is intended to convey the fact that God as the *antarātmā* of all that exists in the universe is the controller (*niyantā*) of all human activities. Thus, there is no room for the view that the Āḻvārs subscribe to the theory of determinism without allowing the freedom of an individual.

III. *Jīva and Īśvara*

Now we come to the theory of the ontological status of *jīvātman* in relation to *Paramātman*. The *Vedānta-sūtra* points out that *jīva* is *aṁśa* or an integral part of Brahman.[1] The word *aṁśa* is interpreted by Rāmānuja in terms of *śarīra* or body in the technical sense as that which is wholly supported (*ādheya*) and controlled (*niyāmya)* and that which is dependent (*śeṣa*) on Brahman which is *śarīrin*. In the epistemological sense, it is an essential attribute (*prakāra* or *viśeṣaṇa*) of the substance (*prakārin* or *viśeṣya*), like the luminosity is an inseparable attribute of the luminous entity. Nammāḻvār describes *jīva* as a part of the glory of the Supreme Being (*Īśaṉ eḻil*) who abides in all sentient beings and non-sentient entities and controls them from within as its *antarātmā*.[2] All souls belong to God who is the Sovereign of the universe (*Sarveśvara*). In a more specific way, he says in one of the hymns: that soul is the property of the Lord.[3] Elsewhere he states: "My soul is yours."[4] Taking the context in which this statement is made, its implication is that the individual soul is the property of *Paramātman* because its very existence (*sattā*) is derived from the latter and it exists for the sole purpose of serving God. In Vaiṣṇava theology, the soul is regarded as *dāsa* or wholly sub-

---

1. VS II.3.42 *aṁśo nānā vyapadéśāt...*
2. TVM 2.7 *aḍaṅgu eḻil śampattu aḍaṅgakkaṇḍu, Īśaṉ aḍaṅgu eḻil akdu eṉṟu aḍaaguha uḷḷē.*
3. TVM I.2.1 *ummuyir vīḍu uḍaiyāniḍai.*
4. TVM II.3.4 *eṉadāvi āviyum nī.*
   See also TVM IV.3.8 *eṉṉadu uṉṉadāvīyum.*

servient to God.[1] Nammāḻvār as well as other Āḻvārs accord greater importance to this theological aspect of the soul. They frequently employ the Vaiṣṇava terminology *aḍiyēṉ* to signify the fact that the soul is subordinate to God (*dāsa-bhūta*). Nammāḻvār prays that his soul should be accepted by God for the exclusive purpose of offering divine service at all times.[2] Āṇḍāḷ also reiterates the same when she says that we desire to do service for ever exclusively to God.[3] Nammāḻvār expresses his gratitude to God for blessing him with philosophic wisdom and enabling him to serve Him.[4]

These hymns reveal that there is an intimate relationship between God and the individual self. Just as God is very dear to the *jīva* longing to see Him, God also has a special affection towards His devotees and desires to have communion with him. The theistic mysticism which is the dominant subject-matter of *Tiruvāymoḻi* and also the *prabandhams* of Periyāḻvār, Āṇḍāḷ, Kulaśekharan and Tirumaṅgai is developed on such an intimate relationship that exists between the compassionate loving Supreme Lord and the devoted, humble subordinate individual self. The mystic is made to crave for a direct vision of God with His full glory and is also subjected to anguish during the separation from Him, because of God's love to him. The communion with God termed as *saṁśleṣa* and separation from Him named *viśleṣa* are the two important states of *bhakti*. In the former state, the mystic sings the glory of God in different ways out of joy derived from the experience of God. In the latter state, he gives expression to his mental anguish in different forms caused by separation from God. All such mystic outpourings are meaningful in the context of the loving, mutual bondship that exists

1. The soul is also described as *śeṣa* or dependent on God who is the *śeṣin* or Lord. *Śeṣatva* is a wider philosophical concept employed by Rāmānuja to define the ontological relationship between God and the universe comprising both sentient souls and non-sentient entities. The term *dāsa* is more specific and applies exclusively to individual souls to denote the idea that soul by virtue of its nature is wholly dependent on God and subserves Him. The Āḻvārs have perferred this concept.
2. TVM II.9.4 *enakkē āḷ śey ekkālattum eṉṟu...*
   tanakkē āha eṉai koḷḷumīdē.
3. See *Tiruppāvai* 29 *unakkē nām āḷśeyvōm.*
4. TVM V.7.3 *poruḷ allāda eṉṉai poruḷ ākki aḍimai koṇḍāy.*

between the soul and God. We shall deal with this subject in detail in the chapter on Theistic Mysticism. For the present we may take note of the fact that the Āḻvārs conceive the soul as intimately related to God, as a part of His glory (*śampat*) and as a dear entity in the same way as a child is to the loving parents.[1] The religious texts compare the soul to the *kaustubha* or a precious gem worn by Viṣṇu on His chest.[2] It has the intrinsic capacity to be reunited with God but it has to endeavour to attain it after overcoming the obstacles in the form of bondage by the observance of the spiritual discipline laid down by the sacred texts for the purpose.

IV. *The Concept of Bhāgavata-śeṣatva*

Before we conclude we should take note of another important aspect of *Jīva's* relation not only to God but also to the devotee of God. In Vaiṣṇava terminology, this is known as *Bhāgavata-śeṣatva,* which means that an individual self is subordinate to God's devotees. This concept which constitutes a distinctive theory of Vaiṣṇavism finds a clear expression in the hymns of the Āḻvārs. Though there are some references to this idea in the *Mahābhārata, Rāmāyaṇa* and *Vaiṣṇava Purāṇas,* the Āḻvārs appear to have been the forerunner of the theory. Two decads of the *Tiruvāymoḻi* (III.7 and VIII.10) are exclusively devoted to extol the greatness of *bhāgavata-śeṣatva.* Nammāḻvār regards the subordination to God's devotee as an ideal to be aspired for (*parama-prāpya*) by a Vaiṣṇava. He says: "Whoever worships the Supreme Lord with devotion, unto him I bow with respect irrespective of his caste and social status."[3] Such a person is to be accepted as one's *svāmin* or master.[4] Not only a *Bhāgavata* is respected but even his devotees up to a few generations are treated as *svāmin* of a Vaiṣṇava. In a characteristic way he says: "We are the subordinates to the devotees of devotees of devotees of devotees."[5] In the tenth decad of the eight centum to

1. Cp ṚV I.31.10 *tvaṁ pitāsi naḥ.*
   See also BG XI.45 *piteva putrasya.*
2. See RTS Chapter 1 *maṇivara iva śaureḥ nitya hṛdyopi jīvaḥ...*
3. TVM III.7.1 *payilum tiru uḍaiyār evarēlum, avar kaṇḍīr...*
   emmai āḷum paramarē.
4. TVM III.7.3 *emmai āḷuḍai yārkaḷē.*
5. TVM III.7.10 *aḍiyār aḍiyār tammadiyār, aḍiyār tamakku-*
   aḍiyār-aḍiyār taṁ aḍiyār aḍiyoṅgaḷē.

which Vaiṣṇava Ācāryas attach special importance, the worship of the *Bhāgavatas* (*Bhāgavata-kaiṅkarya*) is considered superior to the worship of God Himself. Even the Lordship of the world, (*aiśvarya*), the blissful experience of the soul (*kaivalya*) and the experience of God in the state of *mokṣa* are not comparable to the joy derived from the worship of the true devotees of Viṣṇu.[1]

The *Bhāgavata-kaiṅkarya* is held in such a high esteem that one of the Āḻvārs, Vipranārāyaṇa called himself as *Toṇḍaraḍippoḍi*, which literally means 'wearer of the dust of the feet of devotees'. Kulaśekharāḻvār also extols the dust of the feet of the devotees (*aḍippoḍi*) and regards it as holy as Gaṅgā water.[2] He wishes to be born as the pathway to the Tirumalai hills and the footsteps leading to the temple so that he could have the contact with the *Bhāgavatas* coming to worship the Lord.[3]

Tirumaṅgai Āḻvār has devoted two decads (II.6 and VII.4) to glorify the greatness of the *Bhāgavatas.* He considers them greater than the *nitya-sūris* and would ever cherish to see them, think of them and move with them.[4] He regards them as his masters and worthy of worship.[5] Periyāḻvār also speaks highly about the devotees of God. In one of the decads, while condemning those who do not show respect to such devotees, he goes to the extent of saying that these persons have the right even to sell him.[6]

Thus, we find in the hymns of the Āḻvārs a fuller presentation of the theory of *Bhāgavata-śeṣatva* with an added emphasis. Though this concept can be traced to a few statements in the *Itihāsas* and *Vaiṣṇava Purāṇas,* the credit of developing it into a doctrine goes to the Āḻvārs. The teachings of the Āḻvārs on this subject have definitely influenced Rāmānuja and the Vaiṣṇava Ācāryas of later period who have adopted it as an important theory of Vaiṣṇavism.

---

1. TVM VIII.10.1 to 3 and 5.
2. *Perumal Tirumoḻi* II.2.
3. *Ibid.* IV.8 and 9.
   Cp. BP *ahaṁ kadambo bhūyāsaṁ kundovā yamunā taṭe*
   āsāmaho caraṇareṇu juṣāmahaṁ syāṁ
   vṛndāvane kimapi gulmalatauṣadhīnāṁ.
4. PTM VIII. 4.1 to 9.
5. *Ibid.* II.6.2 to 9.
6. PeriTM IV.4.10 *aḍiyārhaḷ entammai virkavum peruvārhaḷē.*

CHAPTER 5

THE DOCTRINE OF SĀDHANA

The hymns of the Āḻvārs which are primarily devoted to sing the glory of God have also accorded importance to the religious discipline to be pursued for the attainment of God. If God-realization is considered as the supreme goal of life (*parama-puruṣārtha*), it would be necessary to know the ways and means of achieving it. The Āḻvārs have, therefore, included in their teachings the methods to be adopted by an individual to attain the highest spiritual goal. Their views on the subject are scattered in the hymns. We shall attempt to present them in a consolidated form and evaluate their influence on Rāmānuja and his successors.

The term *sādhana* is used in Vedānta for the means (*upāya*) to be pursued by an aspirant for *mokṣa* (*mumukṣu*) to realize Brahman. The third part of the *Vedānta-sūtra* known as *sādhanādhyāya* is devoted to the discussion of this subject. According to Śaṁkara, *jñāna* or the spiritual knowledge of Brahman generated by the study of the Upaniṣads (*śravaṇa*), repeated reflection over what is learnt (*manana*) and contemplation (*nididhyāsana*) is the direct means to *mokṣa*. For Rāmānuja it is the knowledge of Brahman culminating in the unceasing loving meditation on Brahman (*upāsanā*) that leads to *mokṣa*. This is also known as *bhakti-yoga* as explained in the *Bhagavadgītā*. *Prapatti* or the complete surrender of one's self to God as the sole refuge is also laid down as an alternative, easier means to *mokṣa* for those who do not possess the capacity and the requisite eligibility to observe *bhakti-yoga.*

I. *The Views of Nammāḻvār on Sādhana*

In accordance with the teachings of the Upaniṣads and the *Bhagavadgītā* Nammāḻvār upholds *bhakti-yoga* as the means of attaining God. He also lays emphasis on the absolute self-surrender to God (*prapatti*) as a direct means of God-realization. The fact that he himself observed *prapatti* at the feet of the Lord Śrīnivāsa (the presiding Deity of Tirumalai)[1] indicates his preference for *prapatti,* as an easier alternative to the arduous *bhakti-yoga.* In either case the grace of God (*aruḷ* in Tamil) is accorded overriding importance.

Though the hymns of the Āḻvārs do not present the details of either the doctrine of *bhakti-yoga* or *prapatti* as the Vaiṣṇava treatises of later period do, they refer to the different methods of worship (*bhajana*) purely for the pleasure of God and the observance of certain religious duties along with the cultivation of non-attachment to worldly pleasures which are all subsidiary (*aṅga*) to *bhakti-yoga.* They also mention some of the components (*aṅgas*) of *prapatti* and its observance as a means to *mokṣa.* On the basis of these details, we can determine the views of the Āḻvārs on the nature of *sādhana* for *mokṣa.*

In the very opening hymn of the *Tiruvāymoḻi,* Nammāḻvār refers to the divine service as a means to spiritual goal.[2] The Tamil word used here is *toḻudal* which means in Sanskrit *namana* or *namaskāra.* The fuller implication of this term, as explained by the commentators, is the performance of *bhakti-yoga* since *namaskāra* is an essential feature of it as stated in the *Bhagavadgītā.*[3] It also means, as some commentators have stated, *śeṣavṛtti* or divine service which in a broad sense covers *bhakti-yoga.* The word *namaḥ* in a technical sense also stands for *prapatti* or surrender of oneself to God, as explained in the *Ahirbudhnya Saṁhitā.*[4]

The second decad of the first centum of the *Tiruvāymoḻi* is primarily devoted to teach the ways and means of attaining

---

1. See TVM VI.10.10.
2. *Ibid.* I.1.1 *śuḍaraḍi toḻudu eḻu....*
3. BG IX.34 *manmanā bhava madbhakto madyājī māṁ namaskuru.... .*
4. See *Ahirbudhnya Saṁhitā* XXXVII.38.

God. Here Nammāḻvār advocates the surrender of one's self to God by the renouncement of attachment towards all worldly objects.[1] In a later hymn of the same decad he states that one should seek the feet of Nārāyaṇa.[2] *Prima facie,* the hymns in this decad do not indicate specifically whether *bhakti-yoga* is the means to *mokṣa* or whether self-surrender (*prapatti*) is the means to it. Naturally, some commentators have taken the view that Nammāḻvār is advocating *bhakti-yoga* as a means to attain God, while others feel that the emphasis is in favour of *prapatti.* Another interpretation is that Nammāḻvār refers to both *bhakti-yoga* and *prapatti* as means to *mokṣa* but either of the discipline may be adopted in accordance with one's capacity and eligibility. If we go by the authoritative commentary of Piḷḷān, who is the direct disciple of Rāmānuja, the Āḻvār teaches in this decad *bhakti-yoga* as a means to God-realization, whereas self-surrender mentioned here is to be adopted as an aid (*aṅga*) to it along with non-attachment to worldly objects (*vairāgya*).[3]

In a later part of the *Tiruvāymoḻi,* Nammāḻvār states explicitly that *bhakti-yoga* is the means to attain God. The relevant hymn reads:

> The feet of *Dāmodara* (the Supreme Lord) is the only goal to be attained (*śārvē*) by those who follow the path of *bhakti* (*tavaneri*).[4]

Nammāḻvār here uses the Tamil word *tavaneri,* which is the equivalent of the Sanskrit word *tapomārga. Tapas* in the present context is understood as *bhakti*. In one of the hymns,[5] Nammāḻvār himself uses the word *tavaneri* along with *vaṇakkuḍai* which means the path of *tapas* associated with *namana* (*vaṇakku*) or salutation to God. In the context of the teaching of the *Gītā*, to which this particular hymn refers, it implies *bhakti-yoga* as the pathway for the attainment of God. Both Piḷḷān and the author of *Īḍu* support this interpretation.

1. TVM I.2.1 *vīḍumin muṟṟavum vīḍuśeydu ummuyir vīḍuḍaiyāniḍai vīḍu śeymino.*
2. TVM I.2.10 *nāraṇan tiṇkaḻal śērē.*
3. See Piḷḷān AP I.2.1.
4. TVM X.4.1 *śārvē tavanerikku dāmōdaran tāḷhaḷ...*
5. TVM I.3.5 *vaṇakkuḍaittavaneṟi vaḻininṟu.*

The word *tavaneri* is also interpreted in favour of *prapatti* because *nyāsa* (same as *prapatti*) is regarded as a distinctive type of *tapas* in the *Taittirīya Nārāyaṇa Upaniṣad*.[1] But in the context of the teaching contained in this particular hymn, it would be more appropriate to take the view as supported by Piḷḷān and others in favour of *bhakti-mārga*.

In a later decad, Nammāḻvār teaches specifically that one should meditate on the feet of Tirunārāyaṇa without any delay.[2] The word *cintana* used in this hymn means *dhyāna* or meditation and it implies the observance of *upāsanā* or *bhakti-yoga*.

The mystic experience of God and His glory is the dominant theme of *Tiruvāymoḻi*. A large number of the hymns refer to the blissful experience of the mystic saint when he is in communion (*saṁśleṣa*) with God. Similarly, several decads portray the anguish of the mystic when he is separated from God (*viśleṣa*). Both these states are the manifestations of *para-bhakti* or the perfected state of *bhakti* arising from the unceasing meditation on God with loving devotion.[3] Such a mystic experience of God indicates that Nammāḻvār accepts *bhakti-yoga* as the means to *mokṣa*.

The advocacy of *bhakti-yoga* as *sādhana* for *mokṣa* is not to be construed to mean that Nammāḻvār does not teach the theory of *prapatti* or absolute self-surrender to God as an alternative means to *mokṣa*. Tradition regards him with high esteem as the *prapannajana-kūṭastha* or the leader of the *prapannas*. He was the foremost among the Vaiṣṇava Saints and Ācāryas to show the alternative path to *mokṣa* by himself resorting to *prapatti*. There are sufficient number of hymns in the *Tiruvāymoḻi* emphasising the observance of *śaraṇāgati* or *prapatti* for attaining God. Thus in one of the hymns, Nammāḻvār says explicitly that God is the sole protector for all those who seek His feet as the sole refuge and He will confer Vaikuṇṭha to them soon after death.[4] In another decad devoted to emphasise the fact that the Supreme Lord is the sole refuge (*rakṣaka*), Nammāḻvār advocates *śaraṇāgati* as the sure way of attaining Him. The relevant hymn states:

---

1. TNUp 147 *tasmāt nyāsameṣāṁ tapasām-atiriktam-āhuḥ.*
2. TVM IV.1.1 *tirunāraṇaṉ tāḷ kālampera cintittu uymiṉō.*
3. See Chapter 7, pp. 153-57.
4. See TVM IX.10.5 *śaraṇamāhuṁ tanatāḷ aḍaintārkku ellāṁ,*
   maraṇamānāl vaikuṇṭham koḍukkum-pirāṉ...

> No one other than Lord Kaṇṇan is the refuge. He took birth in Mathura to reveal this truth. . . . Surrender unto His feet yourself and all that belongs to you without any hesitation because everything belongs to Him.[1]

More importantly, in the tenth decad of VIth centum Nammāḻvār himself observes *prapatti* at the feet of the Lord Śrīnivāsa, the *arcā* deity at Tirumalai for attaining the cherished spiritual goal. While this fact is evident in the hymn, the question is raised by some modern scholars whether *prapatti* is performed as a ritual act for *mokṣa* as conceived in the later Vaiṣṇava treatises.[2] The basis for this doubt seems to be that all the components of *śaraṇāgati* are not explicitly indicated in the hymn to claim it as a complete *prapatti* for *mokṣa*. The Pāñcarātra treatises describe *śaraṇāgati* as a sixfold ethico-religious discipline. It comprises five subsidiary components (*aṅgas*) and the principal act of self-surrender (*aṅgi*).[3] The hymn which speaks of the observance of self-surrender by Nammāḻvār mentions only the *ananya-śaraṇatva* or not having any other refuge than God. Thus says Nammāḻvār:

> I (the humble dependent on God) who has no other means take refuge totally at Thy feet.[4]

However, this hymn read along with the other hymns in general and the two phrases in particular used in it viz., *puhal illā* (*ananya-śaraṇa*) and *puhundu* (*prapadye*) do imply all the other components of *śaraṇāgati*.[5] That such a *śaraṇāgati* is performed for *mokṣa* or doing the *nitya-kaiṅkarya* in the *paramapada* is also obvious from the concluding hymns of the last decad of the tenth centum, where the Āḻvār prays for total liberation from bondage and an eternal communion with God. The fact that he himself performed *prapatti* for *mokṣa* establishes beyond any doubt

1. TVM IX.1.10 *kaṇṇanallāl illai kaṇḍīr śaraṇ...*
2. See R.D. Kaylor and K.K.A. Venkatachari, *God Far and God Near*, p. 66. See also John Carman, *The Tamil Veda*, p. 119.
3. See p. 154.
4. TVM VI.10.10 *puhal oṉṟu illā aḍiyēn uṉṉaḍikkīḻ amarndu puhundēnē.*
5. See *Īḍu* VI.10.10.
   See also PPS VI.10.10.
   See also DTR, 69 *satprapattavyabhāvāt.*

that Nammāḻvār acknowledges it as an alternative means to *mokṣa*, besides *bhakti-yoga*. As will be shown later, the doctrine of *prapatti* which is a distinctive tenet of Vaiṣṇavism finds full support in the *Tiruvāymoḻi* and also in the poems of the other Āḻvārs which are the earliest extant Vaiṣṇava works.

II. *The Theory of Bhakti-yoga*

We may now examine the nature of *bhakti-yoga* as conceived by Nammāḻvār. The *Vedānta-sūtra* is the most important work that discusses the various types of *upāsanās* or *vidyās* enjoined by the Upaniṣads as *sādhana* for Brahman-realization. It also speaks of the prerequisites to be fulfilled for performing meditation on Brahman. The *Bhagavadgītā* explains in detail the various features of *bhakti-yoga*, which according to Rāmānuja is the same as *upāsanā* enjoined in the Upaniṣads. *Bhakti-yoga* is the direct means to *mokṣa*, whereas *karma-yoga* and *jñāna-yoga* referred to in the *Gītā* serve as subsidiary to it.

According to the *Bhagavadgītā*, as interpreted by Rāmānuja, *bhakti-yoga* as a spiritual discipline (*sādhana*) for *mokṣa* comprises not only *karma-yoga* and *jñāna-yoga* as its subsidiary (*aṅga*) but it also includes the development of *vairāgya* or non-attachment to worldly objects by achieving complete control over sense organs including mind along with the observance of *varṇāśrama-dharma*. These are the preliminary requisites for the practice of both *jñāna-yoga* as well as *bhakti-yoga*. The *bhakti-yoga*, in a broad sense, covers the *aṣṭāṅga-yoga* or the eightfold ethico-religious discipline of *Pātañjala-yoga*. But Nammāḻvār does not present all these details in the *Tiruvāymoḻi*. However, there are several hymns in which he refers to the different features of *bhakti-yoga*. In one of the hymns, he says that he attained right in this birth and in a short duration the fruit of the arduous penance (*tapas*) normally to be achieved by observing the spiritual disciplines over several epochs.[1] The term *tavam* (Tamil word for *tapas*) referred here is interpreted as *bhagavadanubhava* or God-realization which is the goal of penance. The epithet *eṉaiyūḻi* used with the word *tavam* imply that such a penance is to be performed over a long period (*ūḻi* literally means epoch). The words *kurikkoḷ jñānaṅgaḷ* are in-

1. TVM II.3.8 *kurikkoḷ jñānaṅgaḷāl eṉaiyūḻi śeytavamuṁ...*

terpreted as *jñāna* in the form of *nididhyāsana* preceded by *śravaṇa* and *manana* including the observance of *yama, niyama* etc.[1] Piḷḷān interprets it as *bhakti-yoga* preceded by *karma-yoga* and *jñāna-yoga*. The word *jñāna* used in plural implies all the various *vidyās* or *upāsanās*.[2]

Elsewhere Nammāḻvār, while seeking refuge in God, pleads that he has not performed any rituals (*nōṉbu*) and he also does not possess the subtle knowledge of the self (*nuṇṇarivu*).[3] All the commentators interpret the terms rituals (*nōṉbu*) and *jñāna* (*arivu*) as *karma-yoga* and *jñāna-yoga* respectively and by implication, *bhakti-yoga* as well. Considering the context of the hymn, it is clear that Nammāḻvār is expressing his utter inability to observe the prescribed *sādhana* for God-realization in the form of *bhakti-yoga* aided by *karma-yoga* and *jñāna-yoga*.

In one more hymn, Nammāḻvār speaks in a similar strain:

> I have not got rid of the sins that cause suffering; nor have I performed unceasing meditation on your feet.[4]

Sins refer to the beginningless *karma* firmly associated with the *jīva* and its removal is effected only through the observance of *karma-yoga* and *jñāna-yoga*. The unceasing meditation on the feet of God refers to *bhakti-yoga*. In view of this, Piḷḷān explains that this hymn speaks of the inability of Nammāḻvār to observe the *karma-yoga, jñāna-yoga* and *bhakti-yoga*. All these statements reveal that Nammāḻvār acknowledges that *bhakti-yoga* as aided by *karma-yoga* and *jñāna-yoga* as taught in the *Gītā*, is the direct *sādhana* for *mokṣa*.

The *Tiruvāymoḻi* as well as the other *Prabandhams* do not contain the details regarding the practice of *bhakti-yoga*. They, however, cover adequately its important features and certain easy methods of worship. As stated in one significant verse of the *Bhagavadgītā*, the essential features (*svarūpa*) of *bhakti-yoga* are: (a) unceasing meditation on God (*manana*), (b) worship of God in all possible ways (*yajana*), (c) divine service such as salutation

---

1. See *Īḍu* II.3.8.
2. See ŚS II.3.8. *sadvidyā daharavidyādibhedāt bahuvacanam.*
3. TVM V.7.1 *nōṟṟa-nōṉbilēṉ nuṇṇarivu ilēṉ....*
4. TVM III.2.8 *mēvu tuṉpa viṉaikaḷai viḍuttumilēṉ,*
   ōvudal iṉṟi uṉ kaḻal vaṇaṅgiṟṟilēṉ.

(*namana*).[1] The *Bhāgavata Purāṇa* mentions nine modes of *bhakti* which subserve *bhakti-yoga*.[2] These are: *śravaṇa*, listening to the glory of God, *kīrtana*, singing His glory, *smaraṇa*, contemplation on His greatness, *pādasevana*, divine service, *arcanā*, offering flowers with recitation of His names, *vandana*, prostrating before God, *dāsya*, feeling the utter dependence on God, *sakhya*, friendly disposition towards God and *ātma-nivedana*, surrendering oneself to God. The three features of *bhakti-yoga* mentioned in the *Gītā* and the nine modes of worship referred to in the *Bhāgavata* are fully covered in the hymns of the Āḻvārs.

In the decad which teaches *bhakti-yoga*, Nammāḻvār emphasises the importance of *yajana* or worship of God. He says:

> In accordance with the teachings of the sacred texts one should develop the concentration of mind and focus it on Mādhavan (*Śriyaḥpati*) and offer worship daily to Him with fresh flowers, incense, light and water; this is the only way open to the devotees to attain God.[3]

In another hymn devoted to teach the easy manner of propitiating God, the Āḻvār advises to serve Him with pure water, burn incense and offer any flower that is easily available.[4] The material chosen by the devotee may be trifle but the same, if offered to God with devotion and without any selfish purpose purely for the pleasure of God will be acceptable to Him with great delight as is stated in the *Bhagavadgītā*.[5] Elsewhere, he commends the worship of God in the same manner as the *Bhāgavatas* (God's devotees) and other enlightened individuals

---

1. See BG IX.34 *maṇmanā bhava madbhakto madyājī*
maṁ namaskuru; māmevaiṣyasi
yuktvaivam-ātmānaṁ matparāyaṇaḥ.
2. BP VII.5.23 *śravaṇaṁ kīrtanaṁ viṣṇoḥ smaraṇaṁ pādasevanam;*
arcanaṁ vandanaṁ dāsyaṁ sakhyaṁ-ātmanivedanam
iti puṁsārpitā viṣṇau bhaktiścen-navalakṣaṇā...
The nine forms of *bhakti (nava-lakṣaṇa bhakti)* do not constitute *bhakti-yoga*, but on the other hand, they serve as aids to it.
See the commentary of Veeraraghavīya on this verse.
3. TVM X.4.10 *vakaiyāl manam oṉṟi mādhavanai*
nāḷuṁ pukaiyāl viḷakkāl pudumalarāl
nīrāl... tahaiyāṉ śaraṇam tamarkaḷku ōr paṟṟē.
4. TVM I.6.1 *parivadil īśaṉai pāḍi, nannīr tūy, purivatuvuṁ pukai pūvē.*
5. BG IX.26.

by offering worship to Acyutan (God) with flowers, incense, sandal-paste and water and by reciting the Vedic hymns[1] without deviating from the prescribed *bhakti-mārga*.

Manana or the contemplation on the glory of God is the second important feature of *bhakti-yoga*. It is the same as *dhyāna* or meditation on God. Nammāḻvār makes pointed references to it. While emphasising the permanent eternal character of God as supreme goal (*parama-puruṣārtha*), he advocates that one should without delay live a religious life by meditating on the feet of the Lord Tirunārāyaṇa.[2] In another hymn he says that he implanted God in his mind permanently with the desire to have His vision.[3] He advises the devotees to meditate (*niṉaimiṉ*) on the Supreme Lord and worship Him with fragrant flowers.[4] The word *niṉaimiṉ* means ceaseless meditation with loving devotion (*prītipūrvaka-dhyāna*) which is the same as *bhakti-yoga*.

Pāda-sevana, which is the same as *namaskāra* referred in the *Gītā* finds equal emphasis in the hymns of the Āḻvārs. In a direct way Nammāḻvār advocates that in order to cross the ocean of bondage one should bow one's head to the feet of the Lord.[5] In another hymn, he addresses his own mind to offer salutation to the feet of the presiding Deity of Tiruvāttār[6] (a pilgrim centre in Kerala). The salutation to the feet of the Lord is understood in its broad sense as *śeṣa-vṛtti* or the devoted service to be rendered by an individual to God. The term generally employed by the Āḻvārs to denote it is *toḻudu*. In several hymns, he teaches that one should live a religious life by doing divine service with *bhakti*.[7] This helps to overcome bondage by getting rid of all evils.[8] In this connection he asserts that what he teaches is true.[9]

From the foregoing analysis of the hymns, it may be observed that the different features of *bhakti-yoga* have been presented in

---

1. TVM V.2.9.
2. TVM IV.1.1 *tirunāraṇan tāḷ kālaṁperaccintittu uymiṉō.*
3. TVM IX.4.6 *uṉṉai kāṇakkarudi eṉ neñjattu iruttāha iruttiṉēṉ.*
4. TVM X.5.10 *śuṉai nāṉ-malariṭṭu, niṉaimiṉ neḍiyāṉē.*
5. TVM I.6.7 *taḷhaḷ talaiyil vaṇaṅgi, nāḷkaḍalai kaḻiminē.*
6. TVM X.6.1 *nī maḍaneñjē vāṭṭāṟṟāṉ aḍi vaṇaṅgē.*
7. TVM IX.10.1 *mālai naṇṇi toḻudu eḻumino viṉaikeḍa...*
   See also V.2.9 *mevittoḻudu uyminīrhaḷ...*
8. TVM IX.10.8 *aṇiyanāhum tanatāḷ aḍaindārkellāṁ,*
   piṇiyum śārā piravi keḍuttu āḷuṁ.
9. TVM X.2.3 *tīruṁ nōyvinaihaḷellāṁ tiṇṇam nāṁ ariyac coṉṉōm.*

the *Tiruvāymoḻi*. The practice of *bhakti-yoga* for the purpose of attaining God is to be preceded by *vairāgya* or non-attachment to worldly objects. Nammāḻvār, therefore, exhorts the devotees to renounce everything in the universe other than God.[1] This is an essential requirement even for *jñāna-yoga,* because as long as the sense organs are attached to worldly pleasures, the concentration of mind and unceasing meditation either on the *jīvātman* or *Paramātman* is well nigh impossible. If one realises the transitory character of worldly pleasures as compared to the eternal bliss of God, it becomes easy to develop the spirit of non-attachment. The root cause of bondage is the false notion of ego (*ahaṁkāra*) and mineness (*mamakāra*). This is to be totally uprooted by realizing the truth that the individual self is the property of the Supreme Lord. Nammāḻvār emphatically asserts that unless one renounces all the attachments to the worldly objects, it is not possible to attain God.[2]

Besides *bhakti-yoga* as taught in the *Bhagavadgītā,* Nammāḻvār also mentions the easy methods of worship such as *nāma-saṅkīrtana, arcanā, vandanā* and *smaraṇa* referred to in the *Bhāgavata Purāṇa*. He often lays greater emphasis on the easy methods of worship than the arduous *bhakti-yoga*. The relevant hymns and the comments of Piḷḷān thereon give the impression that the former are the substitutes for the latter. On careful study of the Āḻvār's hymns against the background of the teachings of the Upaniṣad and also *Bhagavadgītā* on *sādhana,* as interpreted by Rāmānuja, we can notice the difference between the two. The *bhakti-yoga* is a rigorous religio-spiritual discipline (*sādhana*) to be practised for the lifetime until the *mokṣa* is attained along with the prescribed *karma-yoga* and *jñāna-yoga* including the scrupulous observance of *varṇāśrama-dharma.* The easy methods of worship which do not require any such requirements cannot, therefore, become the substitute for *bhakti-yoga*. They are intended to promote *bhakti* in a devotee to enable him to undertake the prescribed *sādhana* for *mokṣa.* They do not serve as direct means to *mokṣa*. Both the Āḻvārs and the commentators

1. TVM I.1.1 *vīḍumin muṟṟavuṁ...*
2. TVM VII.2.8 *kaḍaiyara pāśaṅgaḷ vittapiṉṉai aṉṟi avaṉ avai kāṇkoḍāṉ.*

are aware of this difference between easy modes of *bhakti* and *bhakti-yoga*.[1]

III. *The Theory of Prapatti*

We may now examine the views of Nammāḻvār on the doctrine of self-surrender (*śaraṇāgati*) as a direct means to *mokṣa*. Nammāḻvār is regarded by tradition as *prapannajana-kūṭastha* or the leader of the *prapannas*. All commentators on *Tiruvāymoḻi* are of the opinion that he advocates *prapatti* as a means to *mokṣa* and that he himself performed it. There is no evidence in the *Tiruvāymoḻi* to prove that he observed the *bhakti-yoga* as a *sādhana* for the purpose of attaining *mokṣa*. As he was born as a *yogi* blessed with *para-bhakti*[2] which is the higher state of *bhakti*, there was no need for him to practice *bhakti-yoga*. He himself says in more than one place that he did not observe either *karma-yoga* or *jñāna-yoga* or even *bhakti-yoga*. Another important reason for his not observing *bhakti-yoga* is that he was not eligible for it on the ground of his caste. According to the Upaniṣadic teaching only persons born in the first three castes—Brāhmaṇa, Kṣatriya and Vaiśya—are eligible and since Nammāḻvār was born in *śūdra* caste though a saint was ineligible for it. However, all individuals are potentially eligible for *mokṣa*. Since Nammāḻvār was an ardent aspirant for *mokṣa*, he resorted to the pathway of *prapatti* (*prapatti-mārga*) which is open to all irrespective of caste and creed. Besides non-eligibility on the ground of caste, he ardently yearned to attain *mokṣa* without any delay in this very life. This is evident from the hymns in which he expresses the impatience to wait longer for attaining God. According to the doctrine of *prapatti*, the unbearability to wait for a long period (*kālakṣepākṣamatva*) is one of the eligibility requirements for *prapatti*.

Though he did not practice it as a *sādhana*, he adopted the various modes of *bhakti* for the purpose of experiencing the glory of God and rendering divine service as a goal in itself (*puruṣārtha*). As rightly observed by the author of the *Īḍu*, in reply to a query whether Nammāḻvār is a *prapanna* or *bhakti-yogi*,

Namalvar e prapatti *

1. See Piḻḻān, AP I.6.1.
2. TVM I.1.1 *matinalam aruḷinaṉ yavaṉ avaṉ*.

it is said that he is a *prapanna* who performed *prapatti* but adopted *bhakti* as a way of life (*dehayātrā*).[1] This is evident from the numerous spontaneous out-pourings conveying his anguish when separated from God (*viśleṣa*) and his joy of experience, while in communion with God (*saṁśleṣa*). The several facets of mystic experience of Nammāḻvār are nothing but external manifestation of different aspects of *bhakti* observed for the purpose of rendering divine service purely for the pleasure of God and not as a *sādhana* for achieving any specific goal.[2]

We may now consider whether Nammāḻvār observed *prapatti* as a ritual act for *mokṣa*. The philosophy of *prapatti* is based on two principles: (1) that God as the Supreme Being (*Sarveśvara*) endowed with the attributes such as compassion (*dayā*), omniscience (*sarvajñyatva*) and omnipotence (*sarvaśaktitva*), is the sole refuge (*śaraṇya*) for those desirous of escaping bondage and attaining God; (2) that the individual souls caught up in the ocean of bondage from the time immemorial is utterly incapable of resorting to any means other than Him to overcome bondage. These two points are manifestly brought out in the hymns. Nammāḻvār repeatedly emphasises the fact that the Supreme Being is the sole refuge. Thus he says:

> Oh Lord of the eternal souls, Thou has vouchsafed unto me your feet as my sole refuge.[3]

Elsewhere he states as a message to the people: "Take note that there is no other refuge than His feet."[4]

More specifically he points out that the feet of the Lord is the supreme goal for those following the religious discipline (either *bhakti-mārga* or *śaraṇāgati*).[5]

According to the doctrine of *prapatti*, as explained in the

---

1. See *Īḍu* I.1.1 *āḻvār prapannar, bhakti ivarukku dehayātrā viśeṣam.*
2. In Vaiṣṇava Theology, *bhakti* is conceived in two ways: *sādhana-bhakti* and *phala-bhakti.* When *bhakti* is adopted as a *sādhana* for *mokṣa,* it is known as *sādhana-bhakti* or *upāya-bhakti.* When the same is observed for rendering divine service purely for the pleasure of God, as in the state of *mokṣa,* it is regarded as *phala-bhakti* or more correctly *phalarūpa-bhakti.*
3. TVM V.7.10 *āru eṉakku ninpādamē śaraṇāhat tandu oḻindāy...*
4. TVM VI.3.10 *pirāṉ kaḻaḷhaḷaṉṟi maṟṟōr kaḷaikaṇ ilam kāṇmiṅgaḷē.*
5. TVM X.4.1 *śārvē tavanerikku dāmodaraṉ tāḷhaḷ.*

Pāñcarātra treatises, there are special requirements to be fulfilled by an aspirant for *mokṣa*. The first one is known as *ākiñcanya* or the absolute inability on the part of the individual to adopt any other *upāya* for *mokṣa* such as *bhakti-yoga* aided with *karma-yoga* and *jñāna-yoga*. The second qualification needed is *ananya-gatitva*, that is, not having any other refuge than God. Nammāḻvār has not only referred to these two requirements but also exhibited the same when he himself adopts *prapatti* as a *sādhana* for *mokṣa*. In the 10th decad of sixth centum, which speaks of his performing *prapatti*, he says that he is devoid of other means (*puhaloṉṟu illā aḍiyēn*).[1] When he states openly that he is incapable of observing either *karma-yoga* or *jñāna-yoga* or *bhakti-yoga*, he exhibits his *ākiñcanya*. The reference to the mythological episode of *gajendra* (the mythical elephant), who was rescued by the Lord from the clutches of the mythic crocodile is intended to illustrate the fact that those who solely seek the refuge of God is sure to be protected.[2]

Prapatti is a sixfold ethico-religious discipline. It comprises six components: (1) *ānukūlya-saṅkalpa*, a determined will on the part of the aspirant to perform only such acts as would please God; (2) *prātikūlya-varjana*, to refrain from acts which would cause displeasure to God; (3) *kārpaṇya*, the feeling of humility arising from the helplessness of an individual to resort to other means of salvation; (4) *mahā-viśvāsa*, the absolute and unshakable faith in God as the sole protector; (5) *goptṛtva-varaṇa*, to make a request to God seeking His protection; (6) and *ātma-nikṣepa*, entrusting the burden of protecting the individual self to the care of God along with an ardent prayer. The last one constitutes the principal component (*aṅgi*), which consists in the mental act of actual surrendering of one's self to God, whereas the first five are the subsidiary components (*aṅgas*) of *prapatti*.[3] Though the doctrine of *prapatti* with all the above details is not discussed in the *Tiruvāymoḻi* at one place, particularly in the

1. TVM VI.10.10.
2. TVM VII.10.8 *aṉṟi maṟṟu oṉṟu ilam niṉ śaraṇē eṉṟu,...*
ānaiyin nêñjiḍar tīrta pirān...
3. See for details *Vaiṣṇavism—Its Philosophy Theology and Religious Discipline*, Chapter 13, pp. 269-74.

hymn related to the observance of *prapatti,* we can find reference to them in various hymns in the sixth centum, the main theme of which is *śaraṇāgati.* As a God-intoxicated saint craving for the direct divine vision without a delay and as one who has unshakable faith in the protective power of God as evidenced in the hymns, the Āḻvār exhibits the first two *aṅgas* and also the fourth one. The repeated references to his ardent prayers to bless him with liberation from bondage reveal the third and fifth *aṅga.* Regarding the *ātma-nikṣepa,* which is the principal component, it is fully demonstrated in the manner in which Nammāḻvār totally surrenders his soul to the feet of God. It does not involve a physical transfer of the soul to God, since the soul is not a commodity. On the contrary, it implies the specific mental notion (*buddhi-viśeṣa*) in the form of realization that the soul does not belong to oneself but it is the property of God. At the very outset in the second decad of first centum, Nammāḻvār teaches, while abandoning the attachment to the worldly objects, that one should surrender his soul to the Lord who is its real owner.[1] In interpreting this hymn, Piḷḷān explains the word *samarpaṇa* or surrendering the soul, as the realization of the fact that the individual is the property of the Lord.[2] As Nammāḻvār himself says, all along one had developed the false notion that the soul is one's own due to the beginningless *avidyā-karma*[3] and now with the dawn of spiritual knowledge one realizes the philosophic truth that the soul is the property of God and that it is, therefore, to be surrendered to Him since the individual is helpless in liberating it from the bondage. This is the true meaning of *ātma-nikṣepa* and this fact has been amply demonstrated by Nammāḻvār. As a saint he is sinless but often regards himself as sinner (*pāviyēṉ*) which is an expression of modesty. He uses the word subservient (*aḍiyēṉ*) to signify that as an individual he is utterly dependent on God, who is the Supreme Ruler. The mystic out pourings in the guise of a consort (*nāyakī*) of God also exhibits

---

1. TVM I.2.1 *ummuyir vīḍuḍaiyāniḍai vīḍu-śeyminē.*
2. Piḷḷān, AP I.2.1 *ivvātmā avanukku śeṣameṉṟu saṁvadikkai.*
3. See TVM II.9.9 *yānē eṉṉai ariyahilādē,*
   yānē entanadē enrirundēn
   yāne nī ennuḍaimaiyuṁ nīyē...

the idea of absolute dependence on God (*pāratantrya*). Thus there is enough evidence in the *Tiruvāymoḻi* to uphold the view that Nammāḻvār performed *prapatti* for the purpose of attaining God.

The question whether or not *prapatti* can confer *mokṣa,* is answered in one significant hymn. It says that for those who seek refuge at His feet, He is the saviour in all ways; soon after death He is the benefactor by way of conferring *mokṣa.*[1] While elucidating the meaning of this hymn, Piḷḷān makes it clear that for those who seek the feet of the Lord, being unable to resort to *bhakti-yoga,* God stands as the sole protector in all possible ways and He is ready to grant them *mokṣa* either at that very moment or at the end of the present life when the physical body is cast off.

We have discussed the doctrine of *sādhana* mostly on the basis of Nammāḻvār's *Tiruvāymoḻi* since this poem presents it in greater detail than the other *prabandhaṃs.* The other Āḻvārs too have acknowledged, either implicitly or explicitly that both *bhakti* and *prapatti* are the *sādhanas* for *mokṣa.* As God-intoxicated saints they have all accorded importance to the different modes of *bhakti* such as *smaraṇa, nāma-saṅkīrtana* and *arcanā.* Some have referred to the *bhakti-yoga* as the direct *sādhana* to attain God. Poygai, the earliest Āḻvār, states clearly that the ceaseless knowledge (*aviyāda jñāna*), the performance of prescribed religious deeds (*vēḻvi*) and the cultivation of good virtues (*nalla aram*) along with the control of the sense organs are the means to attain God.[2] This hymn implies that *bhakti-yoga* as aided by *karma-yoga* and *jñāna-yoga* is the *sādhana* for *mokṣa.* In another hymn, he emphasises the importance of *jñāna, vairāgya* and *bhakti* as means of God-realization.[3] He also exhorts the worship of God with flowers, incense, recitation of His names and other forms of divine service.[4] Both Pūtattāḻvār and Peyāḻvār advocate the meditation on the feet of the Lord after securing control of the mind and five sense organs as the means of attaining God.[5]

1. TVM IX.10.5 *śaraṇamāhuṁ tanatāḷ aḍaintārkku ellām,*
   maraṇamānāl vaikuṇṭham koḍukkum pirān.
2. MTi 12 *aviyāda jñānamuṁ vēḷviyuṁ nallaṟamuṁ*
   eṉparē ēṉamāy niṉṟārku iyalvu.
3. MTi 32.
4. MTi 58.
5. ITi 6, 26, 31 and 41.
   MunTi 12, 79 and 88.

Tirumaḻiśai Āḻvār also states explicitly that only those who focus their mind on the Supreme Lord and meditate continuously with loving devotion would attain *vaikuṇṭha* without delay.[1] The remaining Āḻvārs have indirectly hinted the practice of *bhakti-yoga*. There is no indication in their poems whether or not they actually practised *bhakti-yoga* as a *sādhana* for *mokṣa*. Since they were all blessed by God with *parabhakti*, which is the higher state of *bhakti*, there was thus no need for them to observe *bhakti-yoga* as a *sādhana*. *Bhakti*, was however, adopted by them as a goal in itself (*puruṣārtha*) for rendering divine service purely for the pleasure of God.

If *bhakti-yoga* was not practised as a *sādhana*, the question arises as to whether they observed *prapatti* for attaining *mokṣa*. Obviously they would have followed the *prapatti-mārga*, since according to *Vaiṣṇavism* this is the only alternative means to *mokṣa*. Except Tirumaṅgai Āḻvār, Poygai, Periyāḻvār and Kulaśekharan, the other Āḻvārs do not mention explicitly that they actually performed *prapatti* as a ritual act, as is stated by Nammāḻvār. However, there are a large number of hymns in which they emphasise that the Supreme Being is the sole refuge and that they have no other means to attain God. All the Āḻvārs plead that they are totally dependent on God and that they are incapable of helping themselves to escape from the ocean of bondage. These statements reflect the two important eligibility requirements for *prapatti* viz., *ākiñcanya* and *ananyagatitva*. As explained earlier, Nammāḻvār uses these terms in the hymn covering his *śaraṇāgati* at the feet of the Lord of Tirumalai.[2] Both Āḻavandār and Rāmānuja use the same expressions in connection with the *prapatti* observed by them.[3] On the basis of these facts, it may be inferred that all the other Āḻvārs not only advocated the path of *prapatti* but also adopted it for themselves. Thus, Poygai Āḻvār states that if one were to get rid of the sins

1. NanTi 79.
2. See TVM VI.10.10.
3. See *Stotraratna, akiñcano ananyagatiḥ śaraṇyaḥ tvatpāda mūlaṁ śaraṇaṁ prapadye.*
Śaraṇāgatigadya, aśaraṇya śaraṇya ananya-śaraṇaḥ śaraṇaṁ ahaṁ prapadye.

and afflictions totally, one should seek the refuge of God.[1] Periyāḻvār advocates *prapatti* as a direct means to *mokṣa* [2] and emphasises that none other than God is the sole refuge.[3] He also states that he has surrendered his soul to God.[4] Kulaśekharāḻvār pleads that there is none whom he could approach for a refuge other than the feet of God.[5]

Tirumaṅgai Āḻvār, who has contributed the largest number of poems, presents a clearer account of *prapatti*. According to the Vaiṣṇava Ācāryas, the *Periya Tirumoḻi* is an exposition of *śaraṇāgati*. In several hymns addressed to the *arcā* deities at the religious centres, he states explicitly that he surrenders himself to the feet of the Lord. Thus, in the decad devoted to sing the glory of *Naimiśāraṇya* (a religious centre in Uttar Pradesh), he repeatedly says:

> O Lord of Naimiśāraṇya, I surrender myself to your feet (*uṉ tiruvaḍi aḍaindēn naimiśāraṇyattuḷ endāy*).[6]

In each hymn, he expresses his deep repentence over the evil deeds performed in his early life, seeks God as the sole saviour and submits himself to His feet along with the prayer for protection. These hymns reveal that he observed *sāṅga-prapatti* or the self-surrender with all the requisite components.

Similarly in another decad addressed to the Lord of Tiruveṅgaḍa, Tirumaṅgai Āḻvār speaks of self-surrender as the only means of obtaining the vision of God. He says:

> O Lord, who resides in the Tirumalai surrounded with bamboo trees and creepers with fragrant flowers, I wasted my life by developing attachment to parents, wife, children and relatives; I have now come to you as a humble servant and with the sole purpose of securing your vision. I surrender to your feet. Thou should accept me out of your compassion and enable me to render you service.[7]

---

1. MTi 59 *aḍainda aruviṉaiyōḍuallal nōy pāvaṁ.*
   miḍaindavai mīṇḍoḻiyaveṇḍil... tanvil aṁkai vaittān śaraṇ.
2. PeriTM V.3.4 *un pādaniḻalallāl maṟṟōr uyrpiḍam nāṉ eṅguṁ kāṇginṟilēṉ.*
3. *Ibid.* V.4.1.
4. *Ibid.* V.4.5 *eṉṉaiyum uṉṉil iṭṭēṉ...*
5. PeruTM V.5 *eṅguppoy uykēn uṉ iṇaiyaḍiyē aḍaiyallāl...*
6. PTM I.6.1 to 9.
7. *Ibid.* I.9.1.

In the same strain he pleads:

> I have passed through several births of high and low but I have not found any happiness. Nor have I done any meritorious deeds. As one who has undergone suffering I seek your feet. Thou should accept me with compassion to enable me to offer service exclusively to you.[1]

In a more pathetic way he states:

> O Māyaṉ, Mādhava, the Lord of Tiruveṅgaḍa, I have nothing to fall upon (support myself); I have only done evil deeds and become a worst sinner; I know of no other means to save myself; I have now approached you as one solely dependent on you. You should with compassion accept me.[2]

In the subsequent decad (I.10), he prays to the Lord to remove all the obstacles standing in his way and bless him with the opportunity of rendering eternal divine service (*nitya-kaiṅkarya*), which is the supreme goal of life. These hymns reveal without any shadow of doubt the importance of *śaraṇāgati* taught by Tirumaṅgai Āḻvār for attaining God.

Nammāḻvār has preferred the *prapatti-mārga* to the arduous *bhakti-mārga*, by himself observing the former. Tirumaṅgai Āḻvār has expressed his preference to it by directly advising the aspirants seeking *mokṣa* without delay not to torture their body by following rigorous penance (*tapas*) but to take recourse to the easy alternative method of seeking the refuge of the Supreme Lord. In the decad devoted to sing the glory of Cittirakūṭam, a pilgrim centre in South, he exhorts the people who desire to attain *paramapada* in the following words:

> Do not practise the severe penance (*tapas*) by torturing the five sense organs and by burning the flesh of the physical body to all possible extent; on the contrary, proceed to Cittirakūṭam and seek the feet of the Lord residing there.[3]

In another hymn he says:

1. PTM I.9.4.
2. *Ibid.* I.9.9.
3. *Ibid.* III.2.1.

> You do not have to observe the penance by eating only dry jungle fruits and leaves, by inhaling the hot air and standing at the centre of five consecrated fires (*pañcāgni*); on the contrary, you proceed to Cittirakūṭam which is inhabited by the orthodox Vedic scholars engaged in the recitation of the Vedas and the performance of Vedic rituals.[1]

Realizing the hardship involved in the practice of arduous *bhakti-yoga* and the long period of waiting to attain the spiritual goal, Tirumaṅgai Āḻvār advocates the observance of the easier alternative path of *śaraṇagati*. One other important reason for the advocacy of *prapatti* is the realization of the protective power (*rakṣakatva*) of God and His compassion (*aruḻ*) out of which He readily responds to the devotees who seek His refuge. This point is exhibited in one of the decads (V.8) devoted to sing the glory of the Lord Raṅganātha. In this decad Tirumaṅgai Āḻvār refers to several Purāṇic episodes, which narrate the manner in which God willingly and readily showered His grace and protection. Some of the classic examples cited here are the manner in which God-incarnate Rāma embraced Guha, the hunter, unmindful of his status; the way the mythic Gajendra was rescued from the clutches of the crocodile; the way Lord Rāma expressed his gratitude to Hanumāna with an embrace; the protection extended to Mārkaṇḍeya to escape death and a few other incidents. By citing these episodes, Tirumaṅgai Āḻvār says:

> I seek your feet, because I am convinced that you would never let down a devotee who pray for your protection.

Keeping in mind this noble quality of the Supreme Lord, the Āḻvār exhorts the easy method of self-surrender for attaining the spiritual goal.[2]

IV. *Divine Grace and Sādhana*

Thus, it may be observed that both *bhakti* and *prapatti* are advocated by the Āḻvārs as two alternative direct means to attain the supreme goal. *Prapatti* is intended for those who are not

1. TM III.2.2.
2. See PTM V.8.3 *aṟindu uṉ aḍiyaṉēṉum vandu aḍiyiṇai aḍaindēṉ...*

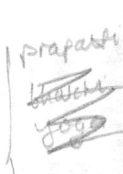

eligible for *bhakti-yoga* and who do not possess the capacity to observe other *sādhanas* such as *karma, jñāna* and *bhakti*. Whatever may be the spiritual discipline to be pursued for the attainment of God, the grace of God (*aruḷ* or *kṛpā*) is reckoned as an important factor. Nammāḻvār accords a greater significance to the unconditioned *kṛpā* of God. In a characteristic way he says:

> I have not performed any good deeds in the past that would take me to you. Nor have I refrained from evil deeds. I have strayed away from you by indulging in sensual pleasures of transitory character. Thou great Lord who is the creator of millions of souls, it would not be too much for you to redeem me and secure for me your feet.[1]

In another hymn he appeals to God:

> Oh Lord, what can I do and who shall be my protector? What indeed do you propose to do with me? I do not crave for means other than you.[2]

The other Āḻvārs also stress the importance of God's grace for overcoming the bondage. Thus Tirumaṅgai Āḻvār in the concluding verse of the *Periya Tirumoḻi* pleads in a pathetic way seeking the *aruḷ* of God to escape from the ocean of bondage (*andō aḍiyērku aruḷāy uṉ aruḷē*).[3] Though *bhakti-yoga* and *prapatti* are taught as *sādhanas* for *mokṣa*, the Āḻvārs feel that such means by themselves cannot secure it. Hence they invoke the grace of God.

The emphasis laid down on divine grace raises the question whether grace alone without the observance of the prescribed *sādhana* can secure *mokṣa*. The *Muṇḍaka Upaniṣad* states that God is the causeway (*sethu*) for immortality (*amṛta*).[4] The *Kaṭha Upaniṣad* expresses the same truth in a different way when it says that God is attained only by those whom He choses

1. TVM III.2.6.
2. TVM V.8.3 *ennān śeykēn yārē kaḷaikaṉ*
   ennai en śeyhinrāy, unnāl allāl
   yāvarālum oṉṟum kuraivēṇḍēṉ...
3. PTM XI.8.9.
4. MUp II.2.5 *amṛtasya eṣa setuḥ*.

(*yamaiveṣa vṛṇute tena labhyaḥ*).[1] These statements as interpreted by Rāmānuja do not imply that grace alone is the cause of *mokṣa* without the observance of the prescribed *sādhana*. On the contrary, *bhakti* or *prapatti* is required to be observed as enjoined in the Scripture, in order to earn His grace, which in the last resort confers the supreme goal (*tasya ca vaśīkaraṇaṁ tat śaraṇāgatireva*).[2] If the relevant hymns of the Āḻvārs are understood in the light of the explanation offerred by Rāmānuja, they convey the idea that divine grace alone without the observance of *sādhana* cannot be the means to *mokṣa*. This view is substantiated by the fact that the Āḻvārs have advocated both *bhakti-yoga* and *prapatti* as *sādhana* for the attainment of God. They themselves have also observed *prapatti* as a ritualistic act. As explained in an earlier chapter, the *jīva*, though dependent on God (*paratantra*) is endowed with the capacity to perform the deeds enjoined by the Sacred texts.[3] The individual seeking *mokṣa* is, therefore, required to observe the prescribed *sādhana*, while the fruit of such an endeavour (*phala*) is finally conferred by the grace of God, as the *Vedānta-sūtra* says.[4] As explained by Vedānta Deśika, following the teaching of Rāmānuja, God is the primary general cause of *mokṣa* (*pradhāna sāmānya kāraṇa*) because His grace confers it, whereas *bhakti-yoga* or *prapatti* serves as accessory cause (*sahakārī kāraṇa*) since that helps to earn His grace.[5] It is in this sense that Nammāḻvār says that God is both the *upāya* or *prāpaka* (means) and *upeya* or *prāpya* (goal).[6] This is the central teaching of the *Tiruvāymoḻi* as pointed out by the commentators.[7]

---

1. KaUP II.23.
2. RB I.4.1.
   See also BG VII.14 *māmeva ye prapadyante māyām etāṁ taranti te.*
3. See Chapter 4, pp. 133-35.
4. VS III.2.37 *phalamata upapatteḥ.*
   See also RB *sa eva hi sarvajñaḥ sarvaśaktiḥ mahodārāḥ*
   yāgādāna homādibhiḥ upāsanena ca ārādhitaḥ...
   sva-svarūpa avāptirūpam apavargaṁ ca dātum īṣṭe.
5. See RTS Chapter XXIII.
6. TVM V.7.10 *āru enakku niṉpādamē śaraṇaha tandoḻindāy.*
   The word *aru* means *upāya* and *śaraṇa* means *upeya*. See Piḷḷān AP and PPS V.7.10.
7. DTR 7 *devaḥ śrīmān svasiddheḥ karaṇamiti vadan ekamarthaṁ sahasre...*

CHAPTER 6

THE DOCTRINE OF SUPREME GOAL

We have discussed the theory of *sādhana* or the means of God-realization as conceived by the Āḻvārs. We shall now examine their views on the nature of the supreme goal of life (*parama-puruṣārtha*).

I. *The Upaniṣadic Theory of Mokṣa*

According to the Vedānta, *mokṣa* or the liberation of the soul from bondage is the highest goal of life. In positive terms, it is described as the realization of Brahman (*Brahma-sākṣātkāra*). It is the direct experience of the blissful Brahman (*Brahmānandānubhava*) by the soul after it becomes totally free from the shackles of bondage. The *Taittirīya Upaniṣad* says that the knower of Brahman attains Brahman.[1] The *Chāndogya Upaniṣad* states that the soul, after it leaves the body and reaches Brahman, manifests itself in its true form.[2] The *Taittirīya Upaniṣad* specifically points out that the individual self-enjoys Brahman together with all its glory.[3] The *Muṇḍaka Upaniṣad* mentions that when the knower of Brahman intuits the

1. TUp II.1 *brahmavid-āpnoti param.*
2. ChUp VIII.12.2 *evamevaiṣa samprasādo asmāt śarīrāt samutthāya paraṁ-jyotir-upasampadya svena rūpeṇa abhiniṣpadyate.*
3. TUp I.11 *so aśnute sarvān kāmān saha, brāhmaṇa vipaściteti.*

Lord, he attains supreme equality with Him.[1] All these Upaniṣadic statements, as interpreted by Rāmānuja, reveal that *mokṣa* is not merely the negative concept of total freedom of the individual soul from bondage but a positive state of the existence of *jīva* in a supramundane realm (*Brahmaloka*) where it regains its true form and enjoys the full glory of Brahman.

The teachings of the Āḻvārs on the nature of the supreme goal of life conform fully to the Upaniṣadic theory. The Āḻvārs generally use the word *vīḍu*[2] for *mokṣa*. This term literally means liberation and in the present context, it denotes the existence of the soul in an eternal abode of God, which is known as *Paramapada* or *Vaikuṇṭha*. Nammāḻvār refers to *Vaikuṇṭha* in several hymns[3] and describes it as a unique place (*nāḍu*) which is free from suffering and full of *ānanda* (bliss) *par excellence*.[4] It is a transcendental spiritual realm constituted of self-luminous *jyotis* (lustre).[5] God is addressed as *Vaikuntā*,[6] implying that He is the Lord of the eternal abode. He is frequently described as the Lord of the eternally free souls (*nitya-sūris*) who dwell in this realm forever.[7]

Regarding the nature of *mokṣa*, Nammāḻvār points out that it is a state of existence for the *jīvātman* enjoying a status equal to that of Brahman, after it is totally liberated from bondage. In one of the hymns he describes it as *śamaṉkoḷ vīḍu*.[8] The word *śama*, as interpreted by the commentators stands for *sāmya* in Sanskrit, which means 'equal to'. The author of the *Īḍu* explains it as *mokṣa*

---

1. MuUp III.1.3 *yadā paśyaḥ paśyate... nirañjanaḥ paramaṁ sāmyam-upaiti.*
2. *Vīḍu* as a verb (*viḍudal*) is also used in the sense of renouncing. See TVM I.2.1.
3. TVM VII.6.10 *ěttrarum vaikuntattai.*
   See also VIII. 6.5 *vaikuntam koyil koṇḍāṉ.*
   IX.3.7 *māka vaikuntam.*
   10.5 *maraṇamānāl vaikuntam koḍukkum pirāṉ.*
   X.9.8 *mādhavan vaikuntam puhavē.*
4. TVM II.8.4 *nalamantamilladu ŏr nāḍu.*
   See DTR 30 *nissīmānanda-deśa.*
5. TVM IX.4.6 *vilaṅgum śuḍarccōti uyarattu oruttā.*
   See also IX.7.5 *teḷiviśumbu tirunāḍā.*
6. TVM II.6.1 *vaikuntā maṇivaṇṇaṉē.*
7. TVM I.1.1 *ayarvarum amararhaḷ adhipati.*
   VI.8.4 *vānavarkōṉ.*
   VI.8.9 *viṇṇavarkōṉ.*
   VI.10.7 *imaiyōr adhipati.*
8. TVM III.3.7 *tiruvēṅgaḍam naṅgaḷku śamaṉkoḷ vīḍu tarum...*

in terms of equality of *jīva* with Brahman (*sāmyāpatti mokṣa*). This view corresponds to the teaching of the *Muṇḍaka Upaniṣad* which says: "The soul free from all defects attains supreme equality with the Lord."[1] In another hymn Nammālvār uses the word *mokkam* (the Tamil word for *mokṣa*) with the epithet *ūṉamil*, which means devoid of imperfection. This implies, as the commentators points out, the eternal experience of the perfect bliss (*yāvadātmabhāva asaṅkucita mokṣānanda*), which is the supreme goal (*parama-puruṣārtha*).[2]

II. The Theological View of Mokṣa

Though Nammālvār acknowledges the theory of *mokṣa* as enunciated in the Upaniṣads, he lays greater emphasis on the theological concept of *mokṣa* as eternal divine service (*Bhagavat-kaiṅkarya*). This view of *mokṣa* is predominantly expressed throughout the *Tiruvāymoḻi* and also in other *prabandhams*. In the decad addressed to the presiding deity of Tirumalai, Nammālvār advocates the performance of uninterrupted appropriate service to God at all times.[3] Commenting on this hymn, Piḷḷān points out that such a service is to be rendered not only at all times (*sarvakāla*) but at all places (*sarvadeśa*) and in all states (*sarvāvastha*). This type of *kaiṅkarya* is regarded as *parama-puruṣārtha*, because it is made available to the *jīvātman* by the Supreme Lord only in the state of *mokṣa*.[4] There are several hymns in which Nammālvār appeals to God to bless him with the eternal divine service. In a characteristic way he asserts that he would not speak of *mokṣa*, however great it might be, but he would prefer the service to the Lord.[5] He goes to the extent of saying that he would never seek at any time any other thing than the ever-

---

1. MuUp III.1.3 *nirañjanaḥ paramaṁ sāmyam-upaiti.*
2. See Piḷḷān AP III.4.7 *paramapuruṣārtha-lakṣaṇa mokṣa.*
   See also *Īḍu* III.4.7, RRB and PPS III.4.7.
3. TVM III.3.1 *oḻuvil kālamellām uḍanāy maṉṉi,*
   vaḻuvilā aḍimai śeyyavēṇḍum nām . . .
4. TVM III.9.3 *oḻivu oṉṟu illāda pallūḻi-tōṛūḻi nilāvappōm,*
   vaḻiyai tarum naṅgaḷ vāṉvaṟīśaṉ.
   See also Piḷḷān AP III.9.3 *anāghrāta-duḥkagandhamāy niratiśayasukharūpamāy*
   nityasiddhamāna bhagavat-kaiṅkarya-lakṣaṇa mokṣam.
5. TVM II.9.1 *emmāvīṭṭu tiṛamum śeppam,*
   niṉ semmāpādaparpuṭ-talai śēṛttu ollai...

lasting divine service.[1]

While speaking of the divine service as the supreme goal, Nammāḻvār refers to the feet of God (*tiruvaḍigal* in Tamil and *caraṇa* in Sanskrit). At the very outset of *Tiruvāymoḻi*, he mentions the *sevā* (*toḻudu*) to the glorious feet (*śuḍaraḍi*) as a means of attaining the spiritual goal.[2] In another hymn, he explicitly states that the Lord's feet is both *upāya* or means (*āru*) and *upeya* or goal (*śaraṇam*).[3] In several hymns, he expresses an ardent desire to attain the feet of God and to offer service to them.[4] In an emphatic manner he says that there is no refuge for any individual other than the feet of the Lord.[5] The feet represent the very spiritual body of the Supreme Being.[6] Hence, all these statements which refer to the feet of the Lord imply the divine service as the supreme goal to be attained (*parama-puruṣārtha*). All the other Āḻvārs have laid equal emphasis on *Bhagavat-kaiṅkarya* as the *parama-puruṣārtha*.

The importance accorded by the Āḻvārs to the divine service (*nitya-kaiṅkarya*) seems to have greatly influenced Rāmānuja. Thus, Rāmānuja in his *Śaraṇāgati-gadya* prays to God to grant him an opportunity to render *nitya-kaiṅkarya* to the Lord (*nitya-kiṅkaro bhavāni*). Following this lead, the Vaiṣṇava Ācāryas of later period, particularly those belonging to the Teṅkalai sect have taken *kaiṅkarya* itself as *parama-puruṣārtha*. It may be justified in the case of Nammāḻvār from a particular point of view viz., that for a mystic saint God's direct vision and everlasting service to the deity is of great significance. If *kaiṅkarya* itself is taken as *mokṣa*, it would run counter to the Upaniṣadic teaching on the *mokṣa*-

---

1. TVM II.9.8 *mattru ekkālattilum yādoṉrum vēṇḍēṉ.*
2. TVM I.1.1.
   See also IX.10.1 *mālai naṇṇi toḻudu eḻuminō.*
3. TVM V.7.10 *āreṉakku niṉpādamē śaraṇāha tandu oḻindāy.*
   See also p. 141 fn 6.
4. TVM V.8.5 *toḻuvaṉēṉai uṉatāḷ śeruṁvakaiyē, śūḻkaṇḍāy.*
   See also V.9.1 *aḍiyēṉ aḍi kūḍuvadu eṉṟurukolō.*
   VI.10.1 *uṉ pādam kūḍumāṟu kūṟāye.*
   VI.10.6 *ennāḷ unnaḍikkaḷ aḍiyēṉ mēvuvadē.*
5. TVM VI.3.7 *pādamallāl illai yāvarkkum vaṉ śaraṇē.*
   VIII.4.3 *emperumāṉ aḍiyallāl śaraṇ ninaipilluṁ piṟidillai enakkē.*
   X.1.6 *tāmarai aḍiyaṉṟi maṟṟilam araṇē.*
   See also PTM VII.7.2 *andō! niṉṉaḍiyaṉṟi maṟṟariyēṉ.*
6. See *Īḍu* I.1.1, p. 135 *niravadhika tejorūpa divyamaṅgaḷa-vigraha.*

svarūpa as explained earlier. Neither the Upaniṣads nor the *Vedānta-sūtra* speak of *kaiṅkarya* in *paramapada* as *mokṣa*. According to the Viśiṣṭādvaita Vedānta, *mokṣa* is the attainment of a status equal to that of Brahman (*sāyujya*) enjoying the blissful Brahman along with His full glory. As Vedānta Deśika has rightly explained on the basis of Rāmānuja's view, *mokṣa* is *paripūrṇa-brahmānubhava* or full and perfect experience of Brahman and the eternal divine service (*nitya-kaiṅkarya*) to which the Āḻvārs refer is to be taken as an outflow of that *ānanda* experienced by the *jīvātman* in the state of *mokṣa*.[1] Nammāḻvār also acknowledges the *mokṣa-svarūpa* as described in the Upaniṣads besides the *nitya-kaiṅkarya*, though the latter receives greater emphasis.

III. *The Theory of Kaivalya*

We come across in the *Tiruvāymoḻi* another theory of *mokṣa*. In one of the hymns, Nammāḻvār uses the term *vīḍu* (*mokṣa*) in respect of the direct vision of the true nature of the individual self (*ātma-svarūpa-sākṣātkāra*). This is a state, which as Nammāḻvār explains, is to be attained by first comprehending the distinction between the soul and body through repeated contemplation; and then develop the spirit of non-attachment towards all worldly objects by gaining complete control over sense organs and thereafter get rid of the *karma* in the form of *puṇya* and *pāpa*.[2] In other words, the direct vision of the soul (*ātma-sākṣātkāra*) is attained by overcoming the bondage caused by the experience of pleasure and pain. "This itself is *vīḍu* (*aduvē vīḍu*)," says Nammāḻvār. The attainment of this state itself is the supreme happiness.[3] This description offered by Nammāḻvār conforms to the state of self-realization *(ātma-sākṣātkāra)* which is the goal of *jñāna-yoga* as enunciated in the *Bhagavadgītā*. Such a state of *mokṣa* is designated as *kaivalya* or the existence of the soul enjoying the bliss of *jīvātman*.

---

1. See *Śaraṇāgati-gadya* 2 *bhagavadanubhava-janita anavadhikātiśaya-prītikārita...nityakaiṅkarya-prāpti.*
   See also RTS XXII, p. 147 *paripūrṇa anubhavattāle piranda prītiviśeṣattukku parīvāhamennum iḍattai gadyattile palakālum aruḷiśeydār.*
2. TVM VIII.8.6.
3. TVM VIII.8.7 *aduvē vīḍu vīḍu pēttru iṉpam tānum adu.*

Though Nammāḻvār refers to *kaivalya* as *mokṣa* (*vīḍu*) in the sense of total liberation of the soul from bondage, he does not admit it as the true state of *mokṣa* proper. He openly condemns it in several hymns for the obvious reason that it is short of God-realization (*bhagvat-sākṣātkāra*). He looks down with contempt those who seek the state of *kaivalya.* He says:

> It is a pity that the gracious Lord is worshipped constantly by those who desire to overcome the suffering of births and deaths and resort to *jñāna-yoga* for the purpose of attaining the blissful experience of the soul (*kaivalya*).[1]

In the opinion of Nammāḻvār, the joy derived from the *ātmānubhava* is of an inferior type (*śittrinpam*)[2] as compared to the *ānanda* derived from the God-realization. It does not, therefore, constitute the supreme goal (*parama-puruṣārtha*).

If *ātma-sākṣātkāra* is not the supreme goal, why then it is called *vīḍu* or *mokṣa* by Nammāḻvār? The answer to this is provided by the commentators. First, it leads to the total liberation of the soul from the bondage without the possibility of its return to mundane existence. Secondly, it is similar to *mokṣa* proper (*muktiprāya*) in terms of the experience of bliss (*ānanda*), which is a common characteristic of both Brahman and *jīvātman. Jīva* is also constituted of *jñāna* and *ānanda* as Brahman is. Further, the state of self-realization (*ātmāvalokana*), as taught in the *Gītā,* can serve as a stepping stone for *bhakti-yoga* by means of which God can be attained. That is, after the completion of *jñāna-yoga* it should be possible for an individual to attain Brahman by meditating on *jīvātman* as a *prakāra* or mode of Brahman. Nammāḻvār acknowledges these facts. In the decad devoted to teach the *sādhana,* he first points out that after one becomes free from all worldly attachments the soul attains liberation from bondage.[3] It is the state in which the soul experiences its blissful true nature (*ātmānubhava*). Such a state is described as *vīḍu* or *mokṣa* insofar as it is equivalent to *mokṣa* in terms of liberation

1. TVM I.7.1 *piravittuyar aṟa jñānattuḷ niṉṟu,*
   turaviccuḍar viḷakkam talaippeyvār,
   aravaṉai āḻippaḍai andaṇaṉai,
   maṟaviyaiyiṉṟi maṉattu vaippārē.
2. TVM IV.9.10.
3. TVM I.2.5 *aṟṟadu paṟṟenil, uṟṟadu vīḍuyir...*

from bondage. Nevertheless, it does not constitute the proper *mokṣa* because it lacks the blissful experience of God. Nammāḻvār, therefore, states in the later part of the same hymn that one should foresake the state of *kaivalya* and seek the eternal bliss of the Supreme Lord by resorting to the steadfast meditation on God.[1] In order to bring out the correct theory of *mokṣa* as taught by Nammāḻvār, Piḷḷān draws a clear distinction between the two views on *vīḍu*. The first one is described as *mokṣa* in the sense of the manifestation of *jīvātman* in its true form (*ātma-yāthātmyāvirbhāva-lakṣaṇa mokṣa*). This is called *mokṣa* in a secondary sense. The second one is designated as *Bhagavat-kaiṅkarya* or uninterrupted service to God in the realm of the eternal abode of God. This is *mokṣa* in the primary sense (*mukhya*).

The theory of *kaivalya* has become a subject of controversy between the two sects of Vaiṣṇavas. The main point of dispute is whether or not the state of *kaivalya* leads to the final state of *mokṣa* in the form of the *Brahmānubhava* and *nitya-kaiṅkarya*. The Tenkalai sect is of the view that the individual souls who attain *kaivalya* are ever denied of *Brahmānubhava*, even though they have escaped from bondage; whereas the Vaḍakaḷai sect believes that they too eventually reach *mokṣa* proper by embarking on *Brahmopāsana*. While Nammāḻvār condemns *kaivalya* as an inferior state of *mokṣa* because it is short of the experience of the blissful Brahman, he does not say that an individual who attains *kaivalya* is for ever deprived of *bhagavat-sākṣātkāra*. Nor is there any mention in the *Divyaprabandhan* that such an individual soul proceeds to a supramundane realm through the *arcirādi-mārga* to enjoy the blissful state of existence so that he cannot come back to the mundane existence to undertake *upāsana* on Brahman. On the contrary, the hymn to which we have referred (I.2.5) indicates the possibility of an escape from *kaivalya* and the attainment of *Brahmānubhava*. The controversial points related to the doctrine of *kaivalya*, as found in the religious treatises of post-Rāmānuja period are not traceable in the hymns of the Āḻvārs.

Thus, the theory of *mokṣa* taught by Nammāḻvār is in conformity with the Upaniṣadic teaching. It is not merely the negative concept of cessation of bondage, as Sāṅkhya and other schools of thought maintain but it is positive state of existence for the

1. TVM I.2.5 *śeṟṟadu maṉṉuril aṟṟu iṟai paṟṟē.*

individual self (*jīvātman*) totally free from bondage enjoying the full glory of God in a transcendental realm and also performing everlasting continuous divine service. This concept of *mokṣa* has influenced considerably the later Vaiṣṇava Ācāryas as is evident in the Vaiṣṇava *sampradāya-granthas* which have accorded greater importance to *nitya-kaiṅkarya* than to the philosophic concept of mere *Brahmānubhava*.

The last but one decad of the tenth centum of *Tiruvāymoḻi* and its two concluding hymns substantiate the view of Nammāḻvār as explained in the preceding paragraph. In this decad, Nammāḻvār offers a picturesque description of the march of the liberated soul (*muktātmā*) through the *arcirādi mārga* (the spiritual path) to the abode of God. The Upaniṣads speak of the presiding deities of the selected celestial beings—*jyotis* or flame, *ahas* or the day, *śukla-pakṣa* or the bright half of the year, *saṁvatsara* or the year, *vāyu* or the air, *mārtāṇḍa* or the sun, *tārakeśa* or the moon and *vidyut* or the lightning accompanied by three deities named as *Varuṇa, Indra* and *Prajāpati*—who serve as guides on the way to the *Paramapada*. Nammāḻvār does not mention each one of it by name but refers in a general way to *vāṉavar* and *imaiyavar*, which imply the celestial deities stated in the Upaniṣads. He excels the Upaniṣadic description by including in his account how the waves of the ocean dance, the thick clouds in the sky roar like drums, the celestial deities hail with offerings, all expressing their great joy for the individual soul proceeding towards the *Vaikuṇṭha* as a dedicated devotee of Viṣṇu (*mādhavaṉ tamar*). In the penultimate hymn (X.10.10) he says that his ardent craving for the direct vision of God (*avā*), which metaphorically is described as greater than the extensive *prakṛti*, the all-pervasive knowledge of *muktātmā* and even that of *Paramātman*, is at last quenched with the direct communion to be attained in the state of *mokṣa* soon after the total liberation from the beginningless *karma*. This sums up the central theme of *Tiruvāymoḻi* viz., that the attainment of God through the total cessation of bondage is the supreme goal of human endeavour and that the means of achieving such a goal is *Paramātman* Himself[1] since He alone can confer it out of His grace.

---

1. See DTR 125 *śrīśaṁprāha svasiddheḥ svayaṁ iha karaṇaṁ svaprabandhe śaṭhāriḥ*...

CHAPTER 7

THEISTIC MYSTICISM

In the preceding chapters we have presented the philosophical theories contained in the hymns of the Āḻvārs. The outpourings of these God-intoxicated saints also manifest vividly their mystic experience of God. In fact a large part of the *Divyaprabandham* covers mysticism of a unique type which provides us a deep insight into an important aspect of *bhakti* as a loving relation between the human soul and God. This subject, therefore, deserves a separate consideration in greater detail.

I. *Meaning of Mysticism*

Mysticism is often identified with certain kinds of psycho-physical states and some supernormal mental experiences. But more commonly it is applied to a variety of religious experiences. In the context of the experience of divinity by the Āḻvārs as portrayed in the Tamil poems, this term bears a different connotation. It is defined by some as the "seeking of intuitive union with the cosmic ground".[1] It is also described as "the quest of the soul or Ātman for the immediate or the intuitive knowledge of God".[2] The quest of an individual for the union with God cannot be treated as mysticism. According to the Vedānta, any individual can develop an ardent desire for *mokṣa* or union with the Supreme Being. Such a person is known as *mumukṣu* and he

---

1. See R.D. Kaylor and K.K.A. Venkatachari, *God Far, God Near*, pp. 72-73.
2. P.N. Srinivasachari, *Mystics and Mysticism*, p. 45.

is not necessarily a mystic. Nor does a direct and comprehensive vision of God constitute mysticism because that kind of vision, which in the Viśiṣṭādvaita Vedānta is known as *paripūrṇa-brahmānubhava*, arises in the state of *mokṣa* only after the soul is disembodied by totally getting rid of the bondage. We come across hundreds of hymns describing a special type of divine experience in which the Āḻvārs convey their feelings of joy whenever they have visions of God and also anguish whenever they feel separation from Him. These expressions of joy and grief which are coached in mystic poetry and which are addressed to God contain mystical element in the form of an irrepressible longing not merely for a direct vision of God but also for an uninterrupted divine service. The mere temporary vision of God obtained either by the grace of God or through the unceasing meditation would not satisfy them. The Āḻvārs also visually see God in the form of an *arcā* (icon) at the temples but even then they continue their restless search for a vision of God in His full glory. Taking these facts into consideration, mysticism with reference to the Āḻvārs may be defined as the spiritual quest of an individual for a direct and comprehensive vision of God culminating in an eternal, uninterrupted divine service.

Mysticism in this sense comprises both a way of life and also a spiritual goal to be achieved. The way of life involves an intense devotional love to God (*bhakti*) and the observance of prescribed religious discipline such as meditation (*dhyāna*) and other methods of worship. It also presupposes, as preliminary requisites, the acquisition of spiritual knowledge (*jñāna*), the development of detachment to worldly pleasures (*vairāgya*) and cultivation of certain ethical virtues. The spiritual goal consists of a state of existence in which the individual soul after being liberated from the bondage enjoys eternally the Supreme Being in His full glory. According to the Viśiṣṭādvaita Vedānta which is upheld by the Āḻvārs, such a goal is regarded as *mokṣa* and the way of life leading to it is *sādhana*. Mysticism understood against this philosophic background becomes meaningful in the context of the life and teachings of the Āḻvārs.

The mysticism of the Āḻvārs is of a distinctive type and it differs from that of other mystics, whether Indian or Western, though they may all share some common characteristics. The Āḻvārs gifted with divine knowledge not only possess a mental attitude of total dedication to God, but also display it in every mode in their thought, word and deed. For Nammāḻvār God is everything, the food for appeasing hunger, the water to quench the thirst and the betel-leaf to satisfy the pleasure.[1] Poygai Āḻvār says: "My mouth will not praise anyone but the Lord; my eyes will not see anything except the image of God; my ears will not hear anything except the name of the Lord; my hands will not worship anyone but the Lord."[2] Periyāḻvār is called *Viṣṇu-citta*, because he has all the time Viṣṇu alone in his thought (*citta*). He says: "I have placed you inside me and I have placed myself within you."[3] It is in this sense that the mysticism of the Āḻvārs has been qualified as 'Theistic' and it is thus distinguished from other types of mysticism such as nature mysticism, spiritual (soul) mysticism, religious mysticism, bridal mysticism, identity or transcendental mysticism.

II. *Theistic Mysticism as Aspects of Bhakti*

The theistic mysticism is closely connected with *bhakti* understood in the sense of total devotion to God as the Supreme Person (*Puruṣottama*). Etymologically the term *bhakti* is derived from the root '*bhaj*' which means *sevā* or meditation (*bhaj sevāyāṁ*). According to the glossary of Vedic terms (*nighantu*), the word *sevā* is synonymous with words *upāsanā* used in the Upaniṣads and *bhakti* in the *Bhagavadgītā*.[4] In common parlance, it is understood in the sense of love (*prīti*) towards one who is higher[5] as distinct from the love on one who is lower, as for example a child. Though the element of *prīti* is common in respect of both the elderly person and the child, it assumes the character of *bhakti* in regard to the former, whereas it is known only as *prīti* in respect of the latter. In the case of God, who is the greatest of all, the love towards Him assuming the form of unceasing meditation is termed as *bhakti* in the technical sense in which it is used in the religious texts.[6]

In the hymns of the Āḻvārs, the Tamil word *patti* is used for

1. TVM VI.7.1.
2. MTi 11.
3. PeriTM V.4.5.
4. See *Śrutaprakāśikā* I.1.1 *sevā bhaktir-upāstiḥ iti naighantukokteḥ*.
5. See *Nyāya Siddhāñjana mahanīya viṣeye prītiḥ bhaktiḥ*.
6. See *Śrutaprakāśikā* I.1.1 *snehpūrvam-anudhyānaṁ bhaktiriti abhidhīyate*.

the Sanskrit word *bhakti*.[1] In the third decad of the first centum, Nammāḻvār mentions this word in the context of describing God as being easily accessible to those who have *bhakti* in Him. In this context *bhakti* is interpreted by the commentators as a specific mental state dominated by a keen desire to see God.[2] That is, for those who earnestly desire to see God, the latter would make Himself accessible, whereas for others (those who despise God), He remains an unattainable mystery.[3] The element of sincere devotion on the part of an individual is a major factor in promoting a close relationship between God and the longing soul. It is this type of *bhakti* which constitutes the seed of mysticism. It must be nurtured and made to grow. When it grows steadily and becomes ripe, it becomes what Rāmānuja calls, *parabhakti* or perfected *bhakti* attained after constant practice of *upāsanā* or meditation along with *karma-yoga* and *jñāna-yoga* as outlined in the *Bhagavadgītā*. The *parabhakti* which is the same as *nididhyāsana* of the Upaniṣad, serves as the direct means to *mokṣa* according to the Viśiṣṭādvaita Vedānta. Thus, there is a difference between *bhakti* used is common parlance and *parabhakti* attained after the practice of *bhakti-yoga* as a direct *sādhana* for God-realization.

This *parabhakti* is the first phase of the mystic experience of God because it is only after attaining it that the mystic can obtain a clear mental vision of God (*mānasa-sākṣātkāra*). Rāmānuja describes it as *darśana-samānākāra jñāna* or an experience which is similar to what one would have actually seen. The main reason for maintaining this view is that according to the Vedānta, God cannot be seen by the visual organ but He can be comprehended only by the mind that has been cleansed of its impurities after the practice of constant meditation with loving devotion.[4] The perception of God through the inner organ during the state of

1. *aṉpu, kādal* and *avā* are the other Tamil words used for *bhakti* in the sense of loving devotion.
2. See ŚS I.3.1 *kāṇa veṇuṁ enhira apekṣārūpamāna jñānaviśeṣam.* See also *Īḍu* I.3.1.
3. See TVM I.3.1 *pattuḍai aḍiyavarkku eḷiyavaṉ, pirarhaḷukku ariya vittahaṉ.*
4. See KaUp VI.9 *na sandṛśe tiṣṭhati rūpamasya na cakṣuṣā paśyati kaścanainam; hṛdā manīṣā manasā abhikliptaḥ. ya ainam viduḥ.*
   See also TNUp 11 and MUp III.1.8.
   See also Mbh *bhaktyā dhṛtyā ca samāhitātmā jñāna-svarūpaṁ paripaśyati.*
   Cp. BG XI.54 *bhaktyā tu ananyayā śakya....jñātuṁ dṛṣṭuṁ ca tattvena praveṣṭuṁ ca parantapa.*

Yogic meditation is not, therefore, the same as the comprehensive, direct vision of God. It is a mere semblance of what one would have seen directly. The fuller and direct vision of God with His full glory which is known in Vedānta as *paripūrṇa-brahmānubhava* arises only in the state of *mokṣa* after the soul is totally liberated from bondage.

The mental perception of God obtained by *parabhakti* produces a craving in the *upāsaka* to see God directly face to face. He then becomes restless and makes repeated appeals to grant him the divine vision. In response to such prayers, he is blessed with glimpses of clear vision of God. This kind of divine vision is known as *para-jñāna*. Even this vision of God does not satisfy the mystic because it lasts only for a limited duration and is soon followed with separation causing intense anguish. Therefore, he yearns ardently for uninterrupted and full vision of God. When this does not bear fruit and becomes unbearable for the mystic, he appeals to God in a state of utter desperation to liberate him from all bondage and grant him the eternal comprehensive vision of God. This phase marks the climax of his spiritual quest and is known as *parama-bhakti*, the most intense *bhakti* leading to the direct realization of God.

Thus, the theistic mysticism comprises four phases: (1) *bhakti* or loving devotion to god; (2) *para-bhakti* or perfected devotion causing mental perception of God; (3) *para-jñāna* or occasional clear glimpses of God followed with joy during communion with God and anguish during separation from Him; (4) *parama-bhakti* or the climax of *bhakti* leading to the direct, comprehensive, eternal communion with God. The last three phases are the *avasthās* or states of the first one.[1] As will be seen presently, Nammāḻvār passes through all these states. In fact Rāmānuja has employed these terms for the first time in his *Śaraṇāgati-gadya* on the basis of the mystic experience of the Āḻvārs.

Some Western Scholars hold the view that the concept of *bhakti* as evolved by Rāmānuja differs from that of the Āḻvārs. Friedhelm Hardy in his book *Viraha-Bhakti*, makes a distinction between emotional *bhakti* and intellectual *bhakti*. The *Kṛṣṇa-bhakti* as depicted in the hymns of the Āḻvārs and the *Bhāgavata Purāṇa*

1. See *Nyāyasiddhāñjana, śaiva avasthā-bhedāt parabhaktyādi-bhedaṁ bhajate.*

which is developed on the theme of *viraha* or separation from God is regarded as emotional *bhakti*. The *bhakti* referred to by Rāmānuja on the basis of the *Bhagavadgītā* as related to *bhakti-yoga* is taken as intellectual *bhakti*. In the opinion of Hardy, Rāmānuja has deviated from the Āḻvār's heritage.[1]

Bhakti as understood in the sense of loving devotion to God is a mental disposition (*jñāna-viśeṣa*). Though it has an emotional element, it is intellectual insofar as it presupposes some knowledge of Divine Being. When such a *bhakti* becomes intense by constant contemplation on God, it assumes different forms characterized by joy during God-experience and anguish during separation from Him. *Viraha* is a mental state which arises in respect of those individuals who have attained *para-bhakti*, either through constant meditation or by the grace of God as in the case of the Āḻvārs and other mystics. As Vedānta Deśika explains, *viraha* is the earlier and later states of *yoga* (*yogāt prāg-uttarāvasthitiḥ*).[2] Yoga here means attainment of mental perception of God (*mānasa-sākṣātkāra lābhaḥ*). *Saṁśleṣa* or communion is the very *sākṣātkāra* and *viśleṣa* or separation is its absence. The two are interdependent. Without *saṁśleṣa*, *viraha* cannot arise and *viraha* in turn leads to *saṁśleṣa*.[3] The two alternate, in view of this, *viraha* itself is not a separate type of *bhakti* in the name of *virha-bhakti*.

Kṛṣṇa-bhakti or devotion to Kṛṣṇa as manifested by Nammāḻvār and the milkmaids in the *Bhāgavata* may be emotional. But when *bhakti* is adopted as a *sādhana* or spiritual discipline for the purpose of *mokṣa*, it would become intellectual since it involves a conscious endeavour in the form of *upāsanā* or *bhakti-yoga* with the scrupulous observance of the prescribed prerequisites as outlined in the Upaniṣads and the *Bhagavadgītā*. As we have seen in the chapter on *Sādhana*, the Āḻvārs have referred to both *bhakti-yoga* and easy methods of worship. They have also dis-

---

1. Friedhelm Hardy, *Viraha-Bhakti*, p. 47.
   See also John Carman, *The Tamil Veda*, p. 187.
2. DTR 3.
3. According to the *Alaṅkāraśāstra*, there is no nourishment of the sentiment of love (*sambhoga*) without the separation (*vipralambha*).
   na vinā vipralambhena sambhogaḥ puṣṭimaśnute
   See Dr. V. Raghavan, *The Spiritual Heritage of Tyagaraja*, p. 186.

played the emotional aspects of *bhakti* as portrayed by the milkmaids of Bṛndāvan. Rāmānuja has acknowledged both the intellectual and emotional aspects of *bhakti,* though he has laid greater emphasis on *bhakti-yoga* as direct means to *mokṣa.*

Patterns of Mysticism

There are different ways in which the mystic-saints experience God. Nammāḻvār and Tirumaṅgai Āḻvār experience God by assuming the role of the consort of God (*nāyakī*), who is separated temporarily from her beloved Lord and convey the pangs of separation either through the media of *nāyakī* or her mother or companions. This type of mystic experience is on the pattern of the love of a maiden to her lover (*nāyaka-nāyakī-bhāva*). The best example of it can be seen in the *Bhāgavata Purāṇa* in which the cowherd maids exhibit their love to God-incarnate Kṛṣṇa. It is one of the modes of *bhakti* described as *kāntāsakti* in the *Nārada Bhakti-sūtra.* The same theme was developed in the later period by the Caitanya School of Vaiṣṇavism under the name of *madhura-bhāva.*

Periyāḻvār takes the role of Yaśodā, the foster-mother of God-incarnate Kṛṣṇa and pours out his sublime love to the divine child. Kulaśekharāḻvār assumes the role of Kauśalyā, the mother of God-incarnate Rāma and also the guise of Daśaratha, the father of Rāma and conveys his devotional feelings to the Lord. In both these cases, the mystic experience of God is on the pattern of the love of a mother or father to the child. This is known as *vātsalya-bhāva* or the loving attitude of a mother to the child. The *Nārada Bhakti-sūtra* describes it as *Vātsalyāsakti* one of the eleven forms in which devotion is expressed.

Āṇḍāḷ, who is the only female mystic among the Āḻvārs, imagines herself as a milkmaid in love with Lord Kṛṣṇa of Bṛndāvan and expresses her devotion to God. Placing herself in the position of a bride, she craves for a spiritual marriage with the Lord. This type of mystic experience conforms to the love of a maiden as a bride towards the beloved bridegroom. This is generally described as bridal mysticism.

The other Āḻvārs experience God in a direct manner. They all have been blessed with the spiritual knowledge and *parabhakti,* as is evident from their hymns. They all have had either the Yogic perception of God (*mānasa-sākṣātkāra*) or the temporary direct visions of God (*parajñāna*). They have sung the glory of God as experienced by them.

III. *Philosophical Significance of Mysticism*

Before we outline the mysticism of each of the Āḻvārs, we should understand the underlying philosophical significance of the different imageries adopted by the Āḻvārs to convey their devotion to God. Why should Āḻvārs pose themselves as *nāyakī* or a maiden and use the motif of the lover and beloved to exhibit their devotion to God? Why should Āṇḍāḷ take the role of a bride and crave for a spiritual marriage with Lord Kṛṣṇa? Why should Periyāḻvār and Kulaśekharan assume the role of a mother or father of God-incarnate Kṛṣṇa or Rāma?

We can find an explanation for the Āḻvārs placing themselves in the position of a mother or father when they adore Kṛṣṇa as a child. The Vedic seers have also adored the higher deities by regarding them as father or mother or a friend. There are several passages in the *Ṛg-Veda* addressing God as father and mother.[1] We find similar references to God in the Itihāsas and Purāṇas.[2] The Vedic seers also conceive God as child and the devotee as a mother, in the reverse order of the soul's relation to God. In one of the *Ṛg-Vedic* passages, Indra is regarded as a child (*vatsa*) and the praying devotee as a mother.[3] The Pāñcarātra treatise also commends the worship of God with an attitude of a mother towards a child.[4] This loving personal relation of a devotee to God in the form of a mother to child is so genuine and intense that both Periyāḻvār and Kulaśekharan adopted this motif to exhibit their devotion to God. As stated earlier, this is known as *vātsalya-bhāva*.

---

1. See ṚV I.31.10 *tvamagne pramatistvaṁ pitāsi naḥ.*
   VIII.98.11 *tvaṁ hi naḥ pitā vaso tvaṁ mātā śatakrato babhūvitha adha te sumnam-īmahe.*
   X.186.2 *uta vāta pitāsi na uta bhrāto uta naḥ sakhā.*
2. See BG *piteva putrasya....*
3. ṚV VIII.95.1 *abhi tvā samanūṣate indra vatsam na mātaraḥ.*
   See also VI.45.25 *imā u tvā śatakrato abhipraṇonuvuḥ giraḥ indra vatsaṁ na mātaraḥ.*
4. See *Śaṇḍilya Smṛti* IV.37 *satīva priya-bhartāraṁ jananīva stanandhyaṁ;*
   ācāryaṁ śiṣyavat mitraṁ mitravat lālayet hariṁ
   ....pitṛtvena tathā bhāvyo matṛtvena ca mādhavaḥ.

We have to seek a different explanation for the adoption of the motif of a lover and the loved. Considering the erotic language used in the hymns to describe the behaviour of the Āḻvārs in the role of a love-stricken maiden (*nāyakī*) towards God as her lover (*nāyaka*), as in the case of two lovers at the human level, it becomes difficult to accept that Nammāḻvār as a born-yogi allows himself to be moved by such erotic feelings. How can we accord to such hymns, which appear to the western scholars as 'love poems' or 'girl poems', the status of a sublime philosophy?

We have to look at this matter in a different perspective with a proper understanding of the underlying philosophic significance of the love motif. The concept of love in itself has a deep philosopical meaning. The Sanskrit term used for love is *kāma* which is used in two senses. *Kāma* in the ordinary sense means desire for any worldly pleasure including the conjugal love. There is yet another sense in which *kāma* is used in the Upaniṣad and the *Bhāgavata Purāṇa*. Here it is understood in the sense of love for *Paramātman* (*Bhagavat-kāma*). The love towards God is wholly spiritual and not carnal, by any means. In view of this, the love exhibited by the Āḻvārs to God, though it is analogous to the sensual love of a maiden towards her lover, falls under the category of *Bhagavat-kāma*. Tirumaṅgai Āḻvār in his *Periya Maḍal* extols it as the highest *puruṣārtha*.[1] The ideal example of spiritual love is depicted in the characters of God-incarnate Rāma and Goddess-incarnate Sītā in the *Rāmāyaṇa* whose relationship is described as similar to the sun (*prabhāvān*) and its luminosity (*prabhā*).[2] This ideal portrayal of love is also found in the *Bhāgavata Purāṇa* in the personality of Lord Kṛṣṇa and the milkmaids.

This motif of a maiden's love for her lover or husband can be traced in the *Ṛg-Veda*. There are passages in the *Ṛg-Veda* in which the Vedic seers adore the higher deity in the same way as a woman loves her husband.[3] The *Pāñcarātra Saṁhitā* also commends the worship of God just as a faithful woman adores her husband.[4] The mystic saints have chosen this metaphor not

1. See *Periya Tirumaḍal, kāmattin maṉṉuṁ vaḻi muṟaiyē niṟṟum nām.*
2. See *Rāmāyaṇa* V.21.15 *ananyā rāghaveṇāhaṁ bhāskareṇa prabhā yathā.*
3. See ṚV IX.32.5 *abhigāvo anūṣata yoṣā jāramiva priyaṁ.*
   See also ṚV I.62.11 *patim na patnīr-uśatīr uśantaṁ spṛśanti tvā...*
4. See fn 1 on p. 184.

so much in the manner of the love poetry found in classical Tamil Literature of Sangam period as assumed by some modern scholars but as a symbol of spiritual experience referred in the Vedas and Purāṇas. The love theme of the Āḻvārs may be similar to that found in the ancient Tamil poetry but it is unlikely that the Āḻvārs who are born yogis gifted with divine vision would have adopted the love motif from the Tamil poets of earlier period.

Further, according to the Vaiṣṇava Theology, the individual soul is dependent on God in the relationship of master and servant (*śeṣi-śeṣa*). But so far as Īśvara is concerned, the soul has no *sattā* (existence of its own) or its *sthiti* (sustenance) and *pravṛtti* (activities). They are all controlled by Him. The soul exists for the pleasure of God and the ultimate goal of the soul is to get united with Him. On the basis of this doctrine of *Jīva*, Nammāḻvār as an individual soul (*jīvātman*) exhibits his absolute dependability on God (*atyanta pāratantrya*), his unshakable faith in not serving anyone else but God (*ananyārha-śeṣatva*)[1] and his conviction that no one else than God is the most enjoyable person (*ananya-bhogya*). All these characteristics are personified in the concept of a consort of God. It is in this sense that both Nammāḻvār and Tirumaṅgai Āḻvār have chosen to act as *nāyakī* and *Āṇḍāḷ* as a bride wedded to the Supreme Lord as *nāyaka* and pour out their heart through mystic songs in praise of the glory of God.

Vedānta Deśika offers another explanation. An episode of Draupadī in the *Mahābhārata* tells that while she was taking a bath in a pond, her female companions were so enchanted by her physical beauty that they wished themselves to be born as males to enjoy her. In this story the females desired to become males. On the same analogy, Vedānta Deśika rationalises Nammāḻvār's desire to seek union with God with himself as a woman. In the words of Vedānta Deśika, the *bhakti* of Āḻvār was transformed into eroticism[2] (*bhaktiḥ-śṛṅgāra-vṛtyā pariṇamati*).

The male preferring the role of a female is also justified on a different ground. It is said in the *Padma Purāṇa*[3] that the sages

---

1. See *Īḍu* I.4.1.
2. DTR 3.
3. *Padma Purāṇa, Uttarakhaṇḍa*, 272.

living in the Daṇḍakāraṇya forest were so enchanted by the bewitching beauty of Rāma, a God-incarnate, that they all desired to be born as maidens to enjoy the communion with Him. According to this Purāṇa, these sages were reborn as *gopikas* or the milkmaids of Bṛndāvan and their attitude to Lord Kṛṣṇa was erotic. Here, erotic play is treated as a spiritual experience. As part of the divine play (*līlā*) of God-incarnate Kṛṣṇa, the love affairs of the milkmaids as *sages* in disguise do not have any sensuality, though outwardly it may look so. On the basis of the same explanation the love exhibited by the Āḻvārs to the *nāyaka*, the beloved Supreme Lord is spiritual in character. The erotic language used in the hymns denoting conjugal union and consummation of love in marriage are all symbolic expressions adopted to convey the idea of deep mutual attachment of God and the individual soul.

During the period of separation from God, the Āḻvārs convey their feelings of grief through birds and objects of nature as messengers. This symbology too is of theological significance. The communication of the thoughts of the loved one to the lover through other media is a normal practice among lovers. Such instances can be found in the Itihāsas and Purāṇas. Lord Rāma sends message to Sītā in captivity at Laṅkā through Hanumān, the friend of monkey King Sugrīva. Similarly, Rukmiṇī, who pines to be united with Kṛṣṇa in wedlock sends her message through an emissary. In the famous Sanskrit poetry, *Meghadūta* of Kālidāsa, the poet uses the cloud (*megha*) as an emissary to convey the message by *yakṣa* (a demi-God) to his lover. Following this example, Vedānta Deśika in his allegorical poetry, *Haṁsa-sandeśa*, uses the swan as the messenger for sending a message by Rāma to Sītā.

The birds and the objects of nature adopted by the Āḻvārs as messengers represent the spiritual preceptors (*ācāryas*) who act as mediators in between God and the individual. In Vaiṣṇava religion Ācāryas play an important role. They serve not only as teachers of spiritual knowledge but also as guides to the disciples to enable them to follow the prescribed spiritual path for *mokṣa* and plead on their behalf to secure the divine grace. They are, therefore, known as *ghaṭakas* or the mediators. The birds with two feathers symbolically represent the *ācāryas* possessing *jñāna* or spiritual knowledge and *anuṣṭhāna* or conduct appropriate to such knowledge—the two important qualifications to become an *ācārya*. Some of the characteristics of birds symbolise the qualities of an *ācārya*. Thus for instance, the white colour of the bird signifies the purity of thought. The melodious voice of a cuckoo symbolises the sweet speech of an *ācārya*. The pet bird implies the modesty of the preceptor. The clouds showering rain represent generosity of the *guru*. Similarly, the cool breeze indicates the calm temperament of an *ācārya*.[1]

The fervent appeals to God to win His sympathy and grace are made directly to God by the *nāyakī*. Whenever such appeals do not find a positive response, the *nāyakī* becomes dejected and depressed to such an extent that she finds it difficult to express her grief in words. In such a situation, an imaginary mother or a close companion is brought into the scene as spokesperson to bring the pathetic condition of the *nāyakī* to the attention of God. This is how the Āḻvār's spiritual craving assumes a poetic fervour to dramatize his state of helplessness. In all these instances it is the same Āḻvār who speaks to convey his inner feelings to God.

Āṇḍāḷ, the only female mystic among the Āḻvārs, takes on a role of a cowherd maid who is in deep love with God Kṛṣṇa. In her case, the craving is for a spiritual marriage with her Lord. As a female she fits well into this role of a typical bride who desires to convey her love to the bridegroom. The erotic emotion (*śṛṅgāra rasa* or *rati-bhāva*) is very common in the religious poetry of the Hindus. We even find this in iconography and miniature paintings of Rajput and Kangra schools which have used the Rādhā-Kṛṣṇa motif freely. In Hindu religion Meera, a female mystic of 16th century, provides an example of deep love to Lord Kṛṣṇa in an erotic form. In Christianity St. Theresa of 16th century stands as an example of bridal mysticism.

IV. *Mysticism of Nammāḻvār*

Nammāḻvār who is considered the greatest of the Āḻvārs, offers an excellent example of the theistic mysticism of a high order. A large part of the *Tiruvāymoḻi* and the *Tiruviruttam* cover his mystic experience. He commences the first two decads of

1. DTR 5.
   See also *Ācārya Hṛdaya*, 150-155.

Tiruvāymoḻi as a philosopher by describing the nature of the Supreme Being and the ways of attaining Him. Soon after this, he resorts to the mystic mood and starts the third decad extolling the quality of *saulabhya* or easy accessibility of God with a pointed reference to the episode of child Kṛṣṇa who was punished by mother Yaśodā for stealing freshly churned butter. Tradition has it that Nammāḻvār fell into a trance at this point and remained unconscious for six months as he could not bear that the Supreme Ruler of the universe could subject himself to be tied with a rope to a mortar by a human being. In the subsequent decad (1-4), the Āḻvār resorts to a mental state in which he pours out his pangs of separation from God with an appeal to Him for communion. Here he poses himself as the consort of God (*nāyakī*) who is separated from her beloved Lord (*nāyaka*) and conveys the grief through the birds and objects of nature and appeals to God for communion. There are serveral decads of this kind in the *Tiruvāymoḻi* containing mystic element with rich poetic imagery. We also come across several decads in which the Āḻvār, after having had glimpses of God, expresses the sense of joy by singing His glory. The two themes—grief induced by separation (*viśleṣa*) and joy caused by temporary union (*saṁśleṣa*) alternate in several parts of the *Tiruvāymoḻi*.

The longing of the soul for communion with God is portrayed throughout the poem. The kind of divine vision sought for is not a temporary vision of God achieved through the Yogic perception. Nor is it the visual perception of God in the form of *arcā* deities in the temples. On the contrary, what he seeks is the direct vision of God in His full form and glory as in His eternal abode (*paramapada*). This kind of divine vision is possible only in the state of *mokṣa* after the soul becomes disembodied. Thus, the mystic saint who longs for such divine vision passes through four states. These are: (1) Mental perception of God (*mānasa-sākṣātkāra*) leading to an ardent desire for an external perception of God (*bāhya-saṁśleṣa*); (2) Mystic experience during the period of separation from God (*viśleṣa*) caused by the absence of communion; (3) Mystic experience during the joyful state of communion with God (*saṁśleṣa*); and (4) Intense yearning for an uninterrupted vision of God leading to eternal communion with God. We shall explain each one of these on the basis of the selected hymns of the *Tiruvāymoḻi*.

Mental Perception of God

The first aspect of Nammāḻvār's mysticism consists in the experience of God through Yogic perception which is distinct from the ordinary visual perception. It arises normally after the practice of Yogic *sādhana* or the *bhakti-yoga* as outlined in the *Bhagavadgītā*. It can also be secured by a few individuals blessed by the grace of God without going through the ordeal of *bhakti-yoga* as in the case of the Āḻvārs and other saints. Nammāḻvār was a born yogi and was blessed with this mental faculty. As one gifted with divine knowledge, he was able to perceive God through Yogic perception as is evident in the opening verse of the *Tiruvāymoḻi*. Piḷḷān, the earliest and authoritative commentator states in his brief preface to the *Tiruvāymoḻi*: "The Āḻvār after having experienced the Supreme Person in His true form through his mental perception speaks out in the way he enjoyed Him out of the unsurpassable joy caused by such an experience." This view has been endorsed by all the Vaiṣṇava Ācāryas.

That Nammāḻvār had visions of God through mental perception becomes evident from the fact that he expresses repeatedly a deep craving for a direct face to face encounter with God and desires to converse with Him. This kind of communion is described as *bāhya-saṁśleṣa* or external physical communion as distinct from *mānasa-sākṣātkāra*, communion through mental perception. A close study of the hymns will reveal this fact. The divine wisdom (*mati*) and the loving devotion to God (*nalam*) together with the taste of divine glory experienced through mental perception thus marks the beginning of the mysticism of Nammāḻvār.

Mystic Experience during Viśleṣa

After experiencing God through the mental perception, the mystic saint develops an urge for a direct communion with God and desires to see Him visually. But this cannot happen for reasons explained earlier and so he suffers in him a frustration and anguish. When he is overtaken by intense grief on account of the separation from God, he gives expression to his inner feelings in different ways. One of the methods which is more often adopted by the Āḻvār is to appeal to God through the media of the birds and objects of nature. The birds selected to serve as emissaries are the stork, the cuckoo, the swan, the *anril* bird (*cakravāka*), the *pūvai* (myna), the heron, the parrot and the bee. The objects of nature are generally the clouds, the sea and the chill wind. The hymns addressed to them are rich with poetic imagery. They contain not only mystical elements but also the description of divine attributes. They are not 'love songs' or 'girl poems' as some western scholars have observed but they are actually intended to convey the different aspects of divine glory.[1]

The 4th decad of the first centum of *Tiruvāymoḻi*, depicts for the first time the pangs of separation. Here the Āḻvār as a grief-stricken *nāyakī* employs the birds as emissaries to carry a message to the Lord. Beckoning a pair of stork he says:

> You young sympathetic stork, with pretty plumes, take pity on me and go on an errand along with your male partner to deliver a message to the Lord who wields the banner with the symbol of the Garuḍa....

Addressing the swan he appeals:

> You lucky pair of swans, with gentle gait, go and tell the Lord, who as Vāmana pervaded the entire universe, that here lies one whose sins are inexhaustible and who is suffering from a disturbed state of mind.....

Looking at the heron he begs:

> You lovely heron, when you see Nāraṇan, the sole sustainer of the seven worlds, tell Him that here is one who is shedding tears; though he may be a sinner, he cannot be thrown away.

In a pathetic tone, the Āḻvār speaks to the bee:

> You bee with lovely hoops, when you meet my gracious Lord, please inform Him that he should shower His grace on me before I lose my life and request Him to pass this way in the street some day riding on His mount (*garuḍa*) so that I may steal a glance at Him.

Addressing the pet parrot he implores:

---

1. See p. 193 fn 1 and 2.

> O my young parrot, go to Tirumāl who only sees my faults and enquire: 'what wrong she has committed so as not to merit His mercy'.[1]

These hymns taken literally refer to the mystic's emotional feelings which are transmitted through the media of birds. Actually they signify one of the ways in which a mystic contemplates on God's noble traits. The main purport of this decad, as the author of the *Īḍu* and Vedānta Deśika have explained, is to emphasise the divine attribute of forgiveness (*aparādha-sahatva*). This idea is implied in one of the hymns (I.4-7) and the divine qualities referred to in the remaining hymns of this decad substantiate this primary divine attribute.[2]

In the later part of the *Tiruvāymoḻi,* Nammāḻvār devotes three more decads (VI-1, VI-8 and IX-7) exclusively to convey the pangs of separation through the birds and other messengers. In all these messages he appeals to the major divine traits such as His willingness to offer protection to the grief stricken devotees (*ārta-rakṣaṇatva*), His loving disposition to have intimate relation with them (*āśrita-ekarasyam*) and His enchanting beauty (*soundarya*) as manifested in His iconic form.[3]

In the first set of verses (VI-1) addressed to the *arcā* Deity at Tiruvaṉvaṇḍūr (a pilgrim centre in Kerala), the Āḻvār appeals to the Lord in submissive tone in order to arouse His sympathy. Thus he says while addressing the birds:

> You herds of heron, go unto my Lord residing permanently in Tiruvaṉvaṇḍūr and convey the depth of this sinner's love with folded hands.
>
> Oh stork of fine complexion, go and report my condition with folded hands.
>
> You swans, go to my Lord wearing the *tulasī* garland and offer worship on my behalf with folded hands.
>
> You lovely cuckoos, meet my Lord and bring unto me heartening news.[4]

---

1. TVM I.4.1, 3, 5, 6, 7.
2. See DTR, verse II.4.
3. See *Ācārya Hṛdaya-sūtra,* 156.
4. TVM VI.1, 1, 2, 5, 6.

In the second set of hymns (VI-8) devoted to convey the message to the Lord through the same media, the Āḻvār touches upon the loving disposition of God to have intimate relation with the devotees (*āśrita ekarasyam*). Thus, addressing the stork he says:

> You, the immaculate stork with flawless white plumes, please spare a day for me, meet the Lord of the celestials and enquire how long this sinner should languish in this condition and tell Him that no one other than He is refuge for me.[1]

In the third set of songs (IX-7) covering the messages to the *arcā* Deity at Tirumūḻikkaḷam (a pilgrim centre in Kerala), the Āḻvār touches upon the enchanting beauty of the Lord to make Him realize the unfairness of forsaking the devotees. Thus he says:

> You flocks of cranes and herons seeking food in the ponds, the Lord resides in cool Mūḻikkaḷam, whose eyes, hands and feet are like lotus, whose lips resemble the red fruit and the complexion matches the lotus leaf; please go there and enquire: 'Are we not fit company for Him?'
>
> You tiny heron, strutting happily in the waters, go and report to my Lord who resides in the Tirumūḻikkaḷam holding discus in the hand, wearing *tulasī* garland on the crown, that it is not fair to have gone away leaving me alone with eyes full of tears and with my breasts shrinking.[2]

The grief caused by separation from God which becomes unbearable for a mystic even for a moment[3] is described in a different manner. In one of the decads (II-1), the Āḻvār in the guise of the grief stricken *nāyakī* imagines that the objects of nature around him are also afflicted with the same kind of grief as his own by developing a desire to enjoy divine glory. In the mystic mood he superimposes his own pathetic condition on the birds (stork and *anril* bird) and objects of nature such as the sea, cool breeze, the clouds, the moon, the dark night, the back water and

---

1. TVM VI.8.8.
2. *Ibid.* IX.7.3 and 9.
3. See DTR 23 *śaureḥ kṣaṇaviraha-daśā dussahatvam jagāda.*

the flame of an oil lamp. The white colour of the stork is looked upon as a decoloration in its body due to separation from its lover as in his own case. The cry of the *anril* bird is treated as a cry of agony on account of separation. The roaring sea is taken to be grief-stricken for not attaining God. The chill wind is imagined to be suffering without sleep day and night and groping in search of God. The clouds pouring rain appear to the Āḻvār as shedding tears for not being able to see Madhusūdan (God). The waning moon is regarded as suffering from mental depression. The heat of the flame of the oil lamp is imagined to have been generated by the separation from the Lord as in his own case.[1]

The mystic saint is also subjected to varying mental dispositions and consequent changes in the physical conditions. Several decads of *Tiruvāymoḻi* depict in a pathetic way these conditions. Generally these descriptive accounts are conveyed by the Āḻvār through the media of the imaginary mother of the maiden or her companions. In the 4th decad of second centum, the mother describes that the daughter afflicted with grief is rattling with a dejected mind and searching for God all over the place. Her body is emaciating like the mẹlting wax. She is crying with hands uplifted and prattling the names of God. While standing speechless she bursts out suddenly with words signifying the glory of God with a choked voice. The mother pleads:

> Neither sunrise nor sunset, my daughter knows and yet her mouth utters, '*tulasī* cool and fragrant, studded with honey' O Lord, holding the discus, what indeed do you propose to do with this innocent girl?[2]

In another decad (VI-6), the physical condition of the God-hungry mystic is graphically presented. The mother speaks:

> My daughter with fragrant locks bedecked with flowers, being engrossed in the thought of the Lord who measured the entire universe with His three strides, has lost her bangles.

---

1. TVM II.1.1-10.
2. *Ibid.* II.4.9.

> Meditating on the Lord possessing lovely lips and lotus colour eyes and also decorated with *tulasī* garland, she has lost her fair complexion.
>
> Steeped in meditation on the Supreme Being, she is thrown into a state of mental imbalance.
>
> Buried in meditation over the enchanting beauty of the divine body, she has lost control over the body.
>
> Engrossed in the thoughts of the Lord who wears the cool *tuḻasī* garland and the majestic crown, she has lost everything that belongs to her.[1]

The best account of the mystic's condition during the state of abject dejection is found in the 2nd decad of seventh centum which is addressed to Lord Raṅganātha, the presiding deity of Śrīraṅgam. The mother of the grief-stricken *nāyakī* speaks:

> This maiden knows no sleep either in the day or night; weeping all the time with handful of tears from the eyes; she utters the words with folded palms, 'O Conch,' 'O Discus,' 'These are the lotus eyes;' she reels all over the floor and searches for her Lord from whom she cannot bear separation. What do you propose to do for her?

This lady with full of tears in her eyes queries:

> What shall I do to get at you, O Lord of Tiruvaraṅgam? Panting and breathing hot, she cries "Come before me" O Lord, is this all the mercy you show to me?
>
> This maiden is motionless sometimes and at times she moves about; she remains insensitive but still is seen with folded palms; she faints exclaiming, 'God-love is indeed hard to endure.' She says, 'O Lord, you are unto me much too severe.'

The mother pleads:

> O Lord of the celestials, the daughter beckons you with joined palms; and gazing at the sky she asks: How and when I can look for you?[2]

1. TVM VI.6.1, 2, 5, 6, 10.
2. *Ibid.* VII.2.1, 2, 4, 8.

The dejected mood of the mystic saint during the period of separation from God is portrayed in a different manner. One of the decads (IV-4) describes in the words of the mother how the Āḻvār as a *nāyakī* behaves in a strange manner by running after the objects which have some resemblance to God or things which are associated with Him even remotely. When he looks at the particles of earth on the ground, he speaks aloud that this is the same earth as trodden by Vāmana. By looking at the sky, he worships it with the thought that it is the eternal abode of his Lord (*Vaikuṇṭha*). The ocean in front of him is spoken as the same milky ocean in which his Lord reposes. By looking at the morning sun with the red hue, he is reminded of the complexion of Śrīdhara. On seeing the red flame of the burning fire, he calls it Acyutan (the name of Supreme Being). The touch of the cool breeze arouses in him the memory of Govinda (Kṛṣṇa) returning from the grazing field with the cows. The bright full moon reminds him *Oḷivaṇṇan* (the name of Kṛṣṇa who possesses the bright complexion). When he sees a hill, he beckons it saying 'Come O Neḍumāl'. The young calves appear to his eyes as the same calves as were tended by Govinda. He runs after the young crawling cobra saying that it is the soft bed of the Lord. The sight of the folk dancers carrying pot on the head makes him imagine that it is the *rāsa-krīḍa* played at Bṛndāvan. The dark blue colour of the clouds bring to his memory the complexion of Hari. The sweet sound of a flute reminds him of Kṛṣṇa playing on the flute and he is thrown into rapture. In a pathetic tone, the mother describes the grief stricken condition of the Āḻvār:

> My daughter looks all around repeatedly for Kaṇṇan; and then looks far across, with her eyes wide open (thinking that He may be standing at a distance); (feeling disappointed) tears roll down in the eyes; she then sweats and wilts; with a deep sigh; she fondly beckons to Kaṇṇa, the Lord.[1]

The strange behaviour of the dejected mystic-saint is presented in an interesting way. In one of the decads (IV-6) Nammāḻvār is depicted as a maiden possessed with an evil spirit.

1. TVM IV.4.10.

On the advice of a gypsy, the imaginary mother and the close relatives of the maiden decide to resort to the worship of the village Goddess to ward off the evil spirit. At this stage a close friend of the maiden intervenes and tells them that this is not a mental disorder caused by any evil spirit but it has arisen as a result of the Āḻvār being deprived of the cherished communion with God. She points out that the performance of ritual dance to appetise the village deity is not the actual remedy; on the contrary, the utterance of words such as *śaṅka* and *cakra* will help to cure the disorder. She strongly advises that the drumbeats with the offer of meat, toddy, cooked colour rice to propitiate the deity would be of no use; but the recitation of the names of the Supreme Being and smearing the body with the dust collected from the feet of the devotees of God would be the appropriate cure for the malady. Thus she says:

> O mothers you are dancing as possessed persons; the illness will only increase but not subside. Instead you smear the body of this young lady with the dust of the feet of devotees of the Lord Viṣṇu; no other remedy would work so well.[1]

These hymns indirectly convey the fact that the exclusive worship of Viṣṇu and His devotees is the sure remedy for the mental affliction of Vaiṣṇavas.[2]

Allied to such a strange behaviour, the Āḻvār during the state of separation craves for the *tulasī* leaf that was placed on the feet of the Supreme Lord at the time He manifested Himself as an infant on the *nyagrodha* leaf. He pines for the fragrant *tulasī* worn by the Lord Kṛṣṇa during the folk-dance with the gopis. He also expresses his madness after the *tulasī* offered to the Supreme Lord during the incarnations as Varāha, Vāmana and Rāma. The deep devotion to God makes him forget that it is impossible to obtain it. The mother complains:

> O Ladies, what shall I do with my daughter? She does not listen to me. Being immature and young, she is well beyond my control. She is getting thinner day by day. She wants

1. TVM IV.6.6.
2. See DTR 40 *devaṁ prācikhyapat svapraṇayiṣu bhiṣajaṁ*.

> to decorate her languishing breast with *tulasī* worn by Kaṇṇan whose broad chest is bedecked with shining jewels.[1]

These hymns indirectly extol the holiness of *tulasī* which is dear to Lord Kṛṣṇa.

When the mystic is overtaken by intense depression accompanied with anger due to the undue delay on the part of the Lord to commune with him, he resorts to a state of defiance and even accuses God for being dishonest. This mental attitude is portrayed in a decad (VI-2) in the form of a dialogue between the Lord as the lover and the Āḻvār as the loved one. A situation is imagined in which the grief stricken maiden becomes dejected after patiently waiting for a long time for the return of the lover and she decides to remain passive even if the lover approaches her voluntarily. As is expected the lover who is also yearning for union, approaches her and makes an effort to enter into a dialogue with his partner indirectly through the media of her pet birds and play things since he is hesitant to talk directly for fear of reproach. The maiden resents every advance made by her beloved Lord and chastises Him for His negligence, deceit and lack of fidelity. The hymns read:

> I fear that your other favourite damsels will scold you (for having come here); I know all your mischief but it no longer matters....You better go away from this place; you may go anywhere you wish but leave my play things here.
>
> O Sir, you better stay away from us and try your pranks on other maidens; I do not know who are those blessed damsels who would enjoy this great person who churned the deep ocean.
>
> O Sir, do not speak to us with pretentious words, because your deceits are well-known all over the world. You should refrain from playing with our mina birds and parrots.[2]

This type of anger which is mixed with love is known as *praṇaya-kopa*. It is a situation which is wantonly created by God

---

1. TVM IV.2.10.
2. *Ibid*. VI.2.1, 3, 5.

Himself as part of the divine play which He enacts for the enlightenment of His devotees.[1]

In a dejected mood the Āḻvār blames himself for the suffering to which he is subjected by the pangs of separation. In moving terms he cries out:

> Devoid of merit, I am indeed a humble person and yet the evil in me looms large; you do not respond to my ardent appeal; neither do you come and let me see your enchanting form; nor do you lift me up into your sweet fold.
>
> I must have committed many sins and you do not, therefore, appear before this sinner though I beckon you often with melting heart and tearful eyes.
>
> I have not given alms, nor did I quench the thirst of others; I have not restrained my five senses; I have not worshipped the Lord with flowers at the appropriate time; I am a hard-hearted and ignorant person; I am a heavy sinner but still I am groping in the fond hope of beholding the Lord. When shall I see Him?[2]

During the state of intense dejection, the mystic saint feels that his body, the physical charm, the ornaments and dress and the very life itself are of no value since these are not of any attraction to God. The Āḻvār as grief stricken *nāyakī* says:

> My lovely complexion is of no use to me if it does not attract the Lord.
>
> I shall discard my docile mind if it is not pleasing to God.
>
> I shall abjure my modesty if it does not get His attention.
>
> My knowledge is futile if it is not useful to offer service to God.
>
> I would not need bangles and garments that are not liked by Him.
>
> I have no need for this body disliked by the Supreme Being.

---

1. See DTR 71 *purṇatvāt gopanārījana sulabhatayā....mokṣasparśecchayā ca svayam abhisarati ityāha kṛṣṇam śaṭhāriḥ.*
   See also p. 257.
2. TVM IV.7.1, 4 and 9.

> Even my soul is hardly of any value if it is not of service to the Lord.[1]

These hymns convey the theological idea that whatever is not of any use for the divine service is to be forsaken.[2]

In an extreme state of such frame of mind, the Āḻvār prefers to die than live in the surrounding of the folks who do not have any love for God and indulge in the pursuit of sensual pleasures. Thus, he pleads in a pathetic manner:

> Pray, take me out of this sprawling world where all creatures are grounded by the wheel of birth, death, disease, old age and hell.[3]

Driven to desperation due to the non-fulfilment of the cherished objective, the mystic reverts to the drastic step of censuring the lover by exposing him in public with the hope of securing reunion with him. It was a common practice among the ancient Tamils to adopt this step known as *maḍal* (riding on a palmyra stem as a horse in the open streets) by the aggrieved lover. Both Nammāḻvār and Tirumaṅgai Āḻvār exhibit their deep love for God by adopting this practice for the purpose of winning His sympathy for communion with Him. The hymns related to this episode (V-3) reveal that Nammāḻvār as a *nāyakī* contemplates to take recourse to *maḍal* but she is dissuaded from it by the imaginary mates on the ground of public reproach. The reaction of the Āḻvār to the pleadings of the mates as stated in the hymns exhibits the remorse and helpless condition of the mystic and also his intense love to God. In the guise of the *nāyakī* he says:

> My Lord with eyes like red lotus has robbed my modesty; my compexion is gone, my body is thinning, the hue of my red lips and black eyes is becoming pale; what indeed would the reproach of these folks do for me?

---

1. TVM IV.8.1 to 9.
   The ideas expressed in these hymns are reflected by Yāmuna in the *Stotraratna*. See verse 57.
2. See DTR 43 *syād-viṣṇoḥ yadyupekṣā tad-idam-akhilam unmūlanīyaḥ tadīyaiḥ.*
3. TVM IV.9.5.

> O my friend, I shall surely resort to *maḍal*; I swear that I shall expose in all possible ways, the Lord of the celestials, who stole my mind, modesty and chastity.
>
> Shaking off all propriety, I shall ride that palmyra stem (like a horse) through every street in town and make all women shout along with me in full sympathy with accusations against Him (by taking recourse to the *maḍal*); I shall procure from my Lord the cool *tulasī* garland and adorn myself with it.[1]

Even in the midst of mental afflictions the mystic-saint seeks to find some comfort for the disturbed mind. There is more than one way in which he attempts to derive mental solace. Quite often Nammāḻvār yearns to visit a holy shrine where the Supreme Lord resides as an *arcā* deity with the fond hope of securing the vision of God in His full splendour. There are several decads in the *Tiruvāymoḻi* which depict earnest desire of the Āḻvār to visit the shrines and his physical inability of reaching the place.[2] His mind runs from one holy place to the other with an ardent appeal to God to grant him direct vision. Thus for instance, the Āḻvār seeks a communion with the Lord Ārāvamudan consecrated at Tirukkuḍandai (a pilgrim centre in South India) but the Lord does not grant him the vision. The Āḻvār pleads:

> My Lord, with eyes like red lotus, you repose in Kuḍandai surrounded with rich and fertile lands; I do cry, worship, sing, dance, prattle and bow my head with shyness; I look for you in different directions loaded with sins; you show me the way to attain you.[3]

In the same way, he pleads before the Lord of Śrīraṅgam and the deities of a few other important Vaiṣṇava centres. Though the Āḻvār finds some comfort in singing the glory of these *arcā* deities, he feels disappointed by not securing the fuller and direct vision of God.

---

1. TVM V.3.2, 9, 10.
2. *Ibid.* V.9
   Here it is depicted that the Āḻvār desires to visit Tiruvallavāy (the pilgrim centre in Kerala) for a communion with the Lord but being unable to reach the place, he assumes the role of *nāyakī* and speaks out his love for the deity.
3. *Ibid.* V.8.5.

Another way in which the Āḻvār attempts to derive comfort is to contemplate on the deeds of the Supreme Lord during His various incarnations in general and in particular the *avatāra* of Kṛṣṇa which is the nearest in point of time.[1] The last decad of the fifth centum speaks of the incarnations on which he contemplates to sustain himself. He takes special pleasure in contemplating on the mysterious deeds of Kṛṣṇa. He says:

> My mind melts like a wax placed on fire whenever I meditate on the Lord's wondrous deeds; how he consumed all the foods to be offered to the chief of the *devas* (Indra), how he did repel the rains holding the hill aloft and how, long ago, He created, swallowed the earth, spanned and pulled it out from the deep water.[2]

Elsewhere he speaks with delight:

> Night and day I sing the wonderful exploits of my Lord Kṛṣṇa, the manner He danced with the milkmaids, the way he lifted the Govardhana hill, the manner he danced on the hood of the serpent in the deep water....[3]

More importantly, the Āḻvār identifies himself with the milkmaid of Bṛndāvan and enjoys the glory of God-incarnate Kṛṣṇa by contemplating on the experience that the gopis had with Kṛṣṇa. There are two decads (IX-9 and X-3) which describe graphically in a mystic language the pangs of separation experienced by the milkmaids on an evening when Kṛṣṇa returns home after grazing the cattle and on a morning when he proceeds to the jungle with the cattle. On certain evenings, Kṛṣṇa would return sounding the bugle with the cattle following him, while on other days he would allow the cattle to go ahead and he himself would come later. The little delay in Kṛṣṇa's appearance would cause them anguish. The fragrance of the flowers, the sounds of the birds, cattle bells etc., and the sights of the evening would intensify their passion and frustration. The Āḻvār in the guise of the milkmaid speaks:

---

1. According to tradition, Nammāḻvār who is claimed to have been born 43 days after the Kaliyuga just missed Kṛṣṇa in His incarnated form by a few weeks and hence his special attachment to this *avatāra*.
2. TVM V.10.5.
3. *Ibid.* VI.4.1, 2.

> Alas, the cool southern breeze laden with the fragrance of jasmine cuts me asunder like the unrelenting shaft; the melodious sound of the evening music pierces my ears; the evening sun puts me into a state of ecstacy; the pretty clouds lit by the crimson sky tear me into pieces. Alas, I do not know where I can resort and survive the lingering memory of my Lord who had embraced me with blooming eyes.
>
> The evening has arrived but not my Lord; the cows mingle with the hefty bulls and their bells do tinkle; alas, the sweet music of the flute is tantalizing; the bees gather honey from the flowers diving deep into them; the roaring sea rends the air; and how can I now put up with these that appear to conspire against me.[1]

In the later decad (X-3) the Āḻvār in the role of the milkmaids dissuades Kṛṣṇa from going to the fields in the early morning to graze the cattle on the pretext that it is unbearable for them to be separated from him for the whole day and that the journey to the desolate jungle is also beset with dangers of attacks by Kaṁsa's spies. In the words of the milkmaid, the Āḻvār cries:

> Alas, my arms which are slender as bamboo have thinned down; I have become weak and lonely but you take no note of it; the pretty koels coo and the peacocks move together in joy; if you go away to graze the cattle, a day seems like a thousand ages; your lotus eyes torment our minds and oppress us. O Kaṇṇa, you do not show us any compassion.[2]

The various steps taken to secure the direct and comprehensive vision of God end up in greater disappointment to the Āḻvār. He often makes pathetic appeals to God to appear before him in His true form with full splendour. Thus he cries:

> O Benefactor Great, My Lord, holding the valiant discus, who churned the deep ocean and delivered the nectar; as I am eager to behold you with your lovely four shoulders, I want you to come up to me right now; greedily I look

---

1. TVM IX.9.1, 10.
2. *Ibid*. X.3.1.

> around with tears flowing in the eyes and the soul drying up.[1]

In a similar strain he pathetically appeals:

> Wondrous Lord, O Vāmana, O Kaṇṇa who is beyond the reach of this sinner, you possess eyes, hands and feet like freshly bloomed lotus; a gait which resembles the huge lotus pond as if in motion. May you please appear before me for a day at least.
>
> I call you many times with dried eyes and parched lips to appear before me but alas, you do not turn up to enable me to behold you at least once....
>
> O Lord, come before me, or else call me into your presence that I may serve your lotus feet.[2]

We have so far presented the different facets of one aspect of mystic experience of the Āḻvār during the period of separation from God. Before we go to the next aspect of mysticism, we may try to understand the underlying significance of these uncommon psychological behaviour of the mystic. We have already explained the significance of the symbology of the lover and the beloved. The specific question with which we are concerned here is whether the mystic saint truly passes through these mental states or whether these are mere poetic imaginations to convey the devotional fervour of God-intoxicated Āḻvār. According to the Vaiṣṇava Ācāryas who have made an indepth study of the hymns, the Āḻvār did actually experience them. The varied mental dispositions and the physical conditions are the outward manifestations of *bhakti*. These are not uncommon for a mystic who longs for a divine vision. These manifold states are described as *sañcārī-bhāva* and *sāttvika-bhāva* by the exponents of the Indian *Alaṅkāra-śāstra* or Science of Rhetoric. These are different ancilliary moods associated with the main *bhāva* known as *sthāyī-bhāva*, which in this case is divine love of *Bhagavat-bhakti*. Among the saints of the modern period, Thyagaraja (18th century), a musical composer and an ardent devotee of Rāma

1. TVM IV.7.5.
2. *Ibid.* VIII.5.1, 2, 7.

has exhibited these *bhāvas*.[1] It is therefore, nothing unusual for the God-intoxicated Āḻvārs to have experienced the varied states depicted in their hymns.

Mystic Experience during the State of Saṁśleṣa

We now take up the next aspect of mysticism depicting the joyful experience of God which takes place as and when the Āḻvār had glimpses of God's vision. As explained earlier, such a vision arises either as a result of the Yogic meditation or it may come to the mystic out of divine grace in response to his ardent prayers. In either case, it lasts only for a short duration. Though the Āḻvār does not openly say when he had such a divine vision, it can be inferred from the tone and the theme of the hymns in a particular decad. Generally, the decad in which the hymns are sung in praise of God with a sense of joy is preceded by a decad in which the hymns are sung in a melancholy tone. This indicates that the Āḻvār first passed through the state of grief caused by separation from God and later he was blessed with brief visions of God in response to his ardent appeals.

Thus, in the first decad of the second centum, Nammāḻvār exhibits his grief caused by separation from God and he unconsciously identifies his own condition with that of the birds and a few objects of nature.[2] In the next two decads he bursts out with delight extolling the glorious divine attibutes. He would have definitely had a glimpse of God's vision as is evident from his own words:

> O, thou mind, dwelling in this physical body, you are indeed good, because of you, this humble subservient person could mingle with Madhusūdan, the chief of the celestials and dissolve into Him like honey, milk, ghee, sugarcane juice and nectar.[3]

---

1. See Dr. V. Raghavan: *The Spiritual Heritage of Thyagaraja,* Chapter VIII.
2. See p. 195.
3. TVM II.3.1 *tānuṁ yānuṁ ellāṁ tannuḷḷē kalandu oḻindōm*. The word *kalandu* indicates communion (*saṁśleṣa*) with God.
   See Piḷḷān AP *tammōḍe kalandu aruḷina paḍiyē śolluhirār*. Here the description of the *saṁśleṣa* in terms of the combination of all the sweetest objects is intended to convey the idea that the experience of God is the most enjoyable.
   See DTR 15 *citrāsvādānubhūti*.

In the subsequent hymns, the Āḻvār expresses with joy his gratitude for securing *saṁśleṣa* by way of praising the Lord:

> There is none above you, O Lord of wonders and none equal to you and yet you would assume different forms like all others; you are the life-giver to one and all, the mother that gave birth to me, the father and preceptor, and I cannot comprehend all the favours done to me.[1]

He acknowledges his achievement in a more specific way:

> Right in this birth and in a short period, I have attained what others achieve by the arduous penance practised over ages.....[2]

In the 5th decad of the second centum which follows immediately after the 4th decad (II-4) in which the pangs of separation suffered by the Āḻvār is described, he speaks with delight that God Himself with His full splendour blessed him with communion. Thus he says:

> The Lord mingled with my soul which He chose as a lovely heaven; He wears a beautiful garland, a shining crown, conch and discus, sacred thread and necklace; His eyes are red like lotus, so also His lips and feet; His body is of golden colour.[3]

In the next hymn, the Āḻvār describes vividly how God with His glory mingled with him in full measure:

> O what a wonder, the Lord in whose chest *Tiru* (Goddess *Śrī*) is seated, in whose naval Brahmā is accommodated and in a part of the body Aran (Rudra) is given a place. His body beams with unique brilliance and His eyes aglow like the red lotus. Such a Lord mingled with me in full leaving no part of my body untouched.[4]

---

1. TVM II.3.2.
2. *Ibid.* II.3.8.
3. *Ibid.* II.5.1.
   See Piḷḷān, AP *divyarūpattōḍe vandu ennōḍe kalandaruḷināṉ.*
   cp. Bhāgavata X.32.2 *tāsāṁ āvirabhūt śauriḥ smayamāna mukhāmbujaḥ*
   pītāmbara-dharaḥ sṛgvī sākṣāt-manmatha-manmathaḥ.
4. *Ibid.* II.5.3.
   See also Piḷḷān, AP ***samasta*** *pradeśattāluṁ kalandu aruḷināṉ.*

Elsewhere (I-9), the Āḻvār expresses the presence of God in every part of his body, thereby implying the divine communion (*saṁśleṣa*) in full measure (*sarvāvayava saṁśleṣa*). He says:

> My Lord is around me....He is near me....He is inside me....He is seated on my hip....He stays in my heart....He has mounted on my shoulders....He rests in my tongue....He has entered into my eyes.....He is right now on my forehead....He is actually on my head itself.[1]

In a later part of the *Tiruvāymoḻi* (VIII-7 and 8), the saint openly states that God Himself on His own has sought a communion with the Āḻvār and revealed to him His true form:

> I invoked the grace of my Lord Vāmana for a long time to lift me up into His golden feet....I now find that He Himself has been very keen to get hold of me; He has now come right inside me and is looking at me, all the time.
>
> He has planted Himself truly in my heart, with His immaculate resplendent form.[2]

The Āḻvār speaks of the grandeur of the divine personality as visualized by him:

> The cloud-hued Lord of unique grandeur, with wide eyes, red lips, sparkling white teeth and wearing pearl pendants, bright crown, having four shoulders with bow, conch, discus, sword and mace, stands inside this humble servant.[3]

In this connection, it is important to know the nature of the communion (*saṁśleṣa*) that Āḻvār had with God. The Tamil words *kalaivi, puṇarci, puhundu*, etc., used in the hymns and the commentaries convey the idea of actual physical contact or the sexual union, as in the case of the lovers. Though the Āḻvārs have adopted the metaphor of conjugal love, the 'union' referred to in the hymns is not to be understood as union of lovers in the erotic sense. In view of the philosophical significance of the

---

1. TVM I.9.1 to 10.
   See also Piḷḷān, AP *īśvaran sātmikka sātmikka sarvāyava saṁśleṣam paṇṇina anubhava-rasattai aruḷa śeyhirār*.
2. TVM VIII.7.1, 4.
3. *Ibid*. VIII.8.1.

imagery of lover and beloved as explained earlier, the consumation of the spiritual love towards *Paramātman* is to be taken as the mental vision of the mystic saint as coming into closer contact with God rather than actual physical union. The justification for such an explanation is that according to the Vedānta, neither the direct visual perception of God nor the physical union of the material body of an individual soul with the transcendental spiritual God is possible. According to the Viśiṣṭādvaita Vedānta such a communion between the *jīvātman* (soul) and *Paramātman* in the sense of *sāmya* or equal status can take place only in the state of *mokṣa* after the soul is totally liberated from bondage.[1] The description of *saṁśleṣa* found in the Āḻvār's hymns is a mental experience (*mānasānubhava*). In the words of Rāmānuja, it is *darśana-samānākāra jñāna* or an experience similar to what one would have actually seen.

It cannot be said that such descriptions about the communion with God and the vision of God's grandeur are poetic imaginations because the hymns portray the divine beauty as actually experienced by the Āḻvārs. In one of the hymns, Nammāḻvār himself states that the divine glory spoken by him is but factual (*Poyyil pāḍal*).[2] He himself admits that he is a blessed soul as he is enabled to offer direct divine service to the Lord and also sing his glory:

> Could there be anything wanting for me for generations to come; blest that I am to prostrate lustily and offer garlands in the form of hymns to the Lord.[3]

Elsewhere he says that it is only by the grace of God (*aruḷ*) that he obtained the communion with God.[4]

Whenever the Āḻvār experiences the vision of God, the joy derived from it manifests itself through certain physical acts and vocal expressions. It is common with God-intoxicated mystics to manifest outwardly their joy by leaping, dancing and singing aloud and by clapping hands. For an outside observer, such a behaviour may appear as madness but in the case of a true

1. See Chapter 6, pp. 167-69.
2. TVM IV.3.11.
   See Piḷḷān, AP *ittanaiyum mey eṅgirār.*
3. TVM IV.5.1.
4. *Ibid.* VIII.7.4, 8.

devotee it is a natural phenomenon. The *Bhāgavata Purāṇa* refers to it in connection with the display of love by the milkmaids towards Lord Kṛṣṇa. It says:

> Of what use is any *bhakti* in which one's voice does not break, eyes do not moisten, hairs do not horripilate and one is not able to move? If one could go about in this divine madness, now weeping, now laughing, now without any shame, sing and dance, verily such a *bhakta* will please the whole world.

The Indian Rhetoric describes these states of experience as *sāttvika bhāvas*, external joyful manifestations of the deep love to God. Such a behaviour is also exhibited by Nammāḻvār. He condemns people who having experienced the divine glory do not act in such a manner. He says:

> What use there can be for those creatures who do not sing the Glory of Kaṇṇan and who do not leap and dance in joy with intense devotion.
>
> Those who do not sing tunefully the glory of Tirumāl and fail to jump up and down in joyous ecstacy will again fall into the trap of bondage.[1]

The overjoy of the mystic is expressed in a different manner. He is so overwhelmed with delight that he wishes to offer his body, mind, soul and everything he possesses as an offering of worship to God. He regards his mind as soothing sandal paste to take off the fatigue caused to the Lord at the time he fought with the demons during the incarnation as Rāma and Kṛṣṇa. The hymns sung by him in praise of the Lord are treated as garland to be used for decorating the divine body. The recitation of the names and the salutations offered to God with folded hands are offered as ornaments to the Lord of Vaikuṇṭha. The very soul is thought as a garland of flowers for the purpose of decorating the crown. The deep love of the mystic is offered as an apparel to the Lord.[2]

Another interesting aspect of joyous experience of a mystic is the yearning to enjoy God not merely by the visual organ but

1. TVM III.5.1, 2.
2. *Ibid.* IV.3.1, 2 and 5.

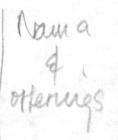

also by other sense organs at all times and in all possible ways. In one of the decads (III-8), Nammāḻvār points out that each of the sense organs vie with the other, even transcending its physical limitation, to enjoy God. The mind desires for a visual perception of God. The tongue wishes to perform the function of the mind. The hands long to praise the Lord. The eyes wish to perform the function of the hands. The ears crave to see the Lord. The vital energy (*āvi*) yearns to possess ears to hear the songs.[1]

In the exalted state of ecstasy, the super-mystic sees God not only within his self but also everywhere. He identifies himself with God and speaks out in the words of God. There is a graphic display of this mood in one of the decads (V-6) in which the Āḻvār as a maiden conveys his vision of God through the media of the imaginary mother. The mother speaks:

> My daughter says that it is she who created this universe with seas surrounding it; she permeated the entire universe; she took it back from Bali; she pulled it out (from the bottom of the ocean); and she retained it in the stomach (during deluge).....[2]

In the same strain, the Āḻvār identifies himself with the divine deeds, Brahmā, Rudra, the celestials, the five elements, the heaven, hell and with every conceivable thing in the universe. All these words of the maiden are regarded by the bewildered mother as the utterances of the daughter possessed with God. Actually, the Āḻvār impersonates as the Supreme Being and tries to derive some consolation by speaking about the divine functions and glory. This behaviour of the mystic saint is analogous to the episode of the milkmaids narrated in the *Viṣṇu Purāṇa* where they enjoy the rapture of *rāsakrīḍa* (the group dance) but in the midst of which Kṛṣṇa suddenly disappears. Unable to bear the separation they impersonate themselves as Kṛṣṇa and imitate his playful deeds to derive some consolation.

According to the Viśiṣṭādvaita Vedānta, the term 'I' or the *Jīvātman*, connotes ultimately *Paramātman* as integrally related to

1. TVM III.8.2 to 6.
2. *Ibid*. V.6.1.

the Jīva (*jīva-śarīraka paramātmā*). Such a philosophical explanation is adopted to interpret the statement of sage Vāmadeva in which he claims: "I am Manu and I am Sūrya etc."[1] The implication of this statement, as interpreted by Rāmānuja is that Vāmadeva perceives that the *Paramātman* indwelling in his soul is the same as the *Paramātman* indwelling in Manu or Sūrya. This is God-vision which the yogis and the great sages acquire. It is in the same sense that Nammāḻvār says that He is God and not in the sense of absolute identity of soul and God.[2]

Final Phase of Mysticism

We have examined two aspects of mystic experience in the state of *viraha* (separation) and *saṁśleṣa* (communion). *Viraha* intensifies the craving for communion with God. The brief spell of communion also does not satisfy the mystic as it is followed with separation from God. He, therefore, becomes restless and craves for a fuller and direct vision of God. Such an eternal communion with God can only be attained after the soul is totally liberated from bondage. Nammāḻvār, therefore, curses himself for being entrapped in the body. He prays God to remove the shackles of bondage since in his opinion the removal of it is to be eventually effected by God's grace. The longer the liberation from bondage is delayed, the greater is the anguish of the mystic. The patience of the mystic-saint has a limit and after a stage it becomes unbearable. This is the state of *parama-bhakti* or the final phase of *bhakti-yoga* which leads to the direct and full vision of God. This is the climax of the Āḻvār's mystic life as is evident from the concluding decad of the tenth centum of *Tiruvāymoḻi*. Here the Āḻvār ardently appeals to God and even takes an oath in the name of God and His beloved consort to liberate him from bondage and bless him with an eternal communion without any further delay. Thus he appeals ardently:

> Pray, do not deceive me any more; I swear upon the fair lady (the consort of God) whose hair is fragrant with flowers and who resides on your chest like a garland of flowers;

---

1. RV IV.25.1 *ahaṁ manurabhavaṁ sūryaśca....*
   See also BrUp III.4.10.
2. See DTR 64 *prabhuḥ ahaṁ-buddhi bodhyo anvabhāvi.*
   cp. VP VI.7.95 *tadbhāva-bhāvam-āpannaḥ tato sau paramātmanā; bhavaty-abhedī....*

> I take an oath on you; you loved me and mingled with me freely as if you and I were one; O come, call me up to your lovely feet and delay no more.[1]

This prayer appears to have been answered as Nammāḻvār himself states in the penultimate verse of the *Tiruvāymoḻi* that at last his ardent craving (*avā*) for an eternal communion with God is fulfilled.[2] In Viśiṣṭādvaita Vedānta such a union is not identity (*aikya*) but it is *sāyujya* or attainment of an equal status with God and enjoyment of the bliss of the Supreme Being for ever without a return to the mundane existence. This is *mokṣa* according to the Vedānta. The Vaiṣṇava theology following the teachings of Nammāḻvār describes it as *nityakaiṅkarya* or eternal divine service in the *paramapada*, the eternal abode of God in an uninterrupted way.[3] This is the final goal of theistic mysticism, as exemplified by Nammāḻvār, which comprises the different phases of *bhakti* commencing with mental perception of God (*para-bhakti*), leading to *para-jñāna* associated with *viśleṣa* and *saṁśleṣa* and culminating with *parama-bhakti* that secures the eternal communion with God after total liberation from bondage.

V. *Mysticism of Tirumaṅgai Āḻvār*

Tirumaṅgai Āḻvār provides another classic example of the theistic mysticism. His voluminous *Periya Tirumoḻi* and the two smaller poems, *Śiriya Tirumaḍal* and *Periya Tirumaḍal*, present vividly the mystic way of God-experience. Though a large part of *Tirumoḻi* covers inspired songs in praise of the glory of individual *arcā* deities or the icons at the various religious centres from Badari in the Himalayas to Tirukkuruṅgudi in the extreme South India, there are nearly twenty-three decads containing significant mystical elements.

The general pattern of mysticism of Tirumaṅgai Āḻvār is same as that of Nammāḻvār. Here also the Āḻvār takes on the role of a *nāyakī* (consort of God) and pours out his devotional love to God who is the *nāyaka*, the Beloved Lord with the usual craving

1. TVM X.10.2.
2. *Ibid.* X.10.10 *śūyndu adanil periya eṉṉavāvaṟa śūḻndāyē.*
3. *Ibid.* III.2.1.
   See also Chapter 6, pp. 167-69.

for communion, followed with the agony during the period of separation and then the joyous experience during the period of communion. The psychological states starting with simple pain, developing itself into distress and depression and later defiance and culminating in irrepressible agony are all portrayed in a dramatic way. The adoption of the practice of *maḍal* to expose the lover to the public is also graphically presented in the two poems, under the titles of *Śiriya* and *Periya Tirumaḍal*. But Tirumaṅgai Āḻvār, unlike Nammāḻvār, was not a born yogi. As we gather from his own *prabandham,* he was, in his younger days, an ordinary individual indulging in sensual pleasures but after he was initiated into spiritual life, he became a mystic saint. Though tradition believes that he is an incarnation of divine weapon (*śāraṅga* or bow), we do not have any internal evidence to show that he embarked on meditation as Nammāḻvār did, to see God through Yogic perception. However, the traditional account of his biography and the opening decad of the *Periya Tirumoḻi* tell us that he had the vision of the Divine Couple in the disguise of a newly wedded couple, who imparted to him the *Nārāyaṇa mantra* containing the quintessence of the Vedānta. The acquisition of this spiritual knowledge by the grace of God marks the beginning of mysticism for Tirumaṅgai Āḻvār. In several later decads of *Tirumoḻi* addressed to the *arcā* deities, he openly says that he beheld the Supreme Being in the form of the icons enshrined at the religious centres.

A close study of the *Periya Tirumoḻi* reveals that Tirumaṅgai's experience of God has two aspects. The first one consists of the actual visits of the Āḻvār to the different Vaiṣṇava centres and singing the glory of the *arcā* deities in the temples. These devotional hymns in praise of God contain vivid description of the natural surroundings of the place, the deity concerned and also the miraculous deeds performed by God during His incarnations on earth. This aspect of the hymns has great theological significance and is covered in an earlier chapter. The second aspect of the experience of God contains a strong mystical element and we shall mainly deal with it now.

In the 7th decad of the second centum of the *Periya Tirumoḻi,* we come acoross for the first time the mystic experience of the Āḻvār. The Āḻvār desires to enjoy God by assuming the role of a maiden (*nāyakī*) and conveys his devotional feelings through the media of the imaginary mother of the maiden who is so grief stricken on account of love for the Lord that she is unable to speak. The mother reports to the Lord the pathetic condition of the daughter with a view to winning His sympathy for her. By way of addressing the Deity at Tiruviḍavendai (a pilgrim centre near Madras), the Āḻvār in the guise of the mother says:

> O Lord of Tiruviḍavendai, this maiden is (no doubt) aware of the Goddess *Śrī* who possesses beautiful face like that of the shining moon, who is born in the milky ocean along with the nectar, who is ever youthful and who resides in your chest; but yet she cannot give up her attachment to you. Please tell me what you intend to do with this lady who possesses lovely eyes and charm and who is also deeply devoted to you.[1]

The mother describes her condition:

> O Lord, this girl who has a sweet tongue has not so far spoken to her friends with a simile; nor does she annoint her breasts with sandal paste; nor does she apply the black eyeline to the eyes; nor does she decorate her curly hair with flowers. But all the times she speaks about the Lord Viṣṇu as one who measured the earth surrounded by the oceans. Tell me what you intend to do with her.
>
> My daughter feels that every moment of her life is like an epoch; she cries with such words as the sun is dead, the cool southern breeze is burning with heat; she wants to pluck her breasts and throw them away.[2]

As in the case of Nammāḻvār, Tirumaṅgai also conveys his agony caused by the separation from God through the emissaries. In the 6th decad of the third centum addressed to the *arcā* deity at Tiruvāli (the religious centre close to Tirumaṅgai's birth place) we have an example of how he expresses his inner feelings. Here he employs the bee as the emissary. He appeals to it:

> O bee, thou trampling on the flowers with your wings stretched and associated with your partner, suck the juice from the freshly blossomed flowers. Would you report my

1. PTM II.7.1.
2. *Ibid*. II.7.2, 4.

condition to the Supreme Lord residing in Tiruvāli which is inhabited by the orthodox devotees engaged in the Vedic rituals.

Though the Lord Himself does not think of me, yet I pine with his memory and languish due to the love pangs. Would you, O bee, approach the Lord Kṛṣṇa, who is now residing in Tiruvāli and tell Him how intense is my agony.[1]

By addressing the Lord directly, the Āl̲vār pleads:

O compassionate Lord, you have made me lose my sleep by attracting me towards you. Is it proper for you to take away also my golden bracelets?

O Lord, though you do not bless me with an opportunity of offering divine service to you, would you at least embrace me with your broad chest.[2]

While enduring the pangs of separation, the Āl̲vār imagines that he is being escorted by the Lord of Tiruvāli to His own abode. This mystical experience is conveyed in an interesting manner through the media of the imaginary mother who speaks about the elopement of her daughter:

I do not know if that person who took away my daughter is a thief or the proper individual. All that I know is a young person of black complexion beckoned my beautiful daughter to go with him; as he held her hand decorated with silver bangles, she fled away with him by deserting me. Have they now arrived at Tiruvāli?

The mother tells the next door lady:

O lady, the person who took away my daughter looked like a cowherd who on many earlier occasions had kidnapped several maidens; such a person entered my house and kissed her lovely red lips and thereafter my daughter with cheerful eyes, followed him willingly by prattling some affectionate words like a parrot. Have they proceeded to Tiruvāli surrounded by fields and trees.[3]

---

1. PTM III.6.1, 4.
2. *Ibid.* III.6.7, 9.
3. *Ibid.* III.7.1, 2.

In the 5th decad of the fifth centum, the physical and mental condition of the grief-stricken mystic is described in the words of the mother. In this instance, the Āḻvār develops a craving to enjoy fully the Lord of Tiruvaraṅga (Śrīraṅga) and being unable to see Him, he is overtaken by grief. The mother narrates:

> My daughter without any fear prattles the words 'Venkaṭa'; she cannot remain restful, I am wondering what havock has been caused to her by that Lord of the Nitya-sūris.
>
> My daughter does not care to cover her breast with clothes; nor does she decorate her arms with bracelets.
>
> The lovely eyes of this girl are filled with tears; the bangles are slipping off from her hands; she cries out seeking the garland of *tulasī*.
>
> She does not heed the words of the mother; she does not mix with her friends; she does not decorate her lovely body. She queries: 'Where is my Lord Raṅga?'
>
> My daughter does not pay any attention to her pet birds; she does not speak anything except the words, 'Where is my Lord Tiruvaraṅga?' I cannot understand what catastrophy has been brought upon her by the Supreme Being who is glorified by the *Chāndogya Upaniṣad*, the *Kauśītikī Brāhmaṇa*, the *Taittirīya Upaniṣad* and the *Sāmaveda*.[1]

The varying mental states through which the God-intoxicated mystic saint passes is graphically presented in the five decads of the eighth centum of *Periya Tirumoḻi* (VIII-1 to 5) in connection with the singing the glory of the Deity of Tirukkaṇṇapuram, a famous Vaiṣṇava centre in South India. As part of his piligrimage tour of Vaiṣṇava shrines, Tirumaṅgai Āḻvār first visits Tirukkaṇṇamaṅgai, another holy centre near about Tirukkaṇṇapuram, to worship the deity at this temple. As he enters the place, he is so inspired by its spiritual atmosphere that he pours out his devotional love by singing the glory of God with epithets that describe the divine deeds and attributes and announces with delight even before actually seeing the deity that he beheld the Lord of Tirukkaṇṇamaṅgai.[2]

The mere mental perception of the Lord of Kaṇṇapuram

1. PTM V.5.1, 2, 3, 4, 9.
2. *Ibid.* VII.10.1 to 9.

kindles in him an intense craving for a direct communion with Him and immediately he resorts to the mood of a *nāyakī* to convey his love to the *nāyaka*. In the words of the mother of the maiden he describes the physical beauty of the deity:

> My daughter exclaims: The Lord possesses such a beauty! He has a powerful bow (*śāraṅga*) in his hand, He holds an attractive discus, the conch and the shapely club; His four hands resemble the four hills. Has she really met the Lord of Kaṇṇapuram?
>
> She admires the ornaments worn by the Lord—the crown decorated with *tulasī* garland, the shining earrings, the golden necklace.
>
> She says that the base of the feet is lotus flower, the two palms are also lotus; her eyes are rivetted on the crown studded with pearls and golden necklace.
>
> She admires the red apparel on the body and the golden belt on the waist. Even the feet and the hands are like lotus flower.
>
> She enquires if the blue colour of the body is solid emerald or it is the dark cloud of the rainy season?[1]

She continues to say:

> I have never seen such a beauty at any time. I do love Him and I cannot remain separated from Him even for a moment.[2]

In the next decad (VIII-2), the Āḻvār who has arrived in the proximity of Tirukkaṇṇapuram bursts out with joy as if he actually beheld the deity. The mother says:

> My daughter (even before reaching Kannapuram) speaks aloud standing in the open street: 'Look at Kaṇṇapuram.' Unconsciously, she mentions the (names of) shrines such as Tiruveṅgaḍa, Tirunīrmalai, Meyyam, but the moment she mentioned Tirukkaṇṇapuram, her heart melted and her body languished. What is the greatness of this particular centre?[3]

1. PTM VIII.1.1, 3, 5, 7.
2. *Ibid.* VIII.1.9.
3. *Ibid.* VIII.2, 2, 3.

In a characteristic way the mother describes the Āḻvār's special devotion to this deity:

> My daughter has not been eating; nor does she sleep; she has not yet attained the full glow of youth; she is very young, yet she wants to come to Tirukkaṇṇapuram to worship the deity. I wonder how she developed such a passion for the Lord of this place.[1]

In the 3rd decad of the VIIIth centum, the Āḻvār conveys his feelings direct to the Lord in the capacity of a *nāyakī*. He says:

> I have given away my bangles to the great Lord who resides in Tirukkaṇṇapuram in full glory; I have lost my entire set of bangles for the Lord who is reposing on Ādiśeṣa.[2]

The climax of the Āḻvār's devotional mood is manifested graphically in the next decad (VIII-4). Here the Āḻvār sees a bee flying towards his head and he imagines that the same is coming to collect the honey from his soft hair. He, therefore, appeals to the bee to blow on him the sweet fragrance of the *tulasī* leaf worn on the shining crown of the Lord of Kaṇṇapuram:

> O bee, it is no use if you merely blow on me the essence gathered from the wild flowers grown in the fields; instead, please touch me with the fragrance of the *tulasī* decorating the crown of the deity at Kaṇṇapuram.[3]

In a more dramatic way the Āḻvār displays his mystic disposition in the next decad (VIII-5). It is pictured here that the night has set in before the Āḻvār could reach the shrine of Tirukkaṇṇapuram. The agony caused by the delay in seeing the deity increases and unable to bear it, he resorts to the contemplation of the anguish suffered by the milkmaids during the period when they were made to wait for the return of Kṛṣṇa in the evening from the field. He assumes the role of the milkmaid and narrates the dialogue that took place between the maids,

1. PTM VIII.2.4.
2. *Ibid.* VIII.3.1 to 9.
3. *Ibid.* VIII.4.8.

while Kṛṣṇa was away. He speaks in the words of one maid:

> I lost my mind when I began to think of that person who manifested Himself in Mathura to release his father imprisoned in the jail; as I am now struggling to sustain the life until I receive His grace. The moonlight which normally unites the lovers burns me with heat and the cool breeze blowing on my breast torments me continuously.[1]

In the words of another maid he speaks:

> My mind was drawn away the moment I developed a desire for that garland which decorates the chest of Kṛṣṇa who has the complexion of dark blue cloud; I do not find anyone offering me help; the moving sun in the sky is disappearing; the whole universe is swept by silence; the directions cannot be recognised; I do not know what I should do now.

Another maid states:

> Whatever He has done to me is the effect of His magical spell. My bangles slipped off from my hands. Would He, who mercilessly extracted the life of Pūtanā, ever show any sympathy to this modest woman? My mind still craves to listen to the melodious sound of the flute.

One other maid speaks:

> The Lord who wielded the bow to destroy the entire Laṅkā surrounded by the ocean has not yet returned; the sun shedding its bright rays has disappeared clamping darkness all over the earth; as a sinner I am unable to sleep; in his absence every moment is like an epoch for me. I do not know how to endure this suffering.[2]

In the next five decads (VIII-6 to 10), the Āḻvār having reached Kaṇṇapuram, expresses his delight mystically in more than one way. As soon as he enters the precincts of the holy shrine, he feels the presence of the divinity and beckons the fellow devotees to join him for the worship of the deity. He then glorifies the place as a centre specially chosen by the Supreme Being for

1. PTM VIII.5.1.
2. *Ibid.* VIII.5.2, 3, 6.

his permanent residence. He sings the glory of the deity and says that he is none other than the very Supreme Being who incarnated Himself as Matsya, Kūrma, Varāha, Vāmana, Narasiṁha, Paraśurāma, Rāma, Kṛṣṇa and Balarāma. He expresses his joy for being a subservient devotee (*śeṣa*) and getting the privilege of exclusively serving the Lord of Kaṇṇapuram. In the concluding decad, he expresses his gratitude for having had the opportunity of enjoying the glory of the Lord in full measure and that he would never think of associating himself with persons who worship any other deity.[1]

There is yet one other manner in which the Āḻvār enjoys mystically the *arcā* deity. An example of it can be seen in the 3rd decad of ninth centum, which is devoted to the singing of the glory of the deity at Tiruppullāṇi (a Vaiṣṇava centre in the extreme South India). Here the Āḻvār imagines himself as the consort of God and conveys his devotional love to the deity through the media of his own mind and an imaginary companion by narrating a few incidents. The Lord is supposed to have that and made love to her under the shade of a *punnai* tree and thereafter disappears leaving her alone. Sometime later He is seen to be resting all by Himself near another tree. One other time He speaks to another maiden in such loving terms as to melt her heart. All this is done in such a secrecy without having any trace of evidence except the presence of the bees. On another occasion, He decorates the hair of a maiden with lovely flowers and forsakes her with the excuse of having some other engagement. In spite of all these events, the Āḻvār as the *nāyakī* speaks that there is no use to pine with grief of separation day and night and that he would offer divine service to the Lord because of his loving disposition to the devotee.[2]

With the onset of night the Āḻvār as a *nāyakī* could not reach the shrine. Unable to bear the waiting, she decides to proceed to Tirukkuruṅguḍi, another Vaiṣṇava centre nearby. In spite of the appeals of the companions to give up the idea of going in the night, she insists on being taken there. The dark night intervenes and without having any patience to wait till morning

1. PTM VIII.10.3 *maṟṟum ōr devyam uḷadeṉṟu iruppāroḍu uṟṟilēn.*
2. *Ibid.* IX.3.9.

she becomes restless. The scent of the jasmine flowers, the new moon, the cool sea breeze all torments her. Every moment of the night is like an epoch for her. In the absence of the communion with the Beloved Lord she cannot notice any difference between day and night. The jingling sound of the bells of the cows returning home from the fields remind her of the sound of the flute of Kṛṣṇa and further intensifies the grief. She suffers with pain as she recalls the meeting she had earlier with the Lord and the sweet words He had then spoken to her. In spite of all the suffering caused to her, the Āḻvār-*nāyakī* insists on being taken to Tirukkuruṅguḍi.[1]

What we have presented so far represents one aspect of the Āḻvār's mystic experience of God on the pattern of the love of the maiden to her beloved. The theological significance of the love motif is explained in the earlier pages. The important point to be noted here is that the individual soul which is sustained by *Paramātman* exists solely for the pleasure of God and none else other than He is the most enjoyable person (*ananya-bhogya*). There is such a loving relationship between the longing soul and God that in spite of the anguish caused wantonly by God to the individual soul, the latter lovingly seeks the union with the former. All these theological ideas are manifestly brought out in the instances we have cited.

There is yet another type of mysticism which is found in the *Periya Tirumoḻi*. In this case the Āḻvār instead of assuming the role of a maiden expresses his loving devotion to God in the capacity of two different characters: (a) as the demons of Laṅkā extolling the victory of Lord Rāma; (b) as Yaśodā, the foster-mother of God-incarnate Kṛṣṇa pouring out the love of a mother to the child. In the first case the Āḻvār in the words of the demons narrates the incidents that compelled Rāma to wage a war with Rāvaṇa and that this catastrophy could have been avoided if only Rāvaṇa had realized the greatness of Rāma and also heeded the advice of his brother Vibhīṣaṇa. The folks of Laṅkā acknowledge the glorious victory of Rāma and appeal to Sugrīva, Lakṣmaṇa and other leaders of the monkeys to offer them protection.[2]

1. PTM IX.5.1-9.
2. *Ibid.* X.3.

In the second case the Āḻvār in the role of Yaśodā pours out the loving devotion in the form of motherly affection to an infant. He speaks as Yaśodā:

> O gracious Lord, come running to me on your own, hold my breasts with your tender hands and suck the milk.
>
> O my beautiful child with wide red eyes resembling the lotus, I have been calling you to suckle. Where are you? Are you playing with cowherd boys?
>
> Come soon, step on to my lap and suck the milk from my breast. I shall fetch for you the moon if you would drink the milk.[1]

He beckons the child to walk towards him with the faltering steps and clasp the palms by clapping the hands.[2]

Each one of the hymns addressed to Kṛṣṇa refers to the childish pranks which reveal the divine glory.

The Āḻvār also poses himself as the milkmaids and enjoys the boyhood deeds of Kṛṣṇa (X-7). The words spoken through the maids are in the form of complaints made by them to Yaśodā regarding the various mischiefs of Kṛṣṇa such as the churning of the curds in the house of the next door neighbour in the disguise of a maid, the toppling of the earthen pots filled with buttermilk in the house of another maid, stealing the butter kept in a vessel in the houses of the milkmaids and the molesting of the young girls. While speaking of these events, the Āḻvār expresses dismay and also a sense of regret for the action of Kṛṣṇa as a child.

In a more interesting way, the Āḻvār enjoys the youthful deeds of Kṛṣṇa. Here again he imagines himself as a young milkmaid who is in love with Kṛṣṇa and who has been eagerly awaiting his return at the appointed time. But Kṛṣṇa comes late and also in an uncommon disguise that arouses the suspicion about his fidelity. The Āḻvār narrates in the words of a maid how she reacts to the lover with contempt for his late appearance. He says:

1. PTM X.4.1, 2, 4.
2. *Ibid*. X.5.1.

> You are wearing in the ears a new earring; you have put on a black dress and a garland of *tulasī*; you have arrived long after the appointed time. Why are you standing outside on the side of the house?[1]

He also states:

> You capture the hearts of several damsels by your enticing tricks; you then forsake them and go to the jungle under the pretext of grazing the cows; you love one, go out with another and converse with a different maiden; you pretend to be nice to all of them. When your own consorts are searching for you, why have you come to my house?[2]

The Āḻvār also poses himself as the mother of the milkmaid and speaks about Kṛṣṇa. In this case, it is imagined that a young milkmaid has loved Kṛṣṇa on an earlier occasion but she has now been deserted by him. The mother expresses her grievance against the lover for cheating her daughter. The statements of the imaginary mother which are in the form of accusations, also contain description of the greatness of God as revealed in his deeds during the incarnations as Kṛṣṇa and Rāma. The hymns read:

> O benevolent Lord, you have snatched away the bangles from the hands of my daughter in such an easy way as plucking the beehive from the small trees grown in the courtyard of my house. I do not know if this is a display of the masculine strength exhibited during the destruction of the seven ferocious bulls and the upliftment of the Govardhana hill to protect the cows and cowherds when they were frightened with the torrential rain.[3]

On the face of it, it appears as an accusation against Kṛṣṇa but in fact, it is aimed to bring out the glory of God through His deeds. Each hymn conveys a specific divine attribute along with the words chastising Kṛṣṇa's deceitful behaviour towards the cowherd maids. Unlike ordinary devotees, a mystic saint

---

1. PTM X.8.1.
2. *Ibid*. X.8.9.
3. *Ibid*. X.9.2.

enjoys the Divine Glory in a characteristic way as in this decad (X-9).

In the case of Nammāḻvār the climax of his mystic experience is reached with the attainment of the *parama-bhakti*, the highest stage of *bhakti* which leads to the realization of the comprehensive, direct, eternal communion with God. The concluding decad of *Periya Tirumoḻi* does not imply *parama-bhakti*. Instead, it presents a graphic description of the unbearable suffering of the human soul caught up in the cycle of births and deaths. Here Tirumaṅgai Āḻvār cites several illustrations to emphasise the magnitude of the human bondage. He compares the life in this universe of suffering to the trees standing on the banks of the flooded river; to the minds of the folks who are sailing on the boat tossed by the storm in the midst of the ocean; to the folks living in a house occupied by a poisonous cobra; to an ant which is caught up in the centre of a faggot burning on both ends; and to a jackal caught up in the midst of a flood.[1] The Āḻvār, therefore, appeals to God ardently to shower His grace on him and protect. He also says that he is ever a subordinate servant to God and would always count on His grace. He ardently prays to the Lord to grant liberation from the bondage and give him an opportunity to render eternal service in the *paramapada*. In a pathetic way he pleads:

> O Benevolent Lord, Thou shower your grace on those who seek you as sole refuge in order to escape forever from the hell-like bondage; O the Supreme Ruler of the universe, O Kaṇṇa with lotus like eyes, Thou art the quintessence of the Vedas. I do grieve, Thou alone should save *us* by your grace (*aḍiyorku aruḷāy uṅ aruḷē*).[2]

The word *aḍiyorku* meaning 'us', indicates that he is offering a prayer on behalf of all devotees.

Though there is no mention in the concluding hymns about the *parama-bhakti* leading to *mokṣa*, it would not mean that the Āḻvār did not achieve *mokṣa*. His biographical account tells us that he attained *mokṣa* at Tirukkuruṅguḍi, a holy centre in the

1. PTM XI.8.1 to 5.
2. *Ibid.* XI.8.9.

extreme South India, where we find even today a monument in memory of his having entered into a *samādhi*.

VI. *Mysticism of Āṇḍāḷ*

Āṇḍāḷ, the only female Vaiṣṇava mystic saint, presents a unique type of mysticism. Though she adopts the symbology of *nāyaka-nāyakī* relation to pour out her love to God-incarnate Kṛṣṇa of Bṛndāvan, she being herself a bride, did not have to assume the guise of a consort (*nāyakī*), as Nammāḻvār and Tirumaṅgai did. According to tradition, she was an *avatāra* or incarnation of *Bhūdevī*, one of the consorts of Viṣṇu. As Sītā, an incarnation of Goddess *Lakṣmī*, manifested herself as an infant in the open field of Janaka, Āṇḍāḷ too manifested herself as an infant in the flower garden of Periyāḻvār. Further as her biography shows, she was God-intoxicated right from her infancy and developed a craving to marry only Lord Raṅganātha, the *arcā* deity at Śrīraṅgam. It, therefore, became very natural for her to exhibit an intense devotional love for God as a *nāyakī* and experience mystically the divine glory in all its aspects.

Āṇḍāḷ's mystic experience of God is described by some scholars as *bridal* mysticism. The word 'bridal' is not an appropriate epithet, because Āṇḍāḷ as a maiden was not an ordinary human being aspiring for matrimonial union with God in the ordinary sense of marriage. She as an incarnation of *Bhūdevī* represents symbolically the individual soul (*jīvātman*) which is inseparably related to God (*Paramātman*). It is temporarily separated from God and it therefore, longs for reunion with Him. Against this philosophic background Āṇḍāḷ yearns for the reunion or to use the symbolic language, the spiritual marriage with her Beloved Lord. She is God-minded; all her deeds and words are directed towards God. The mystic experience of God as exhibited in her poetical composition reflects this theological theme and it should, therefore, be characterised as *theistic* mysticism instead of *bridal* mysticism.

The *Nācciyār Tirumoḻi*, a poetic composition of 143 verses exhibits more predominantly the mysticism of Āṇḍāḷ than the *Tiruppāvai* of 30 songs. The latter is an allegorical poem containing rich philosophical and theological ideas. In this poem, Āṇḍāḷ as a milkmaid in love with Lord of Bṛndāvan, implores the grace of God to fulfil her cherished desire. In the *Nācciyār Tirumoḻi*, she manifests her craving for a spiritual union with God and passes through various mental states of a mystic.

In the opening decad of the *Nācchiyār Tirumoḻi*, Āṇḍāḷ refers to the ritualistic ceremony (*nōṉbu*) undertaken by her in order to achieve her cherished goal viz., the spiritual union with God. In this connection, she makes all the necessary preparations. She first prays to the God of Love named *Kāma-deva* or *Anaṅga-deva,*[1] a celestial deity who can bring together the two lovers. She appeals to him to make use of her soul as an arrow, write on it her name and then shoot it with his bow towards God as the final target. She says that right from her childhood she has been thinking only of Kṛṣṇa and that all her possessions have already been surrendered to Him. In a more specific way she asserts:

> I would not survive if someone were to say that my growing breasts which have been already dedicated to the Supreme Lord are meant for the pleasure of a human being.[2]

She makes food offerings to the God of Love and requests him to have Lord Kṛṣṇa come to her and bless her with the unique opportunity of serving at his feet. In a pathetic way she appeals:

> I would prostrate before you at the prescribed three times of the day, offer lovely flowers and recite prayers. If I cannot have the opportunity to perform divine service to Lord Kaṇṇan, I would be grieving all the times. This would amount to committing as big a sin as causing death to the bullock by not feeding it and this sin would befall on you.[3]

In the next decad, she assumes the guise of a young milk-maid and imagines a situation in which she along with other young maids, are playing in the courtyard by building little houses in the sand. At this time, Lord Kṛṣṇa enters the scene and pretends to interfere in the play. Fearing that he might demolish the sand houses, she appeals to him not to interfere

---

1. The word *Kāmadeva* is also interpreted by some commentators to denote Kṛṣṇa, who is the Lord of Manmatha or Anaṅga (*Manmatha-manmatha*). According to the Vedānta, God is the *antarātmā* of all the devatās including *Kāmadeva*.
2. NacTM I.5.
3. *Ibid.* I.9.

in the play and leave the innocent girls alone. In spite of their appeal, Kṛṣṇa looks at them with a smile, breaks the sand houses and mingles with them without any inhibition.[1] In this manner Āṅḍāḷ enjoys mentally her communion with God.

Āṇḍāḷ visualises another situation to enjoy the communion mentally with Lord Kṛṣṇa. She recalls the episode of *Bhāgavata* in which Kṛṣṇa took away the clothes of the young milkmaids of Bṛndāvan while they were bathing in the river Yamunā early in the morning. The gopis much to their surprise see him perched on the tree and make repeated appeals to return their clothes. Āṇḍāḷ identifies herself with one of the milkmaids and in that capacity makes repeated appeals to Kṛṣṇa. In each of the hymns she refers to the glory of the Lord Kṛṣṇa. Thus she speaks:

> O Lord, who sleep on the soft bed of the Ādiśeṣa, we desired to take a dip in the river early in the morning before the cocks woke up; we are now subjected to great embarrassment; we will never again come to the river; and myself and my companions together offer salutation to you with folded hands; give us back our clothes.[2]

The manner in which Āṇḍāḷ experienced God as a milkmaid did not satisfy her as the joy of such communion was mixed with grief caused by separation. She, therefore, adopts the role of a bride and seeks union with Lord Kṛṣṇa. She thinks that the *arcā* deity in the name of *Kūḍal* (the religious centre at Madurai, South India), can help to secure the communion (*kūḍal*) to those devotees who seek it. She, therefore, prays to this Lord to bless her with divine union.[3]

The prayers offered to the Lord Kūḍal did not help Āṇḍāḷ to have the union with the Lord. She now employs the cuckoo (*kuyil*) as an emissary. She requests the bird to recite the glorious

1. NacTM II.9.
2. *Ibid.* III.1.
3. The word *kuḍal* literally means 'to unite' and the presiding deity of this religious centre is therefore, addressed as *kūḍal*. The word *kūḍal* is also applicable to a game played by young maidens with the wishful thinking of getting united with their cherished lovers. The meaning of the term in favour of the deity of Madurai seems more appropriate, as interpreted by Periya Parakāla Swāmī. See PPS commentary on NacTM IV.1.

names of the Lord, report to Him her pathetic condition caused by separation so that He may be moved to come to her. She goes to the extent of telling the bird that she would prostrate to it and also reward by offering to it her own pet parrot, if it succeeded in securing the union with the Lord.[1] In the final appeal she says:

> O cuckoo bird, living happily in the tree surrounded by humming bees, listen to what I say: "I am caught up in the web of Śriyaḥpati who is shining with lovely complexion of a parrot; if I have to live in this place you either persuade the Lord wearing the conch and discus to come to me or you bring back my bracelet from Him."[2]

In this state of despondency, Āṇḍāḷ derives some consolation from the dream she had about her wedding with Lord Kṛṣṇa. She narrates to her companion all the details of the wedding as she actually witnessed in the dream:

> My dear friend, I saw in my dream that Kṛṣṇa, the Supreme Being, surrounded with thousands of elephants, walked along the street that was decorated with green leaves hanging on the poles and golden pots filled with water placed in front of the houses.[3]
>
> As Kṛṣṇa walked in the street, I saw the young attractive damsels welcoming Him with pots lit with oil lamps.
>
> Amidst the sound of the drums and conch, I also observed Kṛṣṇa holding my hand.
>
> While the qualified priests conducted the wedding ceremony I witnessed Kṛṣṇa going round the sacrificial fire by holding my palm.
>
> I also perceived in the dream that my body was annointed with cool sandal paste and turmeric powder and that I was made to go in a procession round the streets seated on an elephant along with Lord Kṛṣṇa.[4]

---

1. NacTM V.5, 6.
2. *Ibid.* V.9.
3. *Ibid.* VI.1.
4. *Ibid.* VI.5, 6, 7, 10.

This dream is of some significance to Āṇḍāḷ. In the first place, it is a good omen foretelling the future event. It offered some solace to the bride who is craving for an early union with the Beloved Lord. According to the *Vedānta-sūtra*,[1] as interpreted by Rāmānuja, the dreams and what is experienced in them are the creations of God to provide momentarily an opportunity to experience good or bad results according to one's past *karma*. From this point of view, Āṇḍāḷ is made to experience the joy of her wedding with her Beloved Lord.

With the failure to achieve the actual union with the Lord, Āṇḍāḷ becomes desperately mad and desires to enjoy the sweetness of His lips. She addresses the divine conch (*śaṅkha*) which has physical contact with Kṛṣṇa's mouth and enquires fondly whether the red lips of Kṛṣṇa smells like the refined camphor or that of the fresh lotus flower? Or does it have its own taste and fragrance?[2] She extols the glory of *śaṅkha* also known as *pāñcajanya*, which has the good fortune of enjoying the physical contact with Lord's hands and mouth and repeatedly asks for an answer to her query.

As is expected the *śaṅkha* of Padmanābha is passive since it is totally under the control of the Lord. She is now attracted by the dark clouds which have a resemblance to God and conveys her feelings through them. In a pathetic way she implores:

> O compassionate Clouds, I have lost everything—my facial complexion, the colour of the body, the bangles, the mind, the sleep—on account of the depression caused by separation. I am trying to survive by singing the glory of the Lord Govinda residing in the hill (Tirumalai).
>
> O Clouds, please inform the Lord of Tirumalai in whose chest Goddess Śrī is seated permanently that my youthful breasts desire to embrace His body.[3]

The clouds move away as if they went to report to the Lord. Heavy rainfall follows and Āṇḍāḷ then notices around her freshly blossomed flowers, creepers, the cuckoos, peacocks and the

1. VS. III.2.1.
2. NacTM VII.1.
3. *Ibid.* VIII.3, 4.

humming bees. All these remind her of the Beloved Lord and further intensifies her pangs of separation. Naturally, she speaks aloud by addressing these objects of nature to give vent to her anguish. She speaks to her friend:

> The creepers hanging with small white flowers (*mullai*) remind me of His sweet smile; the trees with blooms spread all over appear to me as if they are laughing at me; I cannot sustain the grief caused to me by the Lord.
>
> The lovely flowers of dark blue black (*kāya* and *karuviḷai*) reveal to me the colour of Śriyaḥpati. But they do not tell me the means of survival. She enquires whether it would be appropriate for the Lord of Tirumālirumśolai to enter my house and snatch my bangles?[1]

She addresses in one breath the cuckoos, the peacocks, the lovely colourful flowers, the red fruits hanging on the tree and wonders whether the colour of the divine body of the Lord of Tirumālirumśolai which has been assumed by these objects serves any useful purpose (except to torment me).[2] She appeals to the bees and flowers to find out for her a way of sustaining her life. She takes a vow to offer large quantity of delicious food to the deity at Tirumālirumśolai and prays that her cherished desire be fulfilled.[3]

In the absence of any relief for her suffering, she starts imagining that the flowers whose colour resemble the complexion of God have been commissioned by the Lord to torment her. The red fruits hanging down on the creepers make her feel that they extract her life. She pathetically appeals to the creeper with small white flowers, not to cause her further grief. The sound of the cuckoo bird becomes intolerable. She cannot stand the dance of the peacocks. She requests the rainfall to induce the Lord of Tiruveṅgaḍa to reveal Himself inside her mind. The sea is requested to report to the Lord all about her suffering.[4]

At the sight of the *nāyakī's* mother and companions who have come to see her pathetic plight, Āṇḍāḷ speaks to them about the

1. NacTM IX.2, 3.
2. *Ibid.* IX.4.
3. *Ibid.* IX.5, 6.
4. *Ibid.* X.1 to 9.

miserable condition caused to her by the Supreme Being. She says:

> O Mother, the Lord of Tiruvaraṅga has not looked at my face.
>
> I have lost my bangles for Him. If he wished to take away my bangles, should he not have walked through my street!
>
> The Lord of Raṅga has taken away my soul and all that belongs to me.[1]

In spite of all the pleadings Āṇḍāḷ does not get a response from her Beloved Lord. Nor does she have the patience to wait until God Himself showers His grace on her. In this state of desperate condition, being unable to bear the pangs of separation any longer, she decides to proceed to Mathura where Lord Kṛṣṇa resides. As she is physically weak to walk all the way by herself, she requests the mother and the companions, in spite of their protests, to take her to the environs of Mathura. She tells them:

> You ladies with a different mental attitude, cannot understand my love. After I have developed a craving for Mādhava, my mind is focussed on Him; and whatever you say are like the words spoken to the deaf person. Please, therefore, take me to Mathura where the Lord was born.[2]

She further adds:

> It is no use for me to hide the sense of shame since all the people in the town already know my condition. If you wished to protect me, please escort me to Gokula without any delay.
>
> It does not matter to me if the public criticise me for having run away from home on my own, in spite of my having parents, relatives and friends. Please leave me at the footsteps of the residence of Nandagopāla.[3]

Again she pleads:

> O Mother, nobody can comprehend the intensity of my mental suffering. The remedy for it lies if Lord Kṛṣṇa

1. NacTM XI.1, 4 and 6.
2. *Ibid.* XII.1.
3. *Ibid.* XII.2 and 3.

touched me with His hands. Take me, therefore, to the place where the Lord danced on the head of *Kāliṅga* serpent.

The change of complexion of my body, the mental anguish, the loss of my feminine modesty, the withering of my mouth, the physical weakness caused without food, the lack of courage and all these would disappear if only the garland of *tulasī* worn by Lord Kṛṣṇa were placed on my body.[1]

Āṇḍāḷ does not yet see an end to her mental anguish. The unsympathetic companions decline to take her to Mathura. Instead, the mother and close relatives think that by singing the glory of Lord Kṛṣṇa they would comfort her and make her recover from the state of depression. But Āṇḍāḷ is seeking a direct physical communion with Lord Kṛṣṇa. She, therefore, appeals to them that instead of speaking about his greatness they should fetch for her the garment, the *tulasī* garland and other materials used by Kṛṣṇa which would have some soothing effect on her. She says:

I have known well the greatness of the Lord Kṛṣṇa but yet I am subjected to suffering (on account of His not responding to me); please therefore, refrain from speaking of His charm as these words only intensify my grief like causing more pain by pouring a sour liquid on the open wound. He is the one who does not understand the grief of a woman. Fetch me the wet yellow waist cloth of Perumān (Lord Kṛṣṇa) and place it on my body so that my pain may subside.[2]

I am caught up inside the net of that person who (at one time) swallowed the entire universe and lay Himself as an infant on the *nyagrodha* leaf; please do not torment me with the words about His glory like piercing me with sharp long shaft (*vēl*); get the garland of *tulasī* worn by the Lord lying in Tirukkuḍandai and place it on my dying body to revive its life.

I have been pining with grief after my throat was pierced by the shaft of his charming glances but I have not heard a word from Him to remove my fear; if you would fetch

1. NacTM XII.5 and 7.
2. *Ibid*. XIII.1.

> for me the garland that decorates His chest, please cover my chest with it.
>
> Bring that water used for the Lord Ārāvamuda and sprinkle it on me. Smear on my body the dust particles trampled by His feet.
>
> In order to remove the grief caused by separation make me embrace His body closely.[1]

In an aggressive mood, she cries out:

> While I am pining with grief, Lord Kṛṣṇa has not enquired if I am still alive or dead; He has taken away everything that belong to me; He has been tormenting this woman who loves Him. If I ever meet that Kṛṣṇa, I would pluck my breasts along with the roots and hurl the same at his chest so that I could overcome my grief.[2]

Āṇḍāḷ has now reached a stage, almost the climax of the irrepressible longing for direct communion with Lord Kṛṣṇa. She is perhaps aware that such union with God leading to the uninterrupted divine service can be had only after the soul is disembodied and reaches the transcendental abode of God. Yet she, being the goddess-incarnate *Bhūdevī*, yearns for it in this very cosmic universe. Her ardent craving for it has reached such a stage that her beloved Lord cannot remain passive without responding to the prayer of His own consort. Love has two-sided relation. Just as the soul is deeply in love with God, the latter too loves the former. God who is *āśrita-sulabha*, easily accessible to those who seek Him with love and *āśritavatsala*, one who has a loving disposition towards the devotees, cannot remain passive and subject His devotee to undue suffering. He, therefore, readily condescends to come down and reveal Himself in His full splendour to fulfil the cherished desire of Āṇḍāḷ. The concluding decad of *Nācciyār Tirumoḻi* indicates that Āṇḍāḷ was blessed by Lord Kṛṣṇa with such a God-experience. The hymns in this decad comprise two parts. The first part giving a brief description of the glory of Lord Kṛṣṇa poses a question: 'Have you not seen Kṛṣṇa' (*kaṇḍīrē*)? The second part which also speaks

1. NacTM XIII 2, 3, 6 and 7.
2. *Ibid*. XIII.8.

of the glory of Kṛṣṇa answers with words: 'Indeed we have seen Him in Bṛndāvan' (*vṛndāvanatte kaṇḍōmē*).[1] The implication of the question and answer as explained by some commentators,[2] is that Āṇḍāḷ poses the question to her fellow devotees with the intention that they too should share with her the joy of God-experience. With a view to emphasising the fact that she actually enjoyed the full grandeur of Lord Kṛṣṇa in Bṛndāvan as revealed to her, she gives an answer through the media of these fellow devotees. Actually, it is an experience of God confined to Āṇḍāḷ only. It is a special gift conferred on her by Lord Kṛṣṇa out of His grace yielding Himself to the sincere and ardent prayer of His Beloved Consort in the human guise of Āṇḍāḷ, the adopted daughter of Periyāḻvār. Thus, we have a unique type of mysticism in respect of Āṇḍāḷ whose ardent craving for union with Lord Kṛṣṇa culminates in her spiritual marriage[3] in the philosophic sense of the individual soul being reunited with God.

VII. *Mysticism of Periyāḻvār*

In Periyāḻvār we find a different pattern of mysticism. Unlike Nammāḻvār, this Āḻvār assumes the role of the mother Yaśodā to pour out his devotional love to Lord Kṛṣṇa. His lyrical poem, known as *Periyāḻvār Tirumoḻi* comprising 461 hymns, mostly covers the mystic experience of God in the form of enjoying the glorious deeds (*līlās*) of Kṛṣṇa as a child. In the guise of Yaśodā, he indulges in the pleasure of nursing the baby, feeding it, cradling and playing with it in various ways. The general theme of the poem is the joyful experience of God rather than the melancholy mental disposition caused by the pangs of separation from God. It is the manifestation of the natural love of a mother to the affectionate child (*vātsalya-bhāva*), as compared to the complicated love of an aggrieved maiden to her lover. It will be of interest to take note of the important features of this mysticism.

The opening decad of the *Periyāḻvār Tirumoḻi*, which is des-

---

1. NacTM XIII.1 to 9.
2. See PPS commentary on NacTM XIII.1.
3. According to tradition, Āṇḍāḷ was taken to the precincts of Lord Raṅganātha for a wedding with Him as per the command of the Lord Himself and she then got absorbed into the *arcā* deity.
   See Chapter 1, p. 28.

ignated as *Tiruppallāṇḍu,* indicates that the Āḻvār was blessed with a direct vision of God. Overwhelmed with joy, he hails the Lord: "May Thou live long for many years and millions of years." Being blessed with the divine knowledge, he was able to visualise vividly every detail of the deeds of God during the period of His incarnation as Kṛṣṇa starting from His birth to the final stage. The poetic description of the events excels the narration of the same in the *Viṣṇu Purāṇa, Harivaṁśa* and the *Bhāgavata Purāṇa,* which appear to be the main source for the Āḻvār rather than the mythical folk songs of ancient Tamil poetry as believed by some western scholars.[1]

To begin with the Āḻvār imagines the manner in which the men and women folks of Gokula danced with joy hailing the birth of child-Kṛṣṇa in the house of Nandagopa at Gokula. The people walked across the street sprinkling the oil and turmeric powder (as a symbol of auspiciousness) and ran towards the house of Nanda to look up the infant. Overwhelmed with joy the milkmaids danced and threw in the courtyard the pots filled with milk and curds. Periyāḻvār visualises the miraculous event in which Yaśodā perceived the cosmic universe inside the mouth of the child as it opened its mouth. In the words of the milkmaids, who are also stated to have witnessed this incident, he expresses with dismay that this is not an ordinary child but the very divine being. In the words of the mother Yaśodā he also admires the supernormal power of the infant:

> When I put the baby in the cradle, it kicks the crib so forcefully that it would break; if I carry it on my hip, it kicks it in such a way that I feel like breaking it; if I carry it on my chest, it kicks my stomach and hurts it. I really feel bad when I think how this baby possesses so much power.[2]

While Tirumaṅgai Āḻvār enjoys the enchanting beauty of the *arcā* deity, Periyāḻvār is content with the physical beauty of God as an infant-Kṛṣṇa. In the guise of Yaśodā, he beckons the women folks of Gokula to come and see the charm of every part of its body—the feet, the fingers, the ankles, the knees, the thighs, the

1. See Hardy, *Viraha-bhakti,* Chapter IV.
2. PeriTM I.1.9.

waist, the navel, the stomach, the sex organ (*muttam*), the chest, the arms, the palms, the neck, the red lips, the nose, the eyes, the ears, the face and the curly hairs. In mentioning each part of the body in a separate hymn, he qualifies it with such epithets as would describe the glory of the deeds of Kṛṣṇa. To cite a verse:

> O ladies with heavy breasts, come and see the thighs of this child, who long ago tore the chest of the demon Hiraṇyakaśyapa and who after sucking the breast of the demoness Pūtanā, pretended to be sleeping.[1]

The Āḻvār pours out his love to child-Kṛṣṇa by singing the lullaby to put it into sleep in a cradle.[2] In each hymn of this decad, he imagines that the celestial deities have sent suitable gifts to the child lying in the cradle.

Placing himself as Yaśodā he beckons the moon to come down and see the beauty of the child:

> My precious little baby beckons the moon by pointing his small hand: O Moon, if you desire to play with him, come down without hiding yourself behind the clouds.[3]

He appeals to the child to jump before him at least once with the childish dance. He desires to see the child towards the mother and touch her hands with a clap. He requests the toddler Kṛṣṇa to walk with the faltering steps. He calls the child to come forward to embrace him. He contemplates over the joy derived by Yaśodā when the child touched her back with the tender hands.[4]

More than the infant Kṛṣṇa, Kṛṣṇa as a young boy is of special attraction to Periyāḻvār. He expresses the delight caused to Yaśodā by the playful activities of the boy in chasing the butterflies:

> Look at the child chasing the butterflies who held in his hand the conch, who played the melodious flute, who was the saviour of the Pāṇḍavas, who played the role of a

1. PeriTM I.2.5.
2. *Ibid*. I.3.
3. *Ibid*. I.4.2.
4. *Ibid*. I.5; I.6; I.7; I.8; I.9.

charioteer in the Mahābhārata war.[1]

He delights himself in contemplating over the pleasure that Yaśodā derived by beckoning the child for suckling, for the ear-piercing ceremony, for bathing, for combing its hair, decorating the hair with colourful flowers and annointing its eyes with the eye line.[2] All these hymns addressed to child Kṛṣṇa are couched in such glorifying terms as would convey the glory of God. Thus it reads:

> May you have your hairs decorated with flowers; your lovely eyes are soothing like the cool black clouds; you manifested yourself for the sole purpose of protecting all the living beings in the universe. You are the Lord of the Goddess who is your prosperity; you are lying in the Śrīraṅga temple to save those who seek you.[3]

Periyāḻvār also speaks fondly in the language of the milk-maids complaining to Yaśodā about the mischief of young Kṛṣṇa. In the words of a maid he says:

> Kṛṣṇa hurled mud at me and the other milkmaids, while we were playing in the sand on the river Yamunā. As we were taking our bath in the river keeping aside our clothes and ornaments, he ran away with our clothes and hid himself inside the house; even though we appealed to him by calling his name several time, he kept silent without responding to our request.[4]

The Āḻvār finds greater delight in contemplating over the deeds of Kṛṣṇa as a youth. He speaks fondly about the herioc deeds of killing Pūtanā and other demons and also the romantic activities such as the enticement of the young milkmaids. In the words of Yaśodā, he expresses dismay:

> You are not an ordinary human being but a divine person and I would even fear to suckle you.[5]

---

1. PeriTM II.1.1.
2. *Ibid.* II.2; II.3; II.4; II.5; II.7; II.8.
3. *Ibid.* II.7.2.
4. *Ibid.* II.10.1.
5. *Ibid.* III.1.1.

Posing himself as Yaśodā, he also expresses regret for having sent young Kṛṣṇa to the jungle along with the other cowherds for grazing the cows. In one of the hymns he says:

> O what a pity, after having retained the baby safely in my womb for twelve months and after having fed the child fondly with breast milk, I sent my dear child to the jungle with the cows and allowed him to walk on bare foot in the rugged path.[1]

He also enjoys the grandeur of the return of Kṛṣṇa from the jungle along with the cows. In one of the hymns he describes in the words of a milkmaid:

> My daughter was so enchanted by looking at the lovely face of the boy who is wearing on the right ear the wild flowers, the garland of jasmine flowers on his neck with the curly long hairs hanging in the back and who plays the melodious flute; she stood right in front of him instead of stepping aside his way; her bangles then slipped off and her body too became thinner.[2]

The Āḻvār speaks of the glory of Lord Kṛṣṇa by recalling the deed in which Kṛṣṇa uplifted the Govardhana hill to protect the cows and cowherds from the torrential rain caused by Indra.[3]

He acclaims the melody of the flute:

> When Kṛṣna—the leader of the cowherds, the one without a second, who was decorated with two attractive peacock feathers and the yellow garment on the waist, played the flute, the trees woke up pouring drops of water; the flowers in the branches started falling off; the branches which shoot upward bent down; the trees appeared as if they were turning with folded hands towards *Śriyaḥpati*. What a wonder the trees possess such a noble quality.[4]

The mystic Āḻvār seeks to enjoy the deeds of Kṛṣṇa as a young man by narrating the conversation of the milkmaids relating to

1. PeriTM III.2.8.
2. *Ibid.* III.4.9.
3. *Ibid.* III.5.
4. *Ibid.* III.6.10.

the romantic activities of Kṛṣṇa. In the words of a maid he speaks:

> My daughter who does not know how to converse properly and who only prattles a few pet words like a parrot, stands in front of elderly ladies and tells them unashamed that the Lord possesses lovely hairs and that He would never let down anyone.[1]

In a similar strain, the Āḻvār reiterates the conversation between the cowherd maids expressing their displeasure toward Kṛṣṇa for enticing their daughters.[2]

In another decad, Periyāḻvār assumes the guise of the cowherd maids and speaks the glory of the *avatāra* of Kṛṣṇa along with that of Rāma in the form of a dialogue between the two. One maid says:

> Hail the glory of my Lord Kṛṣṇa who in order to fulfil the desire of His beloved consort, Satyabhāma, took away the blooming *Parijāta* tree from the courtyard of Indra and planted it in the courtyard of Satyabhāma.[3]

The other maid says:

> Hail the greatness of Rāma, the son of Daśaratha, who took away the power and bow of Paraśurāma who challenged Rāma's valour; and (hail that Rāma) who also killed the demoness Tāṭaka by wielding his bow.[4]

Like all other mystic saints, Periyāḻvār too experiences God in the form of *arcā* deities. He is attracted by the deities of only a few selected religious centres—Tirukkottiyūr, Tirumāliruṁśolai, Śrīraṅgam and Tirumalai, all in South India and Tirukkaṇṇangaḍinagar in the Himālayas. The hymns addressed to these deities are mostly devotional in character intended to convey the glory of God.

As we have explained earlier, mysticism is a manifestation of intense loving devotion to God (*bhakti*) leading to the longing

---

1. PeriTM III.7.7.
2. *Ibid*. III.8.
3. *Ibid*. III.9.1.
4. *Ibid*. III.9.2.

of the soul to see God directly in His full splendour. The mystic whose God-thirst is insatiable endeavours in all possible ways to enjoy God and His glory. The manner in which Periyāḻvār finds delight in God-experience represents one pattern of mysticism. Being attracted by the motif of mother-child relation depicting instinctive love and affection, he chose the role of mother Yaśodā to enjoy the deeds of God-incarnate Kṛṣṇa. Though these hymns in praise of Lord Kṛṣṇa contain rich poetic imagery, they are focussed on the divine deeds and divine attributes. Meditation on God which is the pathway to attain communion with God includes the contemplation of *svarūpa,* the essential nature, *guṇa,* the attributes, *rūpa,* the spiritual enchanting body and *līlās,* the deeds of God. The *Bhāgavata Purāṇa* mentions *smaraṇa* or contemplation of Lord as one of the nine modes of *bhakti.* The same is described as *smaraṇāsakti* in the *Nārada Bhakti-sūtra.* Contemplation should include not only God but all His aspects such as *guṇa, rūpa* and *līlās.* The mystic life of Periyāḻvār provides an excellent example of such a contemplation of divinity.

VIII. *Mysticism of Kulaśekharāḻvār*

The mysticism of Kulaśekharāḻvār is of the same pattern as that of Periyāḻvār. His experience is also confined to God-incarnate Kṛṣṇa and Rāma. Unlike Periyāḻvār, he manifests both joy and grief in his mystic experience of God. He assumes the role of the milkmaids to enjoy the playful deeds of Kṛṣṇa. He also puts on the role of Devakī, the mother who gave birth to Kṛṣṇa to express the sense of grief for not having had the opportunity of nursing the baby.[1] Similarly, in the case of Rāma, the Āḻvār imagines himself as Kauśalyā and enjoys God by way of singing the cradle-songs to put the child-Rāma to sleep. At the same time he assumes the role of Daśaratha to express the grief over the banishment of Rāma to the forest.

The *Perumāḷ Tirumoḻi* comprising 105 verses divided into ten decads presents the mystic experience of this Āḻvār. As a God-intoxicated mystic, Kulaśekharan expresses his yearning to

1. Devakī gave birth to Kṛṣṇa but the baby was taken away soon after birth to Gokula for protection where it was reared by Yaśodā, the foster-mother.

worship the Lord Raṅganātha at Śrīraṅgam and the devotees of God residing there. In the very opening decad, he says repeatedly:

> When would be the day, when my eyes can see the Lord of Tiruvaraṅga and enjoy Him? When would be the day, when I shall live with the servants of the Lord at Śrīraṅgam? When would I be able to offer worship with my own hands?[1]

He perceives mentally the glory of the place along with the deity and craves to be physically present there. This marks the beginning of his mystic experience of God.

In the sixth decad, Kulaśekharan actually exhibits his mystic experience of God. Here he assumes the role of different milkmaids and conveys the feeling of anger caused by the misbehaviour of Kṛṣṇa with regard to his love affairs. In the words of a milkmaid he complains:

> O Vāsudeva, though I am aware that in this very town several other gopis with attractive hairdos decked in fragrant flowers do not like to embrace you, yet I entertained some faith in your deceitful words and stood on the sand dune of the river Yamunā until dawn in the expectation of your arrival, with a sense of fear of being seen by others and also enduring the chill fog.

In the words of another maid he says:

> O Dāmodara, I have actually witnessed the way you entered the house on the eastern side where an attractive maid was churning the curd all by herself and by pretending to offer your help you churned the curd along with her and aroused her passion.

In a more sarcastic way it is pointed out:

> O Kṛṣṇa, you exchanged glances with young maid with lovely black hair; you at the same time made another girl believe that you only loved her; you promised one other maid that you would meet her at the appointed hour but

1. PeruTM I.1 to 9.

> actually you made love to another. As you grow, your deceitful affairs also keep increasing.[1]

In the capacity of another maid he expresses wrath:

> I have seen you walking in my own street hand in hand with an attractive damsel by covering your head with a silk cloth and at the same time I also witnessed how you captivated the heart of another girl. Why do you now come to me? You better go back to her.

In a more aggressive tone, the Āḻvār speaks in the words of a maid:

> O Son of Vāsudeva, the moment I fell to sleep, you walked out of my comfortable bed leaving me alone; the next day and the following day, you kept yourself in the company of other ladies. Why do you come to me now? You may get out of this place.[2]

In a similar strain the Āḻvār sings a few more hymns. Outwardly these verses give the impression that the mystic expresses displeasure towards God rather than enjoying His glory. It is not so. It is a manifestation of mild anger mixed with deep love (*praṇaya-kopa*). Theologically the hymns signify the special attachment of God towards the devotees. In order to intensify their devotion, he only provokes them with situations or events that cause disappointment, anger or even grief.[3] Despite the humilation inflicted by God to the devotees, the latter do not give up their attachment to God. In the same way if the devotees push Him out, yet He comes closer to them. These ideas are beautifully presented in the *Bhāgavata Purāṇa* in the love exhibited by the milkmaids to Kṛṣṇa. Against this background Kulaśekharan exhibits his loving devotion to God mystically in these hymns.

As a contrast to the delightful experience of the deeds of the youthful Kṛṣṇa, Kulaśekharan poses himself as Devakī, the mother of Kṛṣṇa and pours out his grief for not being able to enjoy the infant Kṛṣṇa. He cries out through the media of Devakī

---

1. PeruTM VI.1, 2 and 3.
2. *Ibid.* VI.5 and 6.
3. See BP X.30-48 *praśamāya prasādāya tatraiva antaradhīyata.*

by simulating her emotion of motherly tenderness to the child:

> What an unfortunate mother I am that I could not sing the lullabies for my dear child.
>
> How unlucky I am that I could not enjoy the beauty of the infant.
>
> How unfortunate is Vāsudeva, the father of the child, to have not witnessed the delighful gestures of the baby that were enjoyed by the foster-father, Nandagopāla.[1]

The Āḻvār laments in the words of Devakī (expressing both joy and sorrow):

> O Kṛṣṇa, I now enjoy your sight as a young man possessing a face resembling the bright full moon, the soft hands, a wide chest, strong arms, the tender bright eyebrows and the wide eyes resembling the lotus petals; but I grieve for not having had the pleasure of seeing your beauty as a child at that age when the infant cannot recognise anyone but its own mother. How can I endure this life?

He also bemoans:

> O my Child, beautiful and young. I have missed the joy of holding you close in my arms and your looking into my face with lovely eyes and sweet smiles, while one of my breasts is in your mouth.[2]

After enjoying Kṛṣṇa as a child, the mystic-Āḻvār is attracted by Rāma as a child. Posing himself as the mother Kauśalyā, he bursts out with great joy singing the lullabies for Rāma. The ten hymns devoted for this purpose contain a poetic description of the important divine deeds performed during the Rāmāvatāra.[3] This is one of the ways of contemplation of the glory of God.

When Kulaśekharan thinks of Rāma as a prince, he is attracted by the motif of father-son as different from mother-child motif. He identifies himself with Daśaratha, who banished his dearest son Rāma to the Daṇḍakāraṇya forest and suffered the

1. PeruTM VII.1, 2, 3.
2. *Ibid.* VIII.4 and 7.
3. *Ibid.* VIII. 1 to 10.

grief of separation. In order to express his feeling over this tragic event, the Āḻvār in the words of Daśaratha pours out his sorrow in ten hymns:

> O my dearest Son, who is a source of joy to me, who is always obedient and who should have been coronated as the king; what a pity I banished you to the impenetrable forest yielding to the words of your step mother, Kaikeyī.
>
> O Rāma, who is the saviour of all mankinds, how did you choose to go to the forest, after listening to the cruel words of Kaikeyī and forsaking the people of Ayodhyā who are so devoted to you, and also by abandoning the powerful elephants, the horses and chariots? How did you walk through the rugged path followed by the beautiful Sītā decorated with ornaments along with your younger brother?[1]
>
> How can you, who had spent all the earlier years sleeping on soft beds, sleep now in the forest under the shade of the trees on the bed made of dry leaves?
>
> My heart breaks when I think of your entry into the big forest inhabited by wild elephants.[2]

He curses Kaikeyī for being responsible to send Rāma along with his younger brother and Sītā:

> What would you achieve by banishing Rāma to forest, causing my death and sending me to heaven?[3]

These hymns filled with deep emotional feelings are not intended to criticise the action of either Daśaratha or Kaikeyī. They, on the contrary, reflect the devotional love of the Āḻvār to God-incarnate Rāma. The mystic often identifies himself with God or Goddess and any hardship or grief sustained by them during the state of incarnation, is equally taken as his own. Hence they are prompted to speak in the same language as those of the original characters. This represents one of the *bhakti-bhāvas* which is manifested through oral expression. Kulaśekhara Āḻvār

1. PeruTM IX.1 and 2.
2. *Ibid.* IX.3 and 4.
3. *Ibid.* IX.8.

stands as an example of such a mysticism.

We have presented individually the mysticism of the five Āḻvārs namely Nammāḻvār, Tirumaṅgai Āḻvār, Āṇḍāḷ, Periyāḻvār and Kulaśekhara Āḻvār. Each one represents a distinctive type of God-experience. The remaining Āḻvārs except Madhurakavi are also mystics in a general sense, since they too have exhibited an ardent longing for a direct and comprehensive vision of God. But they have chosen to experience God and His glory in a direct manner, like any devoted *bhakta* and hence they do not exhibit in their poems the mental states associated with *saṁśleṣa* and *viraha*. We have not therefore, included their God-experience in the present chapter.

Chapter 8

GENERAL EVALUATION AND CONCLUSION

In the preceding chapters we have attempted a comprehensive presentation of the Philosophy and Mysticism of the Āḻvārs, the twelve Vaiṣṇava Saints of South India under the six headings: (1) Doctrine of Reality, (2) Doctrine of God, (3) Doctrine of Jīva, (4) Doctrine of Sādhana, (5) Doctrine of the Supreme Goal, and (6) Theistic Mysticism. The views of the Āḻvārs on these subjects which are found scattered in the four thousand Tamil hymns have been brought together and discussed in a coherent manner. We have shown that these theories are based on the Upaniṣads, the Pāñcarātra Āgamas, the Itihāsas and Purāṇas. We have also seen that the Philosophical and the religious teachings of the Āḻvārs are in conformity with the Viśiṣṭādvaita Vedānta and the Vaiṣṇava Theology as expounded by Rāmānuja. We have also indicated the distinctive feature of the doctrines and their influences on the Vaiṣṇavism of post-Rāmānuja period. Without repeating what has already been said, we shall now evaluate the contribution of the Āḻvārs to the Viśiṣṭādvaita Vedānta and in this connection, we shall examine the following issues:

I. The Status of the *Divya-prabandham* as Tamil Veda
II. The *Tiruvāymoḻi* as Tamil Vedānta
II. The Theory of *Ubhaya-vedānta*
IV. The Influence of the Tamil *Prabandhams* on Rāmānuja and his Followers
V. The Āḻvārs and the two Vaiṣṇava Sects.

I. *The Status of the Divya-prabandham as Tamil Veda*

Right from the time of Nāthamuni (9th century) the Vaiṣṇava Ācāryas have accorded the status of Veda to the Tamil hymns of the Āḻvārs. They have regarded them as *Tamiḻ marai* or Tamil Veda. Though all the four thousand hymns are generally given the status of the Veda, the *Tiruvāymoḻi* of Nammāḻvār is specially singled out for this distinction.[1] Thus, Nāthamuni, the first and foremost Ācārya to recognise the greatness of the *Divya-prabandham*, describes the *Tiruvāymoḻi* as *Drāviḍa Veda-sāgara* or the ocean of Tamil Veda.[2] Parāśara Bhattar calls it *Drāviḍa Brahma Saṁhitā*.[3] Vedānta Deśika gives it the title of *Dramiḍopaniṣat* and in order to justify this status, he compiled two works in Sanskrit verses under the title of *Dramiḍopaniṣat-tātparya-ratnāvaḷī* and *Dramiḍopaniṣat-sāra*. Vādikesari Aḻakiyamaṇavāḷa Jīyar, one of the commentators on Tiruvāymoḻi, designates his commentary as *Dramiḍopaniṣat-bhāṣyam*. He has also composed a work in Sanskrit verse under the title of *Dramiḍopaniṣat-saṅgati*.

While all these claims in respect of *Tiruvāymoḻi* are unquestionable in view of its philosophical character, it is important to know the correct sense in which the Tamil hymns are Veda or Upaniṣad. *Prima facie*, the very term *Tamil-veda* appears to be a self-contradiction. The term Veda understood in the technical sense, as commonly accepted by the orthodox schools of Indian Philosophy, particularly the Mīmāṁsā and Vedānta, refers to the Revealed Scripture in Sanskrit because it is regarded as *anādi* or beginningless, *nitya* or eternal and *apauruṣeya* or not ascribable to human authorship. If we accept this technical meaning of the term, it would appear to be laudatory to regard the *Tiruvāymoḻi* of Nammāḻvār as Veda for the reason that it does not fulfil the normally accepted criteria for the Veda. Some Vaiṣṇava Ācāryas do, however, claim that Tiruvāymoḻi is also *anādi*, *nitya* and *apauruṣeya* as it was revealed to Nammāḻvār by

1. Aḻakiyamaṇavāḷaperumāḷ Nāyaṅār, the author of *Ācārya Hṛdaya* and Maṇavāḷamāmuni regard the four works of Nammāḻvār as representing four Vedas and the six works of Tirumaṅgai Āḻvār as Vedāṅgas or the six ancillaries to the Veda.
2. See Tanian to *Kaṇṇinun Śiruttāmbu*:
sahasra-śākhopaniṣat-samāgamam namamy-ahaṁ drāviḍa-vedasāgaram.
3. *Raṅgarāja-stava* 6:
sahasra-śākhāṁ yo adrākṣīt drāmiḍīṁ brahma-saṁhitāṁ.

God. The author of *Ācārya Hṛdaya* has advanced a few arguments in defence of this claim.[1] Vedānta Deśika also states that the *Tiruvāymoḻi* is *nitya*.[2] He regards it as a *Saṁhitā* or branch of Veda in Tamil intuited by Nammāḻvār in the same way as the Vedic seers intuited the Veda.[3]

While the orthodox Vaiṣṇavas would not question these authoritative statements, we have to accept the historical fact that Nammāḻvār as the author of the *Tiruvāymoḻi* was born at a particular point of time a few centuries ago, unlike the legendary Vedic seers and sages of the Purāṇas. Even though the Tamil hymns represent the utterances of God through the media of a human being, as stated by Nammāḻvār himself,[4] the fact that God sang them renders it *pauruṣeya* or as a composition of a person. The *Pāñcarātra Saṁhitā* is claimed to have been taught by Lord Nārāyaṇa Himself,[5] although each *Saṁhitā* is ascribed to a legendary sage or divine being and yet it is not accorded the status of Veda. The author of the *Mahābhārata*, Vyāsa, is believed to be an incarnation of Nārāyaṇa (*anupraveśāvatāra*)[6] but this work is not accepted as Veda except in a secondary sense as *pañcama-veda* or the fifth veda. It would not therefore appear justifiable to regard the *Tiruvāymoḻi* as Tamil Veda in the strict technical sense. However, it can be considered as *Veda* as claimed by the Vaiṣṇava Ācāryas on an entirely different basis. It is *Veda* in the sense that it reveals the knowledge of God (*vedayati iti vedaḥ*). It can be treated as Veda or *Upaniṣad* because it contains the essential teachings of the Vedas including the *Upaniṣad*. This view is warranted by the statements made by Madhurakavi Āḻvār, Nāthamuni and Vedānta Deśika. In his short poem of 11 verses written in praise of Nammāḻvār, Madhurakavi says that the essence or purport of the Vedas was taught to him by Nammāḻvār. In his own words:

> Saint Śaṭakopa (Nammāḻvār) has sung and made my mind

---

1. See AH *Sūtras* 45-49.
2. See *Pādukāsahasra* II-9: *nityaṁ jātā śaṭhariputanoḥ niṣpatantī mukhāt te....*
3. *Ibid.* I-3: *āmnāyānāṁ prakṛtim-aparām saṁhitāṁ dṛṣṭavantaḥ.*
   See also DTR 10: *śaṭhajit dṛṣṭa-sarvīyaśākhā.*
4. See TVM VII.9.1: *eṉṉai taṉṉākki eṉṉāl taṉṉai iṉtamiḻ pāḍiya īśaṉ.*
5. *Mahabhārata* XII.359.68: *pāñcarātrasya kṛtsnasya vaktā nārāyaṇaḥ svayam.*
6. VP III.4.5: *kṛṣṇadvaipāyinaṁ vyāsaṁ viddhi nārāyaṇaṁ prabhuṁ.*

> absorbed in his works permanently; has sung them in such a way that the inner meaning *(purport)* of the Vedas, which are recited by the eminent Vedic scholars (*vediyar*), is clearly understood and well-fixed in my mind.[1]

Nāthamuni who has composed a *tanian* in Tamil in praise of Madhurakavi says: Māraṉ Śaṭakopaṉ (Nammāḻvār) has rendered into Tamil the Vedas (*vedam tamiḻ śeyda māraṉ śaṭakopaṉ*).[2] Here the words *vedam tamiḻ śeyda,* do not mean that the Veda was rendered into Tamil for the obvious reason that the *Tiruvāymoḻi* is not either a translation or even a paraphrase of it, but it implies that the essential teachings of Vedas are presented in Tamil. Vedānta Deśika in the concluding verse of his *Prabandha-sāra,* a poetical composition in Tamil giving an outline of the life and works of the Āḻvārs, states explicitly that the Āḻvārs have collected together the purport of the eternal four Vedas[3] and presented it in pure Tamil language out of compassion for the benefit of humanity. In another context, he points out that the Āḻvārs as divine incarnations have given to us the essence of Vedic teachings in a language which is accessible to all in the same way as the clouds gather the moisture from the ocean and pour it down as fresh cool water that is beneficial to all living beings.[4] In view of these authoritative statements, it is but appropriate to regard the Tamil *prabandhams* in general and the *Tiruvāymoḻi* in particular as *Veda* in a restricted secondary sense. It is not actually *Veda itself* in Tamil or Tamil Veda. On the other hand, it enjoys the *status* of Veda, only in terms of the sanctity and authoritativeness (*prāmāṇya*). An appropriate classification of the *Divya-prabandham* would be a *upabrāhmaṇa* or a work which elucidates what is taught in the Vedas. All the *Smṛti* texts such as *Manusmṛti,* the two Itihāsas, *Rāmāyaṇa* and *Mahābhārata* including the *Bhagavadgītā* and the *Vaiṣṇava Purāṇas* such as *Viṣṇu Purāṇa* are regarded as *upabrāhmaṇas,* since they elucidate what

---

1. *Kaṇṇinum Śiruttāmbu* 9, *mikka vediyar vedattin uḷ poruḷ,*
   nirkap-pāḍi en-neñjuḷ niruttināṉ.
2. *Ibid.* 2.
3. *Prabandhasāram* 18, *andamilā āraṇangaḷ nālāy niṉṟa*
   adan karuttai āḻvarhaḷ āyndu eḍuttu śentamiḻāl aruḷ śeyda.
4. RTS, *Guruparamparā-sāra, vedārthaṅgaḷil vēṇḍum sāratamāṁśattai sarvarukkum*
   adhikarikka-lāna bāṣaiyāle sangrahittu kāṭṭi...

is already taught in the Vedas including the Upaniṣads. In the same way, the *Tiruvāyomoḻi* of Nammāḻvār is an *upabrāhmaṇa* but with a difference. As Vedānta Deśika points out, it is a distinctive *upabrāhmaṇa* (*saṁhitā-sārvabhaumi*) since it expounds and elucidates the Vedāntic theories in a better way than the Itihāsas and Purāṇas.[1]

There is yet another reason for according a special status to the *Divya-prabandham*. As we have explained in the earlier chapters, the Tamil poems, though basically devotional in character, present a comprehensive account of Godhead in all its aspects viz., *svarūpa, rūpa, guṇa, vibhava* and *līlā*. It is a superb treatise on the doctrine of God exclusively dealing, unlike the other religious texts, with *Bhagavad-guṇas* in a grand way that would capture the mind of a devotee.

The Viśiṣṭādvaita Vedānta upholds *saviśeṣa-brahmavāda* or Brahman as endowed with attributes as against the *nirviśeṣa-brahmavāda* of Advaita Vedānta and identifies the metaphysical absolute with the personal God of Religion. The *Divya-prabandham* serves as an important source-book for such a system of philosophy. As we shall see later, Rāmānuja and his followers have found sufficient material in the hymns of the Āḻvārs for expounding the fundamental tenets of the Viśiṣṭādvaita Philosophy and Religion. It is, therefore appropriate for the Vaiṣṇava Ācāryas to have accorded, the status of Veda or Upaniṣad to the Tamil *Prabandham*.

II. *The Tiruvāymoḻi as Tamil Vedānta*

We may now examine whether *Tiruvāymoḻi* is Tamil Vedānta and if so, how it is related to the *Vedānta* proper in Sanskrit developed on the basis of the Upaniṣads and *Vedānta-sūtra*. This is an important topic that needs consideration because the concept of *Ubhaya-vedānta* which has gained great importance in the

---

1. See DTR 4, *yattat-kṛtyaṁ śrutīnāṁ munigaṇa-vihitaiḥ*
setihāsaiḥ purāṇaiḥ,
tatrāsau sattva-sīmnaḥ śaṭhamathana-muneḥ
saṁhitā-sārvabhaumi.

See also *Stotraratna-bhāṣya* on verse 5.
paraśara prabandhādapi vedānta-rahasya vaiśadyātiśaya hetubhūtaiḥ sadyaḥ paramātmani cittarañjakatamaiḥ sarvopajīvyaiḥ upabrāhmaṇaiḥ...

post-Rāmānuja period, is based on the assumption that *Tiruvāymoḻi* is *Vedānta.*

The term *Vedānta*, like Veda, bears a special connotation. In a technical sense, it means the end of Vedas (*vedasya antaḥ*) or the concluding portions of the Vedas and as such it refers primarily to the Upaniṣads.[1] It is also used to denote the system or school of thought (*darśana*) developed on the basis of the Upaniṣads. In this sense, it is commonly applied to the *Vedānta-sūtra* of Bādarāyaṇa on the basis of which different schools of Vedānta such as Advaita, Viśiṣṭādvaita, Dvaita have come up. So in the strict technical sense of the term, the Tamil composition of Nammāḻvār cannot be Vedānta. However, it can be treated as *Vedānta* in a secondary sense on the ground that it contains the essentials of the Upaniṣadic teachings on the analogy of the *Bhagavadgītā*. The *Gītā* being part of the *Mahābhārata* is not Vedānta in the technical sense but still it is regarded as a Vedānta treatise because it contains the cream of the Upaniṣadic teachings. The same is the case with the *Tiruvāymoḻi.*

An objection can be raised against this view on the ground of language. Sanskrit is accepted as a sacred language for the reason that the Revealed Scripture (Veda) is in that language. So also the Vedānta texts in Sanskrit developed on the basis of the Upaniṣads are sacred and authoritative source-books for Vedānta. But the hymns of the Āḻvārs are composed in Tamil. Would it be proper to accord it a status equal to the Veda and Vedānta? The Vaiṣṇava Ācāryas who are aware of this objection have provided a suitable answer to it.[2] The Tamil language, according to tradition is propounded by the sage Agastya and thereby it gains as much sanctity as Sanskrit.[3] Besides, for the worship of God and singing His glory, any language is considered

---

1. The term *upaniṣad* is also defined as that which is close to Brahman or that which directly reveals the nature of Brahman (*Brahmaṇi upanisaṇṇeti upaniṣad*). In this sense *Tiruvāymoḻi* is treated as Upaniṣad as it is supposed to reveal the nature of Brahman or God directly. But the more commonly accepted meaning of the Upaniṣad is the concluding portion of the Vedas known as *Brahma Kāṇḍa* because that alone reveals Brahman directly as distinct from the ritualistic portion of the Vedas known as *Pūrva Kāṇḍa* which refers to Brahman indirectly (*sadvāraka*).
2. See Nañjīyar's *Oṉpadināyirappāḍi*, Introduction.
3. See *Ācārya Hṛdaya-sūtra* 41.

appropriate. As the Tamil hymns sing the glory of God, they enjoy equal sanctity with Sanskrit.[1] The Āḻvārs themselves have acknowledged both Sanskrit and Tamil as sacred languages.[2] The content of a work is more important than the language for religious purposes. The fact that the *Rāmāyaṇa* was composed in Hindi or Tamil would not affect its sanctity and value, since the subject-matter which is important is the same.

The important point for consideration is whether or not Tamil hymns represent the Sanskritic Vedānta of the Upaniṣads. In the preceding chapters, we have presented an exposition of the philosophical and theological teachings of the Āḻvārs as revealed in their Tamil hymns. We have also seen that these are also in conformity with the Upaniṣadic teachings. The philosophical theories, though not discussed in systematic detail, are presented adequately at different places in the Tamil hymns. In view of this, the Tamil *Prabandham* can be accepted as a Vedānta work in the sense that it is a composition containing Upaniṣadic teachings.

The Vaiṣṇava Ācāryas have offered a few additional explanations to justify the Vedānta status to the Tamil *Prabandhams* in general and *Tiruvāymoḻi* in particular. In the first place, the Vedānta is primarily devoted to the study of the nature of the Ultimate Reality (*tattva*), the means of attaining it (*sādhana*) and the supreme goal of life (*parama-puruṣārtha*). Accordingly, the *Vedānta-sūtra*, the primary text on Vedānta, deals with these three subjects—the first two *adhyāyas*, with *tattva*, the third and fourth with the other two topics respectively. All the Tamil poems cover these topics either directly or indirectly. The earliest commentary of Piḷḷān on the *Tiruvāymoḻi* in Sanskritised Tamil reveals beyond any doubt the Vedāntic content of this poem. As

---

1. See DTR 1-4, *bhāṣā-gītiḥ praśastā bhagavatī vacanāt rājavaccopacārāt, sāca agastya-prasūtāt....*
2. See *Perumāḷ Tirumoḻi* I.4.
Kulaśekharāḻvār speaks of God as representing the sweetness of Tamil songs and also the northern language, Sanskrit.
aṁ tamiḻin iṉpappāvinai, avvaḍamoḻiyai...
See also Tirumaṅgai Āḻvār's *Tiruneḍuntāṇḍakam* 4,
Tirumaṅgai Āḻvār describes the Lord as the one who is in the form of the sound of Tamil and who is also in the form of the Sanskrit word (*vaḍa śol*).
śentirattamiḻ ōśai, vaḍaśollāhi.

pointed out by Vedānta Deśika, the first twenty and the concluding twenty verses of *Tiruvāymoḻi* present briefly and clearly the substance of Vedānta Philosophy following the same sequence as adopted by the *Vedānta-sūtra* (*śārīraka arthakrama*).[1]

According to the commentators, each centum of the *Tiruvāymoḻi* deals with a specific theory of Vedānta. Thus, Periyavāccān Piḷḷai points out that the first two centums cover the nature of the Ultimate Reality (*parasvarūpa*); the third and fourth with the nature of individual self (*pratyagātma svarūpa*); the fifth and sixth refer to the means of attainment (*upāya*); the seventh and eighth deal with the removal of obstacles in the way of attaining the goal (*prāptivirodhi-nivṛtti*) and the last two with the nature of the goal and its attainment (*phalasiddhi*). The author of *Īḍu* also upholds the view that *Tiruvāymoḻi* deals with these five subjects.[2]

Vedānta Deśika points out that in addition to these five topics the ten centum of *Tiruvāymoḻi* cover the following ten points respectively:[3]

1. God is the Supreme Being to be sought (*sevyatva*).
2. God is the desirable object of worship (*bhogyatva*).
3. God possesses a spiritual body (*śubhatanutva*).
4. God is the highest object of enjoyment (*sarvabhogyādhikatva*).
5. God is the giver of the supreme goal (*śreyaḥ tadhetudānatva*).
6. God is attainable through *prapatti* (*prapadana sulabhaḥ*).
7. God is capable of removing evil (*aniṣṭa vidhvaṁsanaśīlatva*).
8. God exercises His will in disposing His grace in accordance with the desire exhibited by the devotees (*bhaktaśchandānuvṛttitva*).
9. God is friendly to all unconditionally (*nirupādhika suhṛttva*).
10. God assists the individual in leading him to *mokṣa* (*satpadavī sahāyatva*).

---

1. See DTR, I.5, *ādau śārīrakārtha-kramam iha*
viśadaṁ viṁsatiḥ vakti sāgrā.
See also *Vedāntaśāstra, drāviḍāgamādya-daśaka-dvandyaikakanthyaṁ.*
This work is written by one whose name is given as Varadavara Yogi Rāmānuja and who is probably the same one as Aḻakiya Maṇavālaperumāḷ Jīyar. This book expounds how the first twenty verses of *Tiruvāymoḻi* reflects the important *adhikaraṇas* or topics of the *Vedānta-sūtra.*
2. *Īḍu*, Mudal Śriyaḥpati, *ivaindumē tiruvāymoḻiyil pratipādikkiradu.*
3. DTR, verse 1.8, See also *Dramiḍopaniṣat-sāra*, verse 1.

In the opinion of Vedānta Deśika, all that is to be understood in the *Vedānta-śāstra* is contained in the *Tiruvāymoḻi*.[1]

According to the author of the *Ācārya Hṛdaya*, the ten centums of the *Tiruvāymoḻi* deal with the following ten divine attributes respectively:[2]

1. *Paratva* or Nārāyaṇa as the Supreme Being.
2. *Kāraṇatva* or the Supreme Lord as the primary cause of the universe.
3. *Vyāpakatva* or He abides at all times and in all sentient beings and non-sentient entities both within and without.
4. *Niyantṛtva* or He is the controller of all.
5. *Kāruṇikatva* or He is compassionate.
6. *Śaraṇyatva* or He is the sole refuge.
7. *Śaktatva* or He is all powerful.
8. *Satyakāmatva* or God is endowed with *kalyāṇa-guṇas* (auspicious attributes) and *vibhūtis* (glorious property).
9. *Āpatsakhatva* or He is the real friend for the devotees in distress.
10. *Ārtiharatva* or He is the one who can fulfil the ardent craving of the devotee to attain Him.

From the standpoint of Vaiṣṇava Theology, the entire *Divyaprabandham* is an exposition of the inner meaning of the three esoteric Vaiṣṇava *mantras*, known as *mūla-mantra* or *Nārāyaṇa mantra* of eight syllables (*aṣṭākṣara*), the *dvaya* which refers to the *śaraṇāgati* (self-surrender to God), the *carma-śloka*, the verse in the concluding chapter of the *Gītā* enjoining the self-surrender (*prapatti*). These *mantras* contain the quintessence of Vedānta in general and in particular, the *tattva, hita* and *puruṣārtha.* On the strength of the hidden inner meaning of the hymns (*svāpadeśārtha*), the Vaiṣṇava Ācāryas believe that the Tamil *Prabandhams* are an exposition of Vedānta.

In the light of all these explanations it is difficult to deny the status of Vedānta to the *Tiruvāymoḻi*. Though it comprises Tamil hymns in praise of God, it also teaches Vedānta Philosophy.

---

1. DTR II.118.
2. AH 218-228.

III. *The Theory of Ubhaya-vedānta*

What is *Ubhaya-vedānta*? This is a concept which has come into vogue since the time of Nāthamuni. The word *ubhaya* is a pronominal adjective which means two or dual. According to the rule of the Sanskrit grammar this compound word means *ubhau vedāntau* or two Vedāntas. What are the two Vedāntas? The answer is, as generally understood in Vaiṣṇavism, the Tamil Vedānta of *Divyaprabandham* and the Sanskrit Vedānta of the Upaniṣads. The Sanskrit Vedānta taken by itself cannot be *Ubhaya-vedānta*; nor does the *Tiruvāymoḻi* by itself stand for it and the two taken together represent *Ubhaya-vedānta*. They are comparable to the two eyes through which we look at the Supreme Being or God.

The concept understood in this sense presents a difficulty. The subject-matter of the two *Vedāntas* is not considered to be different. Both deal with *Tattva, Hita* and *Puruṣārtha*. If the subject-matter is the same, why then call it *ubhaya* or dual Vedānta? If the Vedānta teachings in Sanskrit are also expressed in Tamil, it would not become a different Vedānta. In order to overcome this problem, the compound word may be expressed as *ubhayaścāsau vedāntaśca* or the system constituted of two Vedāntas namely the Tamil Vedānta and Sanskrit Vedānta. It would then amount to saying that the Vedānta or the Theology which is accepted by the Śrīvaiṣṇavas of South India is *Ubhaya-vedānta*, in the sense that it is a system developed on the basis of two source-books. In other words, the school of thought which embodies the teachings of the Upaniṣads and the Āḻvārs is *Ubhaya-vedānta.*

Even this view presents a difficulty as it would admit the advent of a combined system of Vedānta or Theology, as distinct from the good old traditonal Sanskrit Vedānta. The question arises: when did it come into existence? Was it prevalent at the time of Nammāḻvār? Or did it arise at a later period, either during the time of Nāthamuni or immediately after Rāmānuja. In this connection, some western scholars have taken the view that two diverse traditions viz., the Tamil Vaiṣṇava tradition and the Sanskritic Vaiṣṇava tradition were merged together at the time of Rāmānuja by Piḷḷān (1068 A.D.) in order to project a combined theology as *Ubhaya-vedānta* or dual theology based on both the Sanskrit and Tamil Vedas.[1] Though it is true that for the first time Piḷḷān, a disciple of Rāmānuja wrote a commentary on *Tiruvāymoḻi* in maṇipravāḷa in which he mixed the Sanskrit phrases used in the Sanskrit Vedānta works with the Tamil words used in the *Tiruvāymoḻi* of Nammāḻvār, it cannot be accepted that two diverse Vaiṣṇava traditions or theologies were merged together for more than one reason. In the first instance, it would be wrong to assume the existence of two separate Vaiṣṇava theologies or traditions. Historically speaking, Vaiṣṇavism as a monotheistic religion has been in existence from the time of *Ṛg-Veda* and it has passed through successive stages of development up to the time of Rāmānuja and his successors.[2] The basic tenets of Vaiṣṇavism have remained the same, though there may be doctrinal differences which generally arise in any historical evolution of a religion. Secondly, the Āḻvārs did not preach and practise a Vaiṣṇavism different from that which existed before their advent. Similarly, the *Vaiṣṇavas* who lived during the time of Āḻvārs and those who lived long after them were not different from those who lived during Rāmānuja and post-Rāmānuja period. In connection with the description of religious centres, we come across plenty of references in the hymns of the Āḻvārs, to orthodox Vaiṣṇava Brahmins who are stated to be well-versed in the four Vedas, engaged in the performance of *yāgas* and other prescribed rituals and who scrupulously followed the Vedic tradition.[3] Some of these hymns mention the specific number of Vedic Brahmins as three thousand and describe them as knowers of Sanskrit Veda. They also refer to the smoke emanating from the consecrated fire. Are these Vaiṣṇavas different from the Tamil Vaiṣṇavas of Āḻvār period? They cannot be, as otherwise the Āḻvārs would not speak about them with veneration. Nor are the Vaiṣṇavas of the Āḻvār period following the Tamil tradition

1. See John Carmen and Vasudha Narayanan, *The Tamil Veda* Chapters 1 and 13.
2. See Srinivasa Chari, *Vaiṣṇavism—Its Philosophy, Theology and Religious Discipline*, Chapter I.
3. See TVM V.9.3; VI.1.2, 4 VII.3.3, 6.
   PTM II.10.1, 1, 2; III.6.1; III.2.2; III.2.8; III.8.4; IV.3.2-7; V.9.9; VI.1.7.
   PeriTM IV.4.1, 7; IV.7.8; IV.8.1, 2.
   NacTM II.10.11; PeruTM I.10.2.
   See also Agnihotram Rāmānuja Tatachar, *Āḻvārhaḷuṁ vedaṅgaḷuṁ*.
   This monograph in Tamil explains in detail how the Āḻvārs have adored the Vedas and how they describe the Vedic Brahmins who are well-versed in the Vedas and who have been engaged in Vedic rites and daily rituals.

different from the Vaiṣṇavas of Rāmānuja period to whom he imparted Vedānta. The *Bhāgavata* religion or the religion of the the *Pāñcarātra* Āgama is considered by some modern scholars as different from the Vaiṣṇava religion of the Rāmānuja period. Even this is far from the truth. *Bhagavān* is the same as Viṣṇu or Nārāyaṇa and worshippers of this deity from the early time to the present day are Vaiṣṇavas. The customs and certain religious observances may vary from place to place but basically as devotees of Viṣṇu they are the same irrespective of the places and the period in which they lived. It is, therefore, wrong to assume the existence of two different theologies and their amalgamation at a later period.

We have to look at this matter in the correct perspective. The Āḻvārs who were born long before Rāmānuja taught the same Vedānta Philosophy and Vaiṣṇava Religion that was already prevalent through the medium of Tamil language which was then the principal regional language of South India and understood widely by the common folk. With the *bhakti* movement gaining greater momentum, the common people were greatly attracted by the devotional songs as these had an emotional appeal to them. According to tradition, these hymns were lost for a few centuries and it, therefore, became the task of Nāthamuni in the 9th century to rediscover and introduce them as part of the temple ritual. At that time, there would have been some resentment among the orthodox Brahmins strictly adhering to the Vedic tradition to accept the authority and sanctity of Tamil hymns because of the prejudice towards the language, comparable to the opposition evinced initially by the orthodox Hindus in the North India towards the Tulasī *Rāmāyaṇa* in Hindi language. This is evident from the fact that both Vedānta Deśika (14th century) and Aḻakiya-maṇavāḷa-perumāḷ Nāyanār (the younger brother of Piḷḷailokācārya) have made special effort to establish the *Vedatva* for the Tamil hymns. The Vaiṣṇava Ācāryas from the time of Nāthamuni realized the importance and value of Tamil poems as a Vedāntic work and they have therefore accorded to it a Vedic status to establish its authoritativeness as a source-book for Vedānta. Realizing the value of the *Tiruvāymoḻi* for the study of the Theistic System of Vedānta, Rāmānuja got a commentary written on it by Piḷḷān, his trusted disciple. This undertaking of Piḷḷān is not intended to combine two distinct

Vaiṣṇava traditions or theologies. On the other hand, it was intended to amalgamate. Similar teachings of Vaiṣṇava religion expressed in two different languages. The adoption of *maṇipravāḷa* or the Tamil interspersed with Sanskrit was not, therefore, intended for the purpose of merging together two distinct traditions. Nor is it correct to say that the acknowledgement of dual Vedānta by the Vaiṣṇava Ācāryas lead to the adoption of maṇipravāḷa in order to spread the knowledge of two scriptures in a common language.[1] Actually, it became a necessity to adopt maṇipravāḷa in order to interpret a classical Tamil poem containing Vedāntic concepts because it was easier to explain the philosophical import of the hymns by using Sanskrit phrases instead of the pure Tamil terms. Besides, a philosophical work written in such a style becomes understandable by the common people who are not fully conversant with Sanskrit.

We now comeback to our basic question. What then is *Ubhaya-vedānta*? In the light of the facts, we have so far noticed, the term in a strict technical sense should be applicable to the religio-philosophical works which embody the teachings contained in both the Sanskrit Vedānta and the Tamil Vedānta. The extensive commentaries on the *Tiruvāymoḻi* present manifestly the Vaiṣṇava Philosophy and religion by drawing material from both the sources—the Sanskrit Vedānta texts and the Tamil *Prabandhams* both of which deal with the same subject-matter in two different languages. The *Ārāyirappaḍi* of Piḷḷān and the *Īḍu* of Vaḍakkutiruvīdi Piḷḷai are two best examples of *Ubhaya-vedānta* texts. In both these works we can notice how extensively the contents of *Śrī-bhāṣya* are mixed with those of the *Tiruvāymoḻi*. Among the independent Vaiṣṇava treatises, the *Rahasya-traya-sāra* of Vedānta Deśika and the *Śrīvacana-bhūṣaṇa* of Piḷḷailokācārya offer another example of *Ubhaya-vedānta*. The term *Ubhaya-vedānta* should, therefore, be applicable to the Vedānta or Theology that is embodied in these works and not to any new system of Vedānta or Theology as supposed to have been developed by combining two distinct Vaiṣṇava traditions. In a broad sense even the *Tiruvāymoḻi* can be claimed to contain *Ubhaya-vedānta* as it also incorporate Upaniṣadic teachings. In the same way, *Śrī-bhāṣya* of Rāmānuja is also *Ubhaya-vedānta* work as it contains implicitly

1. See K.K.A. Venkatachari, *Śrīvaiṣṇava Maṇi-pravāḷa*, p. 4.

the Āḻvārs teachings. On the same ground the traditional teaching transmitted orally through the *guruparamparās* from the time of Nammāḻvār, who is the *kulapati* of Śrīvaiṣṇavas, can be treated as *Ubhaya-vedānta*. But in a technical sense, it would be more appropriate to use this title for the *maṇipravāḷa* works which present the same old Vedānta Philosophy and Vaiṣṇava religion by drawing material from the basic Vedānta texts in Sanskrit and the Tamil works of the Āḻvārs. The *Ubhaya vedāntin* is one who has acquired scholarship in both Sanskrit Vedānta works such as *Śrī-bhāṣya* and the commentaries on the *Tiruvāymoḻi* including the maṇipravāḷa Vaiṣṇava treatises dealing with esoteric doctrines (*Sampradāya Granthas*).

IV. *The Influence of Tamil Prabandhams on Rāmānuja and His Successors*

The question has been raised by some Western Scholars as to whether Rāmānuja was influenced by the teachings of the Āḻvārs. The orthodox Vaiṣṇavas accept the *guruparamparā* tradition, according to which Tirumalai Āṇḍān, a direct disciple of Yāmuna taught the meaning of *Tiruvāymoḻi* to Rāmānuja.[1] There are several references in the *Īḍu* to Rāmānuja's views or interpretations of the hymns of *Tiruvāymoḻi* and these indicate that he himself was teaching it to his pupils. It is also believed that the first and foremost commentary on *Tiruvāymoḻi* written by Tirukkurukai Pirān Piḷḷān records what is taught to him by Rāmānuja and that this commentary was prepared at the instance of Rāmānuja. No one in the Vaiṣṇava circle questions about these facts. Nevertheless a doubt arises in this regard since in none of his works Rāmānuja makes any reference either to Nammāḻvār by name or to any of his hymns. For a modern scholar this is a puzzling issue.

That Rāmānuja was acquainted with the Tamil *Prabandham* need not be doubted because as a scholar born in Śrīperumbudur (Tamil Nadu) he would have certainly known it. Tirumalai Āṇḍān was reputed to be an authority on both the Vedānta as recorded by Āndhrapūrṇa also known as Vaḍuka Nambi, a disciple of Rāmānuja in the *Yatirāja-vaibhava*, a biographical poem on

1. See RTS, *Guruparamparā-sāra Tirumalai Āṇḍān śrīpādattile tiruvāymoḻikku artham kēṭṭaruḷinār.*

Rāmānuja.[1] He taught to Rāmānuja what he had learnt from his own teacher, Yāmuna. We could also reasonably guess that Rāmānuja having acquired the knowledge of *Tiruvāymoḻi* would have made use of it in writing his commentaries on the *Vedānta-sūtra*[2] and the *Bhagavadgītā* and also other independent treatises. He has also drawn material from the works of Yāmuna who himself was influenced by the teachings of the Āḻvārs as is evident from several verses in *Stotraratna* which reflect the Tamil hymns of the Āḻvārs. Though Yāmuna does not quote the hymns directly in any of his works, he pays obeisance to Nammāḻvār by name (as *Vakulābhirāma*) at the outset of his *Stotraratna*. Rāmānuja too would have shown similar respect to his spiritual ancestor, Nammāḻvār, following the Vaiṣṇava tradition of paying homage to all the earlier preceptors ending with God who is the *prathama-guru* or the first primary preceptor.

Why then he did not refer to the hymns of Nammāḻvār directly? This is an intriguing question. A plausible explanation for the silence of Rāmānuja can be found. Rāmānuja has written nine works. These are: *Śrībhāṣya* (a detailed commentary on *Vedānta-sutra*); *Vedānta-dīpa* and *Vedānta-sāra* (two smaller commentaries on the same); *Vedārtha-saṅgraha*, which is a treatise primarily concerned with commenting the selected, disputed Upaniṣadic texts; three *gadyas* or prose-lyrics primarily dealing with *Śaraṇāgati* (self-surrender) and lastly *nitya-grantha* on the mode of worship of God. The major objective of *Śrī-bhāṣya* is to interpret the *Vedānta-sūtras* in such a manner as to uphold the theory that Brahman is *saviśeṣa* or qualified with attributes, that the individual souls (*cit*) and the universe (*acit*) are absolutely real and that Brahman as organically related to *cit* and *acit* is one Reality (*Viśiṣṭādvaita*). In this endeavour, it was a major pre-occupation for Rāmānuja to defend his thesis against the theories that had been thus far advanced by the rival schools of Vedānta, Advaita Vedānta of Śaṁkara and the *bhedā-bheda-vāda*

1. See *Yatirāja-vaibhava*, verse 1
śrīmad-yāmuna deśikād-adhigata-śrutyanta-yugmāśayaḥ.
The word *Śrutyanta-yugma* conveys the idea of *Ubhaya-vedānta* (*Śrutyanta* means end of Veda and *yugma* means two). This is the first time that we come across this phrase in the extant Vaiṣṇava literature.
2. See AH *sūtra* 65 *Bhāṣyakārar idai koṇḍu sūtra-vyākhyānaṅgaḷ orunga viḍuvār.* See also the commentary of Maṇavāḷamāmuni on this *sūtra.*

of Bhāskara and Yādava. When he was engaged in a disputation of this kind with a rival school of thought, it is but appropriate that following the traditional convention of logicians, to concentrate on the defence of his theories, on the basis of the very *pramāṇas* accepted by the adversaries which consisted of Scriptural and *Smṛti* texts. In such a situation, he must have felt that it would be inappropriate to bring in the Tamil hymns of the Āḻvārs as a *pramāṇa,* even if it had appeared as valid to him since it was not accepted as a valid *pramāṇa* by the rival schools. In view of this position, Rāmānuja refrained from making any reference to the Āḻvārs in his *Śrī-bhāṣya* as well as the two other commentaries on the *Vedānta-sūtra.* The same principle applies to *Vedārtha-saṅgraha* and the *Gītā-bhāṣya.* We can judge the extent of his intellectual honesty from the fact that Rāmānuja strictly confines himself only to such selected principal Upaniṣads and the Purāṇas such as *Viṣṇu Purāṇa* which were accepted as authoritative by his rival Vedāntin, Śaṁkara.

The three *Gadyas,* the prose lyrics, are theological in character dealing primarily with *prapatti* and incidentally with God and His attributes, *paramapada* and *nitya-kaiṅkarya.* Though there is some scope in these works to refer to the Āḻvārs, he did not make any reference to their hymns for a justifiable reason. In the three *Gadyas,* Rāmānuja speaks in very personal terms in his capacity as a devotee who has totally surrendered to God and describes the manner in which he performed *śaraṇāgati* at the feet of the Supreme Lord associated with Goddess *Śrī,* by expressing his own inability to observe any other *upāya* for *mokṣa,* seeking forgiveness for all offences (*apacāra*) committed by him and invoking divine grace for himself to render *nitya-kaiṅkarya* in the *paramapada.* In such a narration, which sounds like the personal confession and prayer for a higher spiritual goal, the question of quoting the views of Āḻvārs does not arise.

As regards the *nitya-grantha* dealing with daily rituals, including worship of God, its nature and content is such that it does not warrant any material to be drawn from the Āḻvārs.

All these facts explain the absence of any direct references to the Āḻvārs in the works of Rāmānuja. To assume as some American scholars have done,[1] that Rāmānuja being a conservative

1. See John Carman and Vasudha Narayana, *The Tamil Veda,* p. 54.

Brahman did not like to mention in his Sanskrit works anything not written in Sanskrit, would be wrong.

Whether or not Rāmānuja referred to the Āḻvārs and whether or not he commanded Piḷḷān to write a commentary on the *Tiruvāymoḻi*, the fact remains that he has been influenced in several ways by the hymns of the Āḻvārs. Though Rāmānuja primarily owes his allegiance to the sage Bodhāyana and the principal Upaniṣads in writing his *Śrī-bhāṣya*, as is evident from his own words, he has been guided by the teachings of the Āḻvārs in the interpretation of certain crucial Upaniṣadic texts and in formulating certain theological doctrines.[1] We have taken note of these points in the concerned chapters. However, as an epilogue we may recall briefly the nature and extent of the influence of the Āḻvārs on Rāmānuja.

The central doctrine of the Viśiṣṭādvaita Vedānta is that Brahman as the *Śarīrin* or the universal soul is organically related to the universe of *cit* (sentient souls) and *acit* (not-sentient entities) in the same way as the soul is related to the physical body. This is known as *śarīrātma-bhāva sambandha*. The main scriptural authority for the formulation of this theory is the *Antaryāmī Brāhmaṇa* of the *Bṛhadāraṇyaka Upaniṣad* which mentions specifically that the five elements and other entities in the universe including the soul are *śarīra* of body of Brahman as *antaryāmin*. On the strength of this scriptural text Rāmānuja advances his theory of organic relation. In interpreting this particular Upaniṣadic passage in favour of his main thesis, Rāmānuja would have derived both inspiration and support from Nammāḻvār's hymns in which he speaks in clear terms that the Supreme Being pervades everything in the universe on the analogy of body-soul relationship. The *Antarayāmī Brāhmaṇa* would have been noticed by the Vedāntins of other schools of thought prior to Rāmānuja but none of them offered the kind of interpretation that Rāmānuja advanced. From this it may be concluded that Rāmānuja was guided by the teaching of Nammāḻvār in this regard. We have explained in an earlier chapter how Nammāḻvār has presented the details of the theory and the impact of the Āḻvārs' teachings on the same.[2]

---

1. See fn 2, p. 277.
2. See Chapter 2, pp. 51-60.

The keynote of Vaiṣṇavism is that Viṣṇu or Nārāyaṇa is the Supreme Deity (*para-devatā*) who is higher than Brahmā, Rudra and all other *devatās* and Goddess *Śrī* is inseparably related to Him. *Para-tattva* in other words, is *Śriyaḥpati* or *Tirumāl.* Rāmānuja upholds this theory in all his writings. Though this theory is supported by the Upaniṣads, *Viṣṇu Purāṇa* and other religious texts, the Āḻvārs have enunciated it in a clear way on the basis of their intuitive experience of God. Their statements which carry the authority of personal experience have provided support to Rāmānuja in formulating this theory.

The description of Godhead in all its aspects such as *svarūpa, rūpa, guṇa, vibhava, līlā* etc., as provided in the *Gadyas* is superb. Where did Rāmānuja derive these ideas? As we have explained in the chapter on the Doctrine of God,[1] neither the Upaniṣads nor the *Smṛti* texts including the Pāñcarātra Āgamas present all these attributes in such picturesque manner. But these are found in the Tamil poems of Āḻvārs. The description of the glory of God in all aspects is not only vivid but looks so realistic that one cannot fail to notice an element of direct experience of Godhead by these mystic saints. It is therefore very likely that these have had a great impact on Rāmānuja.

The concept of *nirupādhika-śeṣatva* or the absolute unconditioned subordination of *jīva* to *paramātman* and the concept of *Bhāgavata-śeṣatva* or the subordination of an individual to the devotees of God are the two significant features of Vaiṣṇava theology to which Rāmānuja has accorded great importance. Both these ideas are not explicit in the Upaniṣads. There are a few references to them in the Itihāsas and Purāṇas. But as we have noticed in an earlier chapter,[2] several Āḻvārs have placed great emphasis on these concepts. The direct influence of Āḻvārs on Rāmānuja and his followers in this regard can be noticed conspicuously.

Rāmānuja has used three terms, namely *parabhakti, parajñāna* and *parama-bhakti* in his prose lyric. He was the first among the Vaiṣṇava Ācāryas to employ these words. We do not find any mention of these concepts either in the Upaniṣads or the *Viṣṇu Purāṇa* and the *Bhagavadgītā* where *bhakti* as a *sādhana* for *mokṣa*

---

1. See Chapter 3, pp. 79-80.
2. See Chapter 4, pp. 137-39.

finds a prominent place. What could be the source of it for Rāmānuja? Obviously it is the *prabandham* of Nammāḻvār that has provided the basis for it. Though these terms as such are not mentioned in the hymns, the ideas underlying the three concepts are clearly found in them. As we have seen in the chapter on the Theistic Mysticism,[1] these are the phases of *bhakti* which constitute the three facets of mystic experience of God. The influence of the Āḻvārs on Rāmānuja in this regard is undeniable.

The most significant contribution of the Āḻvārs to Vaiṣṇavism as expounded by Rāmānuja and his followers lies in the advocacy of the doctrine of *prapatti* as a direct means to *mokṣa*. Although we can find this doctrine in the Pāñcarātra Saṁhitās and the Itihāsas as well as Purāṇas, the acceptance of *prapatti* as a *sādhana* in preference to the *Bhakti-yoga* and its observance as a ritual for the attainment of *mokṣa* was put into practice by Nammāḻvār for the first time among the Vaiṣṇava saints. Among the extant works, we see that Yāmuna adopted it, and following his example, Rāmānuja too has demonstrated its observance as a direct *sādhana* to *mokṣa* in his *Śaraṇāgati-gadya*. The lead for observance of *prapatti* has thus come from Nammāḻvār and he is, therefore, rightly regarded as *prapanna-jana-kūṭastha* or the leader of the *prapannas*.[2]

The theory of *nitya-kaiṅkarya* or uninterrupted divine service in *paramapada* as the supreme spiritual goal has been incorporated by Rāmānuja into the Vaiṣṇava theology. He refers to it in the *Gadyas* and prays to God to bless him with it in the state of *mokṣa*. Neither the Upaniṣads nor the *Vedānta-sūtra* make any mention of it explicitly. But the Āḻvārs have spoken about it with special emphasis.[3]

These are some of the important doctrines adopted by Rāmānuja on the basis of the teachings of the Āḻvārs. There may be many other ideas which he would have borrowed. According to tradition, the Vaiṣṇava *sat-sampradāya* owes its beginning (leaving out the Divine Beings) to *Nammāḻvār*, who is acknowledged as the *kulapati*,[4] the founder seer of Vaiṣṇava theology. He

---

1. See Chapter 7, pp. 177-80.
2. See Chapter 5, pp. 143-45.
3. See Chapter 6, pp. 167-69.
4. See *Stotraratna*, verse 5: *ādyasya naḥ kulapateḥ vakuḷābhirāmaṁ.*

imparted the esoteric doctrines to Madhurakavi from whom it was transmitted in succession right up to Nāthamuni. Nammāḻvār also taught the Tamil hymns to Nāthamuni in his Yogic state.[1] These teachings were further passed on orally from one Ācārya to another in succession. Following this tradition of *guruparamparā*, Rāmānuja would have definitely received instruction from his own preceptors on the essential teachings of Nammāḻvār.

V. *The Āḻvārs and the Vaiṣṇava Sects*

We are now left with the question whether the controversial doctrines that developed during the post-Rāmānuja period between the two Vaiṣṇava sects—Teṅkalai and Vaḍakaḻai—owe their origin to the teachings of the Āḻvārs. On the philosophical side, there is hardly any room for controversy between the two sects. Both of them owe their allegiance to Rāmānuja and both accept all the tenets of Viśiṣṭādvaita Vedānta as expounded in the *Śrī-bhāṣya*. Both have also acknowledged the authoritative nature of the *Ubhaya-Vedānta*. However, on the theological side there are a few doctrines on which they have some dispute. These have been listed in some of the later Vaiṣṇava works under the title of *aṣṭādaśa-bhedas* or eighteen points of difference.[2] Most of these are of minor character and do not have any philosophical significance. The important ones which have bear-

---

1. See RTS, *Guruparamparā-sāra,*
ivarukku madhurakavihaḻ mudalāha uṇḍāna sampradāya paramparaiyālum tiruvāymoḻi mukhattālum yogadaśaiyile sākṣātkṛtarāyum nammāḻvār ācāryarānār.
2. These are summed up in one single verse:
bhedaḥ svāmikṛpā phala anyagatiṣu śrīvyāpti upāyātyayaḥ
tad-vātsalya dayā-nirukti vacasoḥ nyāse ca tatkartari;
dharmatyāga virodhayoḥ sva-vihite nyāsāṅga-hetutvayoḥ
prāyaścitavidhau tadīya-bhajane aṇuvyāpti kaivalyayoḥ.
The topics mentioned in this verse are: 1. difference in Divine grace; 2. difference in *mokṣa-phala*; 3. types of *upāya*; 4. ontological status of Goddess *Śrī*; 5. Goddess serving as *upāya* for *mokṣa*; 6. meaning of the term *vātsalya*; 7. meaning of the term *dayā*; 8. nature of *prapatti*; 9. eligibility for observing *prapatti*; 10. renouncement of *dharma* as *aṅga* of *prapatti*; 11. incompatibility of *upāya* with the *jīva-svarūpa*; 12. observance of *varṇāśrama-dharma* by a *prapanna*; 13. compliance with the prescribed prerequisites of *prapatti*; 14. *prapatti* as a *sādhana* for *mokṣa*; 15. need to expiate sins committed intentionally by a *prapanna*; 16. the worshipping a low caste *bhāgavata* by a Brahmin; 17. the nature of pervasion of God in souls which are monadic; 18. the nature of *kaivalya*.

ing on the teachings of the Āḻvārs are the following:

1. The ontological status of Goddess *Śrī.*
2. The nature of *prapatti* as a *sādhana* or *upāya* to *mokṣa.*
3. The concept of divine grace (*svāmi-kṛpā* or *aruḻ*).
4. The observance of *nitya-naimittika karma* by a *prapanna.*
5. The theory of *kaivalya.*

We shall examine these briefly with reference to the hymns of the Āḻvārs to find out if they lend any support to the controversies.

The main issue relating to the status of Goddess *Śrī* is whether or not She is an integral part of God. If Goddess is part of the divinity, even though the two are separate ontological entities, She would enjoy equal status with God and as such She has a role in all the important divine functions. If She is not part of divinity, She would remain a beloved consort of God with a subordinate status like an exalted individual soul performing certain limited functions such as *puruṣakāratva.* The Vaḍakalai sect maintains the first view, while Teṅkalai sect subscribes to the second.

The views of the Āḻvārs on the subject of Goddess are fully presented in an earlier chapter.[1] If we go by the hymns without bringing in the interpretations of the later commentators, we can notice that Goddess is inseparably related to God and the two together serve as the *upāya* or means to *mokṣa* by removing the *karma* (*vinai*) standing as the obstacles for God-realization. The hymns also state that both shower grace on the devotees and confer *mokṣa.* These hymns understood in the context in which they are sung do not lend any support to the controversy that has arisen at a later period. Nowhere is there any mention in the poems about *Śrī* being monadic (*aṇu*) like an individual soul and occupying a subordinate position. The commentators on the *Tiruvāymoḻi* also do not express such a view. The source for the controversy surrounding the theory of Goddess is, therefore, to be sought elsewhere.

On the theory of *prapatti,* the main controversy is related to the need of its observance as a prescribed *sādhana* for the purpose of *mokṣa.* If *mokṣa* is to be secured solely by the grace of

1. See Chapter 2, pp. 70-75.

God (*aruḷ*), where is the need of a *sādhana* which involves human effort? The issue finally centres round the subject of divine grace *vis-à-vis* human effort. If eventually the unconditioned *kṛpā*, known as *nirhetuka-kṛpā*, in Vaiṣṇava terminology, is instrumental in granting *mokṣa*, there would be no need to perform *prapatti* as a ritualistic act in the form of surrendering one's self to God with the compliance of the five requisite components (*aṅgas*) or *prapatti*. This is the position taken by the Teṅkalai sect. This view is controverted by Vaḍakalai sect which insists on the observance of the *prapatti* as a ritualistic act in order to secure the grace of God. It contends that if God were to confer a boon like *mokṣa* without a specific prayer or some effort on the part of an individual, He would be open to the criticism of abritrariness.

The views of the Āḻvārs on the subject of *prapatti* as a means to *mokṣa* and the role of Divine grace are stated in the chapter on the Doctrine of Sādhana.[1] The hymns of the Āḻvārs convey the idea of both the *sahetuka-kṛpā* and *nirhetuka-kṛpā* but they do not imply any conflict between the two.[2] The Āḻvārs have no doubt emphasised the need of *aruḷ* to overcome bondage and attain the spiritual goal. But at the same time they have all advocated strongly the observance of a *sādhana* either *prapatti* or *bhakti*. They have also resorted to *prapatti* to attain God. If we examine the relevant hymns dispassionately without bringing in the interpretation of the commentators, we do not find sufficient basis for the view that *nirhetuka kṛpā* of God, without the observance of some *sādhana*, is the means to *mokṣa*.[3]

Regarding the theory of *kaivalya*, the main point of dispute is whether or not it is a permanent state of existence for the individual soul deprived of *Brahmānubhava* for ever. Based on the teaching of the *Bhagavadgītā*, the Teṅkalai sect holds the view that *kaivalya* is a permanent state of existence for the soul and it is ever deprived of *Brahmānubhava*. On the contrary, the Vaḍakalai sect maintains that the soul even after reaching *kaivalya* can attain *mokṣa* proper by doing *upāsanā* on Brahman as in the case of the *upāsaka* embarking on *madhuvidyā* referred to in the

1. See Chapter 5.
2. See Chapter 3, pp. 93-94.
3. See Chapter 5, pp. 102-03.

Vedānta-sūtra.[1]

The views of the Āḻvār on this subject are stated in the chapter on the Doctrine of Supreme Goal.[2] Nammāḻvār looks upon expressly *kaivalya* as an inferior state of liberation, because it falls short of the blissful experience of God. But he does not say categorically that those who attain the state of *kaivalya* after being liberated from bondage proceed to a supramundane realm through the *arcirādi mārga* and ever remain there without an opportunity for *Brahmānubhava*: We cannot, therefore, find any material in the hymns to support the view of Teṅkalai sect on this subject. Apparently, it is a theory that was developed in the post-Rāmānuja period.

On the question of the observance of the *nitya-naimittika karma* or the mandatory daily rituals by a *prapanna*, there is a dispute between the two sects. Taking its stand on the teaching of the *Bhagavadgītā* relating to self-surrender which demands the renouncement of all *dharmas* (*sarva-dharma parityāga*), the Teṅkalai sect holds the view that the prescribed mandatory daily rituals are also to be given up as a prerequisite (*aṅga*) of *prapatti*. The Vaḍakalai sect on the other hand, contends that the renunciation of all *dharmas* do not include the *nitya-naimittika karma* because these are binding on every individual as part of the *varṇāśrama-dharma* and should not be given up under any circumstances. The only difference between a *prapanna* and the one who has embarked on *bhakti-yoga* is that the former observes it as a *kaiṅkarya* or divine service for the pleasure of God, whereas the latter follows it as subsidiary (*aṅga*) to *bhakti-yoga*.

The hymns of Nammāḻvār refer indirectly to the teachings of the *Bhagavadgītā* on both *bhakti-yoga* and *prapatti* but they do not cover this issue. The hymn in which he exhorts the renouncement of everything (*vīḍumin muṟṟavum*), refers to the abandonment of attachment to worldly objects and not to the religious duties. The Āḻvārs have extolled the orthodox Brahmins who scrupulously perform the prescribed daily rituals and Vedic *yāgas*. As part of the mode of worship, Nammāḻvār commends the

1. See RB on VS I.3.32.
2. See Chapter VI, pp. 170-72.

worship of God with the recitation of the Vedic *mantras.* From these statements, it can be inferred that the Āḻvārs have not suggested any dispensation of the prescribed rituals by a devotee following either the *bhakti-mārga* or *prapatti.*

From the foregoing analysis of the views of the Āḻvārs, it may be observed that the existing controversies between the two Vaiṣṇava sects cannot be traced in their hymns. It cannot also be said that the acceptance of the *Ubhaya-vedānta* and the possible undue importance given to the Tamil *prabandhams* as against the Sanskrit Vedānta texts have caused the split of the Vaiṣṇava community into two sects. It is generally believed that the *teṅkalai,* which literally means southern culture, applies to those who give greater prominence to the Tamil *prabandhams,* whereas *Vaḍakalai,* which means northern culture, refers to those who give greater importance to Sanskrit tradition. This is far from the truth. These two terms—*Teṅkalai* and *Vaḍakalai*—have come into usage to represent the followers of Maṇavāḷamāmuni and Vedānta Deśika respectively, the two Ācāryas to whom they owe a special allegiance in addition to Rāmānuja and Nammāḻvār. Maybe a section of Śrīvaiṣṇavas of Teṅkaḻai sect have shown greater devotion to the works of the Āḻvārs since these have greater emotional appeal as compared to the terse Sanskrit Vedānta texts. Similarly, a section of the Vaḍakalai Śrīvaiṣṇavas may have given greater importance to the Sanskrit texts than to the devotional Tamil hymns of the Āḻvārs. But this kind of partial attitude towards the works of *Ubhaya-vedānta* has not given rise to the split of the community, because eminent Vaiṣṇava Ācāryas belonging to both sects have wholly accepted the authority and importance of both *Śrī-bhāṣya* of Rāmānuja and the *Divya-prabandham* of the Āḻvārs. In fact, it is Vedānta Deśika who re-affirmed the Vedic or Upaniṣadic status accorded to the Tamil *Prabandham.* Raṅgarāmānuja, Periya Parakālasvāmi and Sākṣātsvāmi who were the followers of Vedānta Deśika have written scholarly commentaries on the *Tiruvāymoḻi.* They are also scholars in the area or *Śrī-bhāṣya.* Similarly, Nañjīyar, Periyavāccān Piḷḷai and Vaḍakku Tiruvīdipiḷḷai, who have written extensive commentaries on the *Tiruvāymoḻi* have exhibited their deep knowledge in *Śrī-bhāṣya* of Rāmānuja. Further, the Vaiṣṇava Ācāryas of both the sects who have written independent treatises in Maṇipravāḷa known as *Sampradāya granthas* on the esoteric doctrines of Vaiṣṇavism have drawn material both from the Sanskrit Vedānta works and Tamil *Prabandhams*. We cannot therefore attribute the split of the community to the *Divyaprabandham* of Āḻvārs. How and when it arose is a matter that needs further examination. This task falls outside the scope of this book.

To sum up, the period of the Āḻvārs and their rich poetical compositions mark an important stage in the history of Śrī Vaiṣṇavism. Their sublime songs inspired by intense devotion to God and Divine experience contain rich philosophical and theological ideas. Their teachings have had a strong influence on the Vaiṣṇava Ācāryas including Rāmānuja.

GLOSSARY

Ācārya: Spiritual preceptor.

ādhāra: the supporter; that which serves as the ground of the universe.

ādheya: the supported; that which is supported by God.

advaita: non-dualism; system of Vedānta associated with Śaṁkara.

Ādiśeṣa: divine serpent.

Ādipirān: primordial deity; Nārāyaṇa.

Āgamas: Revealed scripture; the treatises dealing with modes of worship of God and matters relating to temples.

aiśvarya: lordship; one of the six principal attributes of God.

Āḻvār: one who is deeply immersed in God's experience; the Vaiṣṇava Saints of South India.

amala: pure; free from defects.

aṁśa: a part; an integral part of the complex whole.

amṛta: immortal.

ānanda: bliss; blissful.

ananta: infinite; countless.

andādi: a poetical composition in which the last word of the preceding verse is used as the first word of the succeeding verse.

antarātmā: the indwelling self; the Paramātman who is immanent in all beings.

Antaryāmin: the inner controller; the immanent Supreme Being.

aṇu: monad; subtle.

apauruṣeya: not ascribed to a human author.

arcā: idol of worship; icon; incarnation of God by entering into

the idols chosen by devotees.
aruḷ: grace; compassion.
ātman: the self; the individual self.
avatāra: descent of God; incarnation of God.
āvirbhāva: manifestation.

Bhagavān: God; Viṣṇu; Nārāyaṇa.
bhāgavata: a devotee of Viṣṇu.
bhajana: worship; mode of worship.
bhakti: loving devotion.
bhakti-yoga: unceasing meditation on God as a means to *mokṣa*.
bheda: difference.
Brahmā: the vedic deity entrusted with the task of creation of the universe.
Brahman: the Ultimate Reality; the personal God according to Viśiṣṭādvaita.

cetana: sentient being; individual soul.
cintana: contemplation.

darśana: direct vision.
dāsa: subordinate; one who is subservient to God.
dayā: compassion.
devatā: vedic deity; celestial being.
dhyāna: meditation.
divya: divine; sacred.
divyaprabandham: Divine compositions of Āḻvārs.

drāviḍa: Tamil.
dravya: a substance.

gadā: mace; Visnu's weapon.
gadya: a prose lyric.
garuḍa: Divine bird; Viṣṇu's mount.
ghaṭaka: a mediator.
grantha (paḍi): a unit of 32 letters.
guṇa: a quality; an attribute.
guruparamparā: the genealogy of preceptors.

heya: defect; evil.
heya-pratyanīka: opposed to everything that is defiling or evil.
hita: means to achieve the supreme goal.

īḍu: the commentary on the Tiruvāymoḻi known as *muppattiyārāyirappaḍi.*
indriya: sense organ.
Īśvara: Supreme Ruler; God.

jīva: individual self.
jñāna: knowledge; consciousness.

kāla: time.
kāma: desire; conjugal love; love towards God.
kāraṇa: cause.
kāruṇya: compassion.
khadga: sword; Viṣṇu's weapon.
kṛpā: compassion; grace.
kalyāṇaguṇa: auspicious attributes of God.
kṣamā: forgiveness.
kaiṅkarya: loving service; divine service.
kaivalya: the state of existence of the self in its true form as free from bondage; a state of liberation.
kulapati: the founder seer of the Vaiṣṇava community.

līlā: divine deed; sport.

manana: logical reflection.
mantra: esoteric syllables or words signifying spiritual ideas; a vedic hymn.
Maṇipravāḷa: a style of writing in which Tamil words are interspersed with Sanskrit words; Sanskritised Tamil prose.
mokṣa: liberation of soul from bondage; a complete and comprehensive experience of Brahman.
mumukṣu: an aspirant for *mokṣa.*

namaskāra (namana): offering salutation; self-surrender.
nāyaka: a lover; the beloved Lord.
nāyakī: a maiden; the beloved consort of God.
nididhyāsana: steadfast meditation.

nimittakāraṇa: instrumental cause.
nirhetuka-kṛpā: unconditioned flow of divine grace or compassion.
nirviśeṣa: devoid of all attributes; undifferentiated.
nitya: eternal.
nitya-kaiṅkarya: eternal divine service.
nitya-vibhūti: eternal transcendental realm.
niyantā: controller of all beings; God.

para: the highest; the supreme.
parabhakti: the perfected stage of meditation serving as direct means to *mokṣa*.
para-devatā: the supreme deity.
parajñāna: vision of God; a stage of meditation giving rise to temporary vision of God.
paramātmā: the Supreme Self; God.
parama-puruṣārtha: the supreme spiritual goal.
paraṁ-jyotis: the transcendental light; Brahman.
paramapada: the supreme abode of Viṣṇu.
parama-bhakti: the highest state of meditation culminating in the liberation of soul.
Paratattva: the Ultimate Reality; Nārāyaṇa.
phala: fruit.
prabandha: a composition of Tamil hymns of Āḻvārs.
prabhā: light; luminosity.
prādurbhāva: manifestation of God.
prapatti: total self-surrender to God as the sole refuge.
prāptā: one who seeks to attain God.
prāptivirodha: obstacle in the way of attaining God.
prāptyupāya: means of attaining the supreme goal.
prāpya: the goal to be achieved; God.
pratikūla: disagreeable.
prīti: love; devotion.
puruṣakāra; an interceder; mediatrix of grace.
puruṣārtha: the goal of human endeavour.
puruṣottama: the Supreme person; God.

rakṣaka: saviour; God.
rasa: blissful.
rāsakrīḍa: a kind of sportive dance practised by Kṛṣna and the

gopis of Bṛndavan.
rūpa: colour; divine personality.
rahasya-grantha: a treatise dealing with esoteric doctrines.
Rudra: a vedic deity entrusted with the task of dissolution of the universe; Śiva.

sādhana: a means adopted to achieve a goal; a spiritual discipline serving as means to attain God.
śakti: power.
sākṣātkāra: direct vision.
saṁśleṣa: communion with God.
sāmya: equality.
śaṅka: conch; Viṣṇu's weapon.
saṅkalpa: will of God.
śaraṇāgati: surrendering to God as the sole refuge.
śarīra: body; that which is necessarily supported and controlled by God.
śarīrin: the owner of the śarīra; God.
sarvajña: omniscient.
satyakāma: ever desired God.
śāraṅga: bow; divine weapon.
sattā: existence.
satyasaṅkalpa: firm resolve of God.
saulabhya: easy accessibility; a divine attribute.
śeṣa: one who exists for the purpose of God; the dependent.
śeṣin: one who utilizes the śeṣa for his purpose; the Lord.
śeṣavṛtti: Divine service.
sevya: to be sought as supreme goal.
Śriyaḥpati: the consort of Goddess *Śrī*.
sauśīlya: gracious condescension.
śubha: auspicious.
svabhāva: essential attribute of an entity.
svarūpa: the essential nature of an entity.

tanian: reverential verse; a verse paying obeiscance to a preceptor.
tapas: austerity.
tattva: the ultimate reality.
tejas: splendour.
Tirumāl: Lord Viṣṇu; Śriyaḥpati.

tulasī: basil leaf considered as holy and dear to Viṣṇu.

upabrāhmaṇa: that which elucidates the meaning of the Śruti texts.
upādānakāraṇa: material cause.
ubhaya: twofold; dual.
ubhaya-liṅga: the twofold characteristic of Brahman.
ubhaya-vedānta: Vedānta developed on the basis of the Upaniṣads and the hymns of the Āḻvārs.
upāya: means; the spiritual discipline adopted for *mokṣa*.

vātsalya: tender affection; an attribute of God.
vaibhava: greatness; glory.
vibhava: one of the forms of avatāra of Viṣṇu.
vibhu: all-pervasive; infinite.
vibhūti: property or glory of God.
vigraha: image of God.
vīrya: valour.
viśleṣa: separation from God.
viśeṣaṇa: a quality; an attribute.
Viṣṇupatnī: the beloved consort of Viṣṇu.
Viśvaksena: the divine angel.
vyūha: one of the five forms of incarnation of God.

yajana: one of the modes of worship of God.
yuga: epoch.
yuva: youth.

SELECT BIBLIOGRAPHY

I. *Tamil and Maṉipravāḷa Works*

1. Basic Source-book

Nālayira Divyaprabandham (collection of the Tamil hymns of the Āḻvārs including the *Rāmānujanūṟṟandādi*).[1]

2. Commentaries

Bhagavad-viṣayam—comprising the following commentaries in maṇipravāḷa on *Tiruvāymoḻi* of Nammāḻvār, 10 Vols.:

(a) Tirukkurukaipirān Piḷḷān, *Ārāyirappāḍi* (6000)
(b) Nañjīyar, *Onpadināyirappaḍi* (9000)
(c) Periyavāccān Piḷḷai, *Irupattunālāyirappāḍi* (24000)
(d) Vaḍakkutiruvīdi Piḷḷai, *Īdu Muppattiyārāyirappaḍi* (36000)
Ed. S. Krishnamacharya, Noble Press, Madras, 1924-30.

Bhagavad-viṣayam—comprising the following commentaries on *Tiruvāymoḻi* besides Piḷḷān's *Ārāyirappaḍi*, 2 Vols.:

(a) Raṅgarāmānuja, *Onpadināyirappaḍi* (9000) in Sanskrit
(b) Periya Parakāla Svāmi, *Padinennāyirappaḍi* (18000)
(c) Sākṣātsvāmi, *Irupattunāḻāyirappaḍi Śabdārtham*

---

1. There are several editions of *Nālāyira Divyaprabandham* but the texts used in this book are:
(a) The edition published by S.S. Iyengar, Madras, under the title *Candamihu Tamil Marai* in 4 vols.
(b) The edition published by S. Krishnaswamy Ayyangar, Puttur, Tiruchy.

(d) Vedānta Deśika, *Dramiḍopaniṣat-sāra* and *Dramiḍopaniṣat-tātparya Ratnāvalī.*
Ed. P.B. Annangaracharya, Conjeevaram, 1941.

Bhagavad-viṣayam—comprising the following commentaries besides Piḷḷān's *Ārāyirappaḍi,* 2 Vols.:

(a) Sākṣātsvāmi, *Irupattunālāyirappaḍi* (24000)—a glossary on Piḷḷān's *Ārāyirappaḍi* along with *Śabdārtham* on *Tiruvāymoḻi.* Ed. Tiruvenkatachar, Sundapalyam, 1912.

Mudalāyira Vyākhyānam (Commentaries on *Tiruppallāṇḍu, Periyāḻvār Tirumoḻi, Tiruppāvai, Nacciyār Tirumoḻi, Perumāḷ Tirumoḻi*) by Periya Parakāla Svāmi. Ed. P.B. Annagaracharya, Conjeevaram, 1942.

Munivāhana-bhogam (a commentary on *Amalanādipirān*) by Vedānta Deśika. Ed. Uttamur Veeraraghavacharya, Viśiṣṭādvaita Pracharini Sabha, Madras.

Periya Tirumoḻi Vyākhyānam by Periya Parakāla Svāmi, Ed. P.B. Annangaracharya, Conjeevaram, 1942.

Periya Tirumoli and other Prabandhams—*Vyākhyānam* (Commentary) by Periyavāccān Piḷḷai.
Published by Srivaisnavagrantha Mudrapaka Sabha, Madras, 1901-2.

Prabandha Rakṣā—a commentary in Tamil on *Tiruvāymoḻi* and other Prabandhams by Uttamur Veeraraghavacharya, Viśiṣṭādvaita Pracarini Sabha, Madras.

Divyārthadīpikā—a commentary in Tamil on *Tiruvāymoḻi* and other Prabandhams by P.B. Annangaracharya, Conjeevaram.

3. Other Works (related to Divyaprabandham)

Aḻakiya Maṇavāla perumāḷ Jīyar: *Ācārya Hṛdayam* with commentary of Maṇavāḷamāmuni
Ed. P.B. Annangaracharya, Conjeevaram.

Garuḍavāhana Paṇḍita: *Divyasūri-caritam*
Ed. Srinivasacharya, Granthamala Office, Conjeevaram, 1953.

Maṇavāḷamāmuni: *Upadeśaratnamālai* and *Tiruvāymoḻi Nūṟṟandādī*
Ed. P.B. Annangaracharya, Conjeevaram.

Pinpaḻakiya Perumāḷ Jīyar, *Guruparamparā Prabhāvam* (Ārāyirappaḍi)

Ed. S. Krishnaswamy Ayyangar, Tiruchy, 1975.
Tṛtīya Brahmatantra Parakāla Svāmi, *Guruparamparā Prabhāvam* (mūvāyirappaḍi) Lifco, Madras, 1968.
Vādikesari Aḻakiyamaṇavāla Jīyar, *Dramidopaniṣad Saṅgati* Ed. P.B. Annangaracharya, Conjeevaram, 1947.
Vedānta Deśika, *Dramiḍopaniṣat-sāra—Dramiḍopaniṣat-tātparya Ratnāvalī*, Srikrishna Sabha, Bombay, 1951.

4. General Works (in Sanskrit and Maṇipravāḷa)

Āḷavandār: *Catuḥślokī* with *Catuḥślokī-bhāṣyam* of Vedānta Deśika.
Gītārtha-saṅgraha with *Gītārtha-saṅgraha-rakṣā* of Vedānta Deśika.
Stotraratna with *Stotra-ratna-bhāṣyam* of Vedānta Deśika.
Nañjīyar: *Śrī-sūkta Bhāṣya*, Ed. A. Srinivasaraghavan, Pudukota, 1937.
Parāśara Bhattar: *Aṣṭaślokī*
Bhagavadguṇa-darpaṇa
Śrī-guṇaratnakośa
Śrī-raṅgarājastatva
Rāmānuja: *Bhagavadgītā-bhāṣya*
Brahmasūtra Śrī-bhāṣya with *Śrutaprakāśikā*, Viśiṣṭādvaita Pracharini Sabha, Madras.
Gadyatrayam with the commentary of Vedānta Deśika, Periyavāccān Piḷḷai and Śruta Prakāśika Bhattar. Śrīvaiṣṇavagrantha Mudrapaka Sabha, Madras.
Piḷḷailokācārya: *Arthapāncakam*
Mumukṣuppaḍi
Śrivacanabhūṣaṇam
Tattvatrayam with the Vyākhyānam of Maṇavāḷamāmuni
Ed. P.B. Annangaracharya, Conjeevaram.
Śrīvatsānka Miśra (Kūreśa): *Pañcastava* with commentary in Tamil, 2 Vols., Viśiṣṭādvaita Pracarini Sabha, Madras, 1968.
Vedānta Deśika: *Rahasyatrayasāra* and other *Rahasya-granthas*
Pāñcarātra-rakṣā
Nikṣepa-rakṣā
Sacaritra-rakṣā
Tattva-muktā-kalāpa with *Sarvārthasiddhi*
Ed. P.B. Annangaracharya, Conjeevaram.

II. *English Works*

Aiyangar, S.K.: A History of Early Vaiṣṇavism in South India, Madras University, Madras, 1920.

Balasubramanian, R.: The Mysticism of Poygai Āḻvār, Vedānta Publications, Madras, 1976.

Bhandarkar, R.G.: Vaiṣṇavism, Śaivism and Minor Religion (Reprint), Asian Educational Services, New Delhi, 1983.

Buitenen, J.A.B. Van: Rāmānuja on the Bhagavadgītā (Reprint), Motilal Banarsidass, New Delhi, 1968.

Dasgupta, S.N.: History of Indian Philosophy, Vol. III, Motilal Banarsidass, New Delhi.

Friedhelm, Hardy: Viraha-bhakti, The Early History of Kṛṣṇa Devotion in South India, Oxford University Press, Delhi, 1983.

Gopinath Rao, T.A.: History of Śrīvaiṣṇavas, Madras University, Madras, 1923.

Govindacharya, Alkondavilli: The Divine Wisdom of the Drāviḍa Saints, Madras, 1902.

Holy Lives of the Āḻvārs (Revised Ed.), Ananthacharya Indological Research Institute, Bombay, 1982.

Hooper, J.S.M.: The Hymns of the Āḻvārs, Association Press, Calcutta, 1929.

John B. Carman: The Theology of Rāmānuja (Indian Reprint) A. Indological Research Institute, Bombay, 1981.

John B. Carman and Vasudha Narayanan: The Tamil Veda—Pillan's interpretation of the *Tiruvāymoḻi*, The University of Chicago Press, Chicago, 1989.

John C. Plott: The Philosophy of Devotion, Motilal Banarsidass, Delhi, 1974.

Kaylor, R.D. and Venkatachari K.K.A.: God Far, God Near, Ananthacharya Indological Research Institute, Bombay, 1981.

Kurattalvar Ayyangar, N.: A Free Translation of Tiruvāymoḻi of Śaṭagopa, Tiruchy, 1929.

Otto Schrader: Introduction to the Pāñcarātra and Ahirbudhnya Saṁhitā (2nd Edn.), The Theosophical Society, Madras, 1973.

Raghavan, V.K.K.S.: The Amalanādipirān
Kaṇṇinum Śirattāmbu
Tiruppallāṇḍu

Tirupaḷḷiyeḷucci
Tiruppāvai
(with translation and notes)
Viśiṣṭādvaita Pracarini Sabha, Madras.

-do- Tirumālai
Tiruvāśiriyam
Tiruveḻukkuṟṟirukkai
(with translation and notes)
Madras University Journal, Madras.

Raghavachar, S.S.: Introduction to the Vedārtha-saṅgraha (2nd Edn.), Ramakrishna Ashrama, Mangalore, 1959.

Ramanuja, A.K.: Hymns for the Drowning—poems for Viṣṇu by Nammāḻvār, Princeton University Press, Princeton.

Ramaswamy Ayyangar, D.: Peeps into the Mysticism, Madras, 1942.

Satyamurthi Ayyangar: Tiruvāymoḻi—English Glossary, 2 Vols., Ananthacarya Indological Research Institute, Bombay, 1981.

Srinivasachari, P.N.: Mystics and Mysticism, Madras, 1951.
Philosophy of Viśiṣṭādvaita, Adyar Library Madras, 1943.

Srinivasachari, S.M.: Fundamentals of Viśiṣṭādvaita Vedānta, Motilal Banarsidass, Delhi, 1988.
Vaiṣṇavism—Its Philosophy Theology and Religious Discipline, Motilal Banarsidass, Delhi, 1994.

Subba Reddiar, N.: Religion and Philosophy of Nālāyiram with special reference to Nammāḻvār, Venkatesvara University, Tirupati, 1977.

Varadachari, K.C.: Āḻvārs of South India, Bharatiya Vidyabhavan, Bombay, 1966.

Varadachari, V.: Āgamas and South Indian Vaiṣṇavism, M. Rangacharya Memorial Trust, Madras, 1982.

Venkatachari, K.K.A.: Śrīvaiṣṇava Maṇipravāḷa, Ananthacharya Indological Research Institute, Bombay.

Vidyarthi, B.P.: Rāmānuja's Philosophy and Religion, M. Rangacharya Memorial Trust, Madras, 1977.

INDEX

Āḻvārs passim, chronology of 9; dates of 10-13; divine origin of 13-15; compositions of 32, 17, 18, 20, 22, 24, 25, 26, 27, 28, 30; their influence on Rāmānuja 234-37; their contribution to Viśiṣṭādvaita Vedānta and Vaiṣṇavism 238-40; see also individual Āḻvārs

amalan, as nature of God 44, 45, 69; as essential divine attribute 29, 71

Amalanādipirān, 29, 44, 86

amṛta (also amuda), God as 85

ānanda, as essential attribute of God 38, 70, 71, 84, 86

Āṇḍāḷ (also Goda), 24-25; as incarnation of Bhū-devī 24; compositions of 25; as female mystic 162; mysticism of 192; vision of Lord Kṛṣṇa by 207

ananta, Brahman as 70

antaryāmī (antarātmā), God as 38, 41, 49, 52, 102

Antaryāmī avatāra *see* avatāra

Antaryāmī Brāhmaṇa 45, 46, 50, 102

Ārāyirappaḍi passim, importance of 33-34

arcā (iconic form), passim, significance of 98-99; spiritual character of 99-100; as avatāra 97-98.

arcirādi-mārga, 150, 243

aruḷ *see* grace

aṣṭādaśa-bheda, 240

aṣṭākṣara, *see* Nārāyaṇa-mantra

aṣṭāṅga-yoga, 126

ātmanikṣepa, 133, 134; *see* also prapatti

attributes, of God, *see* Divine attributes

avatāra (Incarnation), doctrine of 90; five forms of 91; philosophy of 98; views of Āḻvārs on 92-94; para 94-95; vyūha 95; sub-vyūha forms of 93; vibhava 95-96; arcā 97-98; significance of arcā 98-99, 100-101; antaryāmi 101-2; anupraveśa 15, 223

Bhagavadgītā passim, teaching of bhakti-yoga in 121, 126-27, 130

Bhagavad-guṇas, *see* Divine attributes

Bhāgavatas (devotees of Viṣṇu), religion of 232; service to, *see* Bhāgavata-kaiṅkarya

Bhagavat-kaiṅkarya (Divine service) 26, as parama-puruṣārtha 145, 146, 239, *see* also Kaiṅkarya

Bhāgavata-kaiṅkarya, 26, 28, 118-19

Bhagavad-viṣayam, 90, 255

Bhāgavata-purāṇa, antiquity of 12-13; reference to Āḻvārs in 11-12; modes of bhakti in 147-8; mysticism in 184, 214.

Bhāgavata-śeṣatva, theory of 118-19, 238; views of Āḻvārs reg. 118-19.

bhakti, meaning of 153; Nammāḻvār's view on 154; nine modes of 103, 128; higher states of 154-55, 186, 238; emotional aspect of 155-56; as a goal 132, 136.

bhakti-yoga, theory of 126; as sādhana to mokṣa 121; the feature of 127; aṅgas of 126, 127, 128, 130; views of Nammāḻvār on 122-23; views of other Āḻvārs on 135-39

Bhūdevī, as consort of God 65, as personification of *kṣamā* 64, 66; relative ontological status of 64-65, 67

Brahmā, caturmukha, origin of 54-55; subordinate status of 18, 54, 55-57; cosmic function of 58-59

Brahman, *see* paratattva and Nārāyaṇa; definition of 39
Brahmānubhava, also Brahmasākṣātkāra, 143, 147, 148, 149, 155, 242-43

carama-śloka, 33, 229
commentaries, on Divyaprabandham 33-34; *see* also Ārāyirappaḍi and Īḍu muppattiyārāyarappaḍi

devotion, *see* bhakti
Divinity, *see* God
Divine attributes (bhagavad-guṇas), infinite number of 71; classification of 71, 72; essential 37-38, 42, 71; secondary 71, 74-83; as related to Sarveśvara 73-74, 77; as related to divine body (*vigraha*) 86; as revealed during avatāras 96, 97; as exhibited in the deeds (līlās) 105, 106, 107; ānandatva 38, 71; anantatva 70; amalatva 29, 44, 71; aparādhasahatva 166; āśritarakṣatva 166; āśritaikarasya 167; aiśvarya 77; audārya 82; bandhutva 82-83; bala 76; jñāna 74-75; Kṛpā, also Kāruṇya 80-82; paratva 106; śakti 75; saulabhya 78, 96, 107, 163; sauśīlya 78-79; tejas 76; vātsalya 79, 80, 107
Divine body (vigraha), 83; spiritual character of 84; beauty of 85-86, 87-88 justification for 90; ornaments and weapons on 88-89
Divine deeds (līlās), 103, 106.
Divine incarnations, *see* avatāra
Divine hymns, *see* Divyaprabandham
Divine service, *see* kaiṅkarya
Divyaprabandham, also prabandham passim, meaning of 2; names and classification of 32-33; distinctive character of 2; topics covered in 5-6; as source-book for Viśiṣṭādvaita Vedānta 3, 225; as Tamil Veda 221-25; as an exposition of Vaiṣṇava doctrines 33, 229; its influence on Rāmānuja 234-240; commentaries on 33-34
Divyasūricaritam, 10
Dramiḍopaniṣat-tātparya-ratnāvalī, 21-34
Drāviḍa Veda also Dramiḍa Upaniṣad, 3, 21, 222
dvaya mantra, 39, 229

gadyas, of Rāmānuja 236, 238
God, doctrine of 79; 53; as Nārāyaṇa 61; as Śriyaḥpati 60; as Sarveśvara 54, 73; as jagat-kāraṇa 39-40; as Lord of nityavibhūti 73; attributes of 74-82; as giver of mokṣa 59, 74; cosmic functions of 39, 104-105; deeds of 103, 106; incarnations of 95-97; as means and goal 146; *see* also Nārāyaṇa, Paratattva and Divine attributes
Goddess, the doctrine of 60; *see* also Śrī, Bhū and Nīla
grace (aruḷ), the concept of 139; its relation to sādhana 140-41; *see* also kṛpā
guruparamparā, works relating to 10; tradition of 234, 240

heya-pratyanīka, God as 42-43
hita (means of attainment), *see* sādhana

icon, also idol of worship, *see* arcā
Īḍu Muppattiyārāyarappaḍi passim, as important commentary on Tiruvāymoḷi 35; see also Vaḍakkutiruvīdi Piḷḷai
individual self, *see* jīva
Iraṇḍām-tiruvandādi, 17, 32

jīva, also jīvātman (individual self), doctrine of 109; types of 111; cause of bondage to 111-12; removal of bondage of 114-16; as agent of action (*kartā*) 115; freedom of 115-16; relation of Īśvara to 116-18; as *aṁśa* of God 115; as *śeṣa* to bhāgavatas 118-19; see also bhāgavata-śeṣatva
jñāna, as svarūpa of God 74; as an essential attribute of God 74-75; as svarūpa and attribute of soul 110
jñāna-yoga, 126-27, 130, 147

kāruṇya, *see* kṛpā
kaiṅkarya (divine service), in the state

of mokṣa 145-46, 147, 186 for bhāgavatas 28, 118
kaivalya, the theory of 147; views of Nammāḻvār reg. 147-48; Piḷḷān's view reg. 149; controversy reg. 149, 242-43
kalyāṇa-guṇa, *see* Divine attributes
kaṇṇinum-śiruttāmbu, 22, 32
karma, as cause of bondage 111-12, 114, 115
karma-yoga, 126-27
kṛpā (also kāruṇya), as an attribute of God 80-81; as sahetuka and nirhetuka 81-82, 96, 115; controversy reg. 81, 242; see also grace
Kṛṣṇa-bhakti 155-56
Kṛṣṇa-līlās 176-77, 196-97
Kulaśekhara Āḻvār, life and works of 25-26; mysticism of 214-19.

līlās, *see* Divine deeds

maḍal, concept of 31, 174; observance of by Nammāḻvār 174-75; Tirumaṅgai's presentation of 187
Madhurakavi Āḻvār, life and works of 22; as an example of *ācārya-bhakti* 22
mānasa-sākṣātkāra (yogic perception), 163, 164
maṇipravāḷa, meaning of 3; purpose of the adoption of 233; works in 10, 33, 34, 234
mokṣa also vīḍu, upaniṣadic theory of 143-44; theological concept of 145-47; Nammāḻvār's view on 144-45; as sāyujya 145, 186
Mudal tiruvandādi, 17, 32
Mūṉṟām-tiruvandādi 17, 32
Mysticism theistic, definition of 151-52; as different aspects of bhakti 153-54; patterns of 157; philosophic significance of 158-62; symbologies in 159-162; of Nammāḻvār 162-65; of Tirumaṅgai Āḻvār 186-87; of Āṇḍāḷ 199; of Kulaśekharāḻvār 244; of Periyāḻvār 208; mental perception of God in 164; state of separation (*viraha*) from God in, 164-179, 187-90, 192-93, 203-4; state of communion (*saṁśleṣa*) with God in 179-85; final phase of Nammāḻvār's 185-86; final phase of Āṇḍāḷ's 207-8; nāyaka-nāyakībhāva in 157, 159-60; vātsalya-bhāva in 158, 186, 196, 208-217; mystic's physical and mental conditions in 168-70, 190-92, 205-6; joyful experience of a mystic in 179-80, 182, 183, 209-11, 212-13; contemplation of the deeds and glory of God in 176-77, 193-94, 201-2, 211-13

Nācciyār Tirumoḻi, 25; mysticism in 199-200
Nālāyira-divyaprabandham, *see* Divya-prabandham
Nammāḻvār (also Śaṭakopan, Parāṅkuśa) passim, life and works of 18-22; as incarnation of Viśvaksena 13, 18; as nitya-saṁsāri 18; as prapannajana-kūṭastha 124; mysticism of 239; his influence on Rāmānuja 134-35; Vaiṣṇava sects and 240, 241-44
Nāṉmukaṉ-tiruvandādi, 18, 32, 56
Nārada-bhakti sūtra, 157, 214
Nārāyaṇa (also Viṣṇu, Brahman), implication of the term 53, 54; as Supreme Being (paratattva) 54, 55; as Śriyaḥpati 60; his place among trinity of Gods 54-56; as *jagatkāraṇa* 58; as inner controller (antarātmā) of all deities 58-59; as Lord of Nityasūris 94; as sole refuge 94; as giver of mokṣa 59, 73-74; *see* also Paratattva and God
Nārāyaṇa-mantra (also aṣṭākṣara), 30, 33, 229
Nāthamuni, 19, 22, 232
Nāyaka-nāyakībhāva, theological significance of 159-60; *see* also mysticism
Nīlā (also Goda and Ayarmaḍamakal), as consort of Viṣṇu 64; as incarnation of Bhūdevī 66; ontological status of 64
Nitya-kaiṅkarya, as spiritual goal 145-47, 150, 184, 236, 239
nitya-naimittika karma, 243
nitya-sūris, 73, 89, 94, 111; Āḻvārs as incarnation of 15

nitya-vibhūti, 73

organic relation, *see* śarīra-śarīrabhāva

pāda-sevana, *see* kaiṅkarya
para-brahman, *see* Brahman
parabhakti, 154-55, 156, 238
parajñāna, 155, 238
parama-bhakti, 155, 185, 238
paramapada, 91, 94, 95, 102, 144, 147, 163; *see* also Vaikuṇṭha
paramātmā, *see* God
paramapuruṣārtha (supreme goal), the doctrine of 145; *see* also mokṣa
paratattva (ultimate Reality), the doctrine of 37; Nammāḻvār's view reg. the nature of 37-38, 39-42 43-45; as Nārāyaṇa 39, 52-53; as Śriyaḥpati 60; as material cause 40; as free from defects 42-45; as universal soul (śarīrī) 45; as antarātmā 41-42; *see* also God and Nārāyaṇa; *see* also Vaikuṇṭha
parāṅkuśa, *see* Nammāḻvār
Periyāḻvār also Viṣṇucitta, life and works of 23-24, 32; mysticism of 208-14
periya-tirumaḍal, 31
periya-tirumoḻi, 30; mysticism in 186-87
Periyāḻvār Tirumoḻi, 23, 24, 208
periya-tiruvandādi, 20, 32
Perumāḻ Tirumoḻi, 26, 32, 208
Peyāḻvār, 13, 16, 32
Poygai Āḻvār, 13, 16, 32
Pūtattāḻvār, 13, 16, 32
Piḷḷān, Tirukkurukaipirān passim, his commentary on Tiruvāymoḻi 33-34
prapatti (also śaraṇagati, nyāsa), theory of 131, 132-33; components of 133; prerequisites of 133; observance of by Nammāḻvār 125, 132-35; views of Nammāḻvār on 122-25, 126; views of Tirumaṅgai and other Āḻvārs on 135-39; controversy reg. the theory of 241-42
puruṣakāratva, the concept of 62

Rāmānuja passim, works of 235-36; influence of Āḻvārs on 237-40
Rāmānuja-nūṟṟandādi, 33
Reality, the Ultimate, doctrine of 37; *see* paratattva, Nārāyaṇa
Rudra (Śiva) origin of 56; subordinate status of 56-57; his place among Trinity; cosmic function of 58

Sādhana, also upāya (means to mokṣa), doctrine of 121, *see* also bhakti-yoga and prapatti
Śaivism, works of Śaiva devotees 2, 17
saṁśleṣa (communion with God), 156, 164; mystic experience of God during, 179-185; *see* also mysticism
Śarīra-śarīribhāva (organic relation), theory of 45; Nammāḻvār's exposition of 46, 48-51, 52, 237
Śaraṇāgati, *see* prapatti
Saulabhya, *see* Divine attributes
Śauśīlya, *see* Divine attributes
śeṣa-vṛtti (divine service), *see* kaiṅkarya
śiriya-tirumaḍal 32; enumeration of verse in 33
Śrī, Goddess (also Lakṣmī), as consort of Viṣṇu 60; her inseparability from God 60-61; as *upāya* to mokṣa 61-62; her role as puruṣakāra 62-63; 241; as giver of mokṣa 61; ontological status of 63-64, 65; doctrinal difference of Vaiṣṇava sects reg. 241
Śriyaḥpati, *see* Nārāyaṇa
Śuddhasatva 84, 101
Supreme Being, *see* Paratattva
Supreme goal, *see* paramapuruṣārtha

Tamil Veda, *see* Divya-prabandham and Tiruvāymoḻi
Tenkalai, implication of the term 288; doctrinal difference with Vaḍakalai 90-91, 149, 242-43
Tiruccanda viruttam, 18, 32
Tirukkuruntāṇḍakam, 31, 32
Tirumālai, 27, 32
Tiruneḍuntāṇḍakam, 32
Tiruppaḷḷāṇḍu, 23, 24, 32, 209
Tiruppaḷḷiyeḻucci, 27, 32
Tiruppāṇāḻvār, 14, 28-29
Tiruppāvai, 20, 32, 199
Tiruvāciriyam, 20, 32
Tiruvāymoḻi passim, contents of 20-21,

228-29; commentaries on 3, 33-34, 35; as drāviḍa veda 3, 21, 222; as Tamil Vedānta 225-29, 230; as upabrāhmaṇa 225; *see* also divya-prabandham
Tirumaṅgai Āḻvār (also Parakālan, Kaliyan), life and works of 29-32; mysticism of 186
Toṇḍaraḍippoḍi Āḻvār, 26-27; his contribution to Vaiṣṇava theology 28
Tirumaḻiśai Āḻvār, 13, 17, 32, 56
Tiruveḻukūṟṟirukkai, 31
Tiruviruttam, 20, 32

ubhaya-liṅgatva, 45
ubhaya-vedānta, the concept of 230; implication of the term 233-36; maṇipravāḷa works of 236
ultimate Reality, the doctrine of 37; *see* paratattva
upāsanā, *see* bhakti-yoga

Vaḍakkutiruvīdi piḷḷai passim, his commentary on Tiruvāymoḻi 34, 35; his view on status of Goddess Śrī 63
Vaḍakalai, implication of the term 244; doctrinal difference with Tenkalai 93-81, 240-41, 242-43
Vaikuṇṭha *see* also Paramapada
vairāgya, 150, 176
Vaiṣṇavism (also Vaiṣṇava theology) passim, phases in the historical development of 2; tenets of 1, 81, 84, 90, 91, 95, 118, 132, 238
Vaiṣṇava Saints *see* Āḻvārs
Vaiṣṇava sects, *see* Tenkalai and Vaḍakalai
vātsalya-bhāva 157, 158; 184; *see* also mysticism
vīḍu *see* mokṣa
viraha-bhakti, 155, 156
viśleṣa (also viraha), 156, 164; *see* also mysticism
Viṣṇu, *see* Nārāyaṇa
Viṣṇucitta, *see* Periyāḻvār
Viśvaksena, as a nityasūri 89; Nammāḻvār as an incarnation of 13
Vedānta, Viśiṣṭādvaita passim, fundamental topics of 7, 37, 70, 121, 227; central doctrine of 45, 237
Vedānta Deśika passim, his view on the divine nature of Āḻvārs 12 his recognition of Tiruvāymoḻi as Drāviḍa Upaniṣad 21, 34, 222; on Madhurakavi 22; on Pāṇāḻvār 29; on Tirumoḻi 30; his view on the main topics of Tiruvāymoḻi 228-29
Vedānta-sūtra passim, on the nature of Brahman 39, 40, 43, 104; on the nature of jīva 115, 116; on sādhana 121; on Supreme goal 143
Viśiṣṭādvaita Vedānta, *see* Vedānta
vyūha, *see* incarnation

worship, modes of 128, 130; *see* also bhakti

Yāmuna (Āḷavandār) 235
yatirājavaibhava, 235